CHILDREN'S
LITERATURE
IN CHINA

Studies on Modern China

CHILDREN'S LITERATURE IN CHINA
From Lu Xun to Mao Zedong
Mary Ann Farquhar

CHINA'S LAST NOMADS
The History and Culture of China's Kazaks
Linda Benson and Ingvar Svanberg

HAKKA CHINESE CONFRONT PROTESTANT CHRISTIANITY, 1950–1900
Jessie G. Lutz and Rolland Ray Lutz

IMAGINING THE PEOPLE
Chinese Intellectuals and the Concept of Citizenship, 1890–1920
Edited by Joshua A. Fogel and Peter Zarrow

INDUSTRIAL REFORMERS IN REPUBLICAN CHINA
Robin Porter

THE KWANGSI WAY IN KUOMINTANG CHINA, 1931–1939
Eugene William Levich

"SECRET SOCIETIES" RECONSIDERED
Perspectives on the Social History of
Early Modern South China and Southeast Asia
Edited by David Ownby and Mary Somers Heidhues

THE SAGA OF ANTHROPOLOGY IN CHINA
From Malinowski to Moscow to Mao
Gregory Eliyu Guldin

MODERN CHINESE WRITERS
Self-Portrayals
Edited by Helmut Martin and Jeffrey C. Kinkley

MODERNIZATION AND REVOLUTION IN CHINA
June Grasso, Jay Corrin, and Michael Kort

PERSPECTIVES ON MODERN CHINA
Four Anniversaries
Edited by Kenneth Lieberthal, Joyce Kallgren,
Roderick MacFarquhar, and Frederic Wakeman, Jr.

READING THE MODERN CHINESE SHORT STORY
Edited by Theodore Huters

UNITED STATES ATTITUDES TOWARD CHINA
The Impact of American Missionaries
Edited by Patricia Neils

Studies on Modern China

CHILDREN'S LITERATURE IN CHINA

From Lu Xun to Mao Zedong

MARY ANN FARQUHAR

AN EAST GATE BOOK

M.E.Sharpe
Armonk, New York
London, England

An East Gate Book

Copyright © 1999 by M. E. Sharpe, Inc.

Library of Congress Cataloging-in-Publication Data

Farquhar, Mary Ann.
Children's literature in China : from Lu Xun to Mao Zedong / by
Mary Ann Farquhar.
p.   cm.—(Studies on modern China)
"An East gate book."
Includes bibliographical references and index.
ISBN 0-7656-0344-6 (alk. paper).—
1. Children's literature, Chinese—20th century—History and criticism.
2. Lu, Hsün, 1881–1936—Contributions in children's literature, Chinese.
I. Title.   II. Series.
PL2449.F37   1998
895.1′099282′0904—dc21   98-39817
CIP

Printed in the United States of America

BM (c)   10   9   8   7   6   5   4   3   2

For my mother, Peggy, and in memory of my friend, Dianne

Contents

Figures

Tables

Illustrations

Acknowledgements

This book has been researched and written over two decades. I express sincere thanks to the many people who have contributed to its production, though it is impossible to name everyone. There are several exceptions. My son Vishal deserves a special 'thank you' from me for growing up with this manuscript in its various forms.

I give particular thanks to the following people:

Colin Mackerras, doctoral supervisor, colleague and friend; Maureen Todhunter, who edited this book; Jennilyn Mann, who painstakingly put the manuscript into desktop publishing format; Sue Jarvis, for preparing the index; Liz Wilson, Macs at Work, for cover design; Sang Ye, for organizing copyright permission for the illustrations; and Patricia Loo and Doug Merwin at M.E. Sharpe.

I also acknowledge my teachers at Beijing University in the mid-seventies, who gave me a thorough grounding in Lu Xun's writings and in Mao Zedong's 'Thoughts', the beginning and the end of this work.

I am grateful to the following publishers for permission to publish illustrations in this book: Foreign Languages Press, Beijing; New World Press; Shanghai Renmin Chubanshe (formerly Shaonian Ertong Chubanshe) and Zhongguo Shaonian Ertong Chubanshe.

CHILDREN'S
LITERATURE
IN CHINA

Introduction

From its beginnings in the early twentieth century, modern Chinese children's literature was cast as an ideological tool to reshape China. It aroused deep controversies over concepts of childhood, education and language. At the core of the controversy was its role in China's push for modernization. Revolutionaries—from Lu Xun to Mao Zedong—insisted that the future of China would be decided by Chinese children themselves. To this end, they needed their own distinctive literature.

Children and children's literature, therefore, emerged as serious political concerns in modern Chinese history. In a China racked by national disintegration and spiritual crisis early this century, children became a symbol of hope for the future. In the past, children represented a continuity of family and traditional values. Early reformers reinterpreted this ideology within an evolutionary framework and fashioned a new image of children: they represented national, not family, continuity, and evolutionary change, not unchanging tradition. Lu Xun was the spokesperson for this position. The Marxists adopted this position but substituted revolutionary struggle for evolutionary change, calling children 'revolutionary successors' (*gemingde jiebanren*). In a society that valued literature as the primary source of moral values, children's literature was to be a powerful means to educate the future masters of a modern state.

Yet for all its significance in China's recent political and cultural history, in China there are only fragmented and frequently polemical studies of children's literature despite the wealth of available material. In the West the subject itself has been barely acknowledged. It is not that Chinese themselves attribute little significance to children's literature. A cursory reading of the relevant twentieth century literature reveals the opposite; renowned Chinese thinkers insisted on the crucial importance of children and their books for Chinese society.

The first modern short story in China, 'A Madman's Diary' (1918) by Lu Xun, ends with the now famous cry, 'save the children'.[1] The first children's magazine in Mao Zedong's guerilla base area exhorted children, in Mao's own words and handwriting, to 'rise up. . . and learn to be free, independent citizens of China'.[2] In the fifties, Mao told Chinese youth that both the world and China's future belonged to them[3] and then, as if to prove it, he mobilized them as the energetic 'red' vanguard of the Cultural Revolution that swept China in the sixties. Both liberal reformers and Marxist revolutionaries clearly considered children's literature an important aspect of any long-term modernization strategy. The cry to 'save the children' meant, ultimately, to 'save' China itself.

Ironically, the absence of systematic study of children's literature in China is due *precisely* to its ideological importance. In the period before 1949, the year the Chinese Communist Party gained control over the Chinese state, the major political factions had considered control of children's literature indispensable in their struggle for power. The conflict was so intense that discussions of the subject were usually conducted in quick-fire succession through the newspapers and magazines of the day. This environment was not conducive to rigorous scholarly inquiry.

In the period after 1949, the political potency of children's literature begged an authoritative Party delineation of the field, commensurate with the importance that the Party had bestowed on it. Yet tentative explorations were discouraged, and frequent swings in Party policy towards literature denied any opportunity to publish a definitive work.[4] Nonetheless, children's literature is a serious subject in modern Chinese history. It is overtly political, and offers valuable insights into contemporary China. As such, it merits special consideration. This book takes up that task, mapping the tumultuous, formative period of modern Chinese children's literature this century: from Lu Xun to Mao Zedong.

In the West there has been only one serious study of modern Chinese children's literature, published in 1971: Jean-Pierre Diény's *Le Monde est à Vous, La Chine et les Livres pour Enfants* (*The World Belongs to You, China and Children's Books*, 1971).[5] This is a study of children's literature under Mao. Diény's opening sentence comments on the then prevailing Western view of children's literature. To write on such a subject, he said then, seems a 'bizarre eccentricity'. Indeed, he continued, 'some Western specialists of children's literature deny that China has any books worthy of the name'.[6] Diény treats these views with some disdain, using Mao Zedong's catchphrase, 'the world belongs to you', in his title to emphasize the significance of this subject. He points out the musings that prompted his study—about the decisive political role of the young Red Guards in the Cultural Revolution and the reading matter that may have influenced them, about the eager young readers whom he saw filling China's bookshops and libraries. 'It is worth the trouble to stoop over these books, whatever they are, that they read so carefully.'[7] In end-of-millennium China, poised to become an economic and political powerhouse of the Pacific region, it is especially worth the 'trouble'.

Diény is modest about the limitations of his work. At the personal level, it was a means of prolonging his stay in a China which captivated him. In scope, it relies on only 180 books (most published in the early sixties) collected while he worked there between 1964 and 1966. In depth, it is bereft of bibliographic research into histories of Chinese children's literature. Yet this work is pioneering. It points to an unexplored field which yields new perspectives on twentieth century China, not just in its children's literature but also in education, cultural policy and political control. Diény claims:

> In China. . . there is no break in continuity between the literature for children, adolescents and adults. All three, being three branches on the single trunk of official ideology, resemble each other: China treats children as adults and adults as children. To have a knowledge of children's literature, therefore, is to know something of all forms of literary activity.[8]

Diény's work identifies three key problems that serve as useful starting points for this study. The first is the extent to which Chinese children's literature is an identifiable field with its own distinguishing characteristics. The second is the basic task of classifying the major literary texts in each historical period and assigning them to the main currents, or schools, of children's literature. The third problem is tracing the development of these schools and explaining their dominance or decline. Diény's analysis, for example, shows how the majority of the children's books that he collected on the eve of the Great Proletarian Cultural Revolution (1965) conform to the primary function then assigned to children's literature by the Chinese Communist Party: political education of the young who must assure the continuity of the revolution. But he also discerns a dissident 'counter-current' which challenges the 'cement block of propaganda' dominating the cultural scene in these years. He claims that an inquiry of any depth 'should explain how this heretical stream evolved and then lost ground during the rectification campaigns', which successively assailed literature after Liberation in 1949.[9] These three problems in analyzing Chinese children's literature—its distinguishing characteristics, the major texts in the field, and the evolution of the main schools of literature—are central issues examined in this book.

The purpose here, however, extends beyond the problems outlined by Diény and derives from a reading of the Chinese sources. The central proposition here is that the Chinese, in the twentieth century, have attempted to develop a canon of children's literature. In literature, a canon variously refers to major authors, major literary works or fundamental rules governing standards of literary criticism.[10] Early this century, China's first generation of modern writers produced a vernacular children's literature to displace the key texts of the Confucian canon in the classical language that traditionally children memorized as part of their education. At the end of this century, we can confidently say that these Confucian texts are relegated to history. Vernacular children's literature is now institutionalized as part of children's reading and part of the education system.

The purpose of this book, therefore, is four-fold. First, we seek to identify the hallmarks of Chinese children's literature. Second, we seek to identify and classify the major literary texts for Chinese children, beginning with the first work in 1921. Third, we relate these texts to the historical conditions that produced and privileged them. On this basis we can, fourth, assess the development of a canon in the field of children's literature in China.

The proposition that there *is* a canon of children's literature in China rests on two assumptions. The first is that there is a literature specifically for children. Diény's contention that 'in China. . . literature for children, adolescents and adults. . . resemble each other' does not mean that these literatures are the same, however solid are the continuities between them. Chinese distinguish children's literature from that for adults, but do not differentiate within this literature between works for children and works for adolescents. Children's literature is called *shaonian ertong wenxue* which means literally 'literature for adolescents and children'. This study adopts the inclusive Chinese usage. It examines a literature in China which, from its inception, has catered for children from five years (kindergarten) to fifteen years (the end of junior middle school).

The second assumption is that children's literature in China is now an identifiable field. The sources reveal that Chinese children's literature has:

- a clearly constituted audience of vast proportions. Population statistics show that the potential readership for children's literature has grown rapidly this century. The total population of 387.89 million in 1911 grew to 1.008 billion in 1982. By far the most significant factor is the very high proportion of young people, with approximately 300 million then under sixteen years of age, according to Chinese census statistics;[11]

- a wealth of books, some of which are considered classics, and a range of genres, some of which are considered particularly suitable for children, such as fairytales and children's songs;

- specialized professionals, such as writers and critics, and organizational support such as libraries, publishing houses, a writers' federation, congresses and prizes. The organization extends from national through provincial to local levels;
- a history filled with its own particular debates, such as those on the role of children's literature, the nature of childhood and the social function of fairytales and comic books; and
- conscious, even mammoth, efforts by Chinese to enrich their own literature with translations, especially in the 1920s, 1950s and 1980s.

Given the magnitude of this field, how do we approach it? The approach taken here is that of the Chinese themselves, using the texts of writers, critics, educators, theoreticians and political leaders. Chesneaux has stated that:

> China has become an active subject which in itself defines the restrictions and approaches that determine the area in which they must think and work. . . there is still some room for speculation. . . but this margin. . . remains narrow, for it is defined by the Chinese themselves which means that the questions we ask are in some sense predetermined.[12]

The sources for a study of children's literature in China are many and various. Indeed, there is an over-abundance of material. Newspapers and magazines, including children's magazines, have featured articles on the subject since its genesis in the twenties. Major debates, reviews and discussions of policy change are conducted continuously in the main newspapers and adult magazines on literature. For the contextual materials I have utilized sets of newspapers and magazines covering the entire period under study. The exception is almost a decade (1938–47) in the war period when literary production was low and paper was scarce; in this case I have relied on later reports and reviews. In the mid-fifties, and again since the late seventies, many important essays and reports have been published in book form for easy access. These include reports on congresses, book reviews and essays on writers, as well as theoretical articles and debates.

Most of the major literary texts reviewed in the press during the period under review here were located for this study. The May Fourth or inter-war period (1918–36) is the formative period of modern children's literature in China as Lu Xun and others set about to produce the first vernacular children's works. This period takes its name from Chinese demonstrations over the Versailles Treaty on May 4, 1919, and ends with the Japanese attack on China in 1937. It is the period of greatest Western influence on China and is particularly well documented, as the main writers for children were also major figures in the literary world. Again the exception is the war periods, which include the Anti-Japanese War (1937–45) and the Civil War between the Nationalists and Communists (1946–49). However, the first two anthologies of the 'best' children's literature cover the civil war period (1946–49) and many works from this period have been republished. It should be restated that commentators agree that there was not much published in this period, partly because the Japanese, as colonizers, had taken over the publishing centres on the eastern coast. Nevertheless, despite this relative paucity, fair generalizations about pre-Liberation children's literature will be offered here, based on a sample which represents the range and diversity of the works produced during that time. This sample is itself based on an analysis of both the literary works which the Chinese consider important, and the contextual material in the press.

The range of works published after 1949 is available to Western researchers. These are found in books, newspapers and literary magazines for both adults and children. The most important source is the anthologies of children's literature published periodically since 1949 with the exception of the Cultural Revolution period (1966–76). During the first phase of the Cultural Revolution (1966–69) most publication ceased. Works published in the seventies were collected while I lived in Beijing for three years from 1974. The publication record was so pitiful in this period that it was possible to collect and digest almost everything available on this subject. The situation changed dramatically in the late seventies with a publishing explosion, which has included works of, or on, children's literature. From 1978 to the mid-1980s, for example, more anthologies were published than during the three decades of the preceding period, and these include not only annual or biennial anthologies but specialized collections, such as fairytales and pre-school literature. Most cover literature originally produced in the period 1949 to 1979 but some begin with twenties selections. They therefore come within the period under study. Although the titles, *Ertong Wenxuexuan* (*Anthologies of Children's Literature*), suggest they do not include adolescent literature, many of the works are selected from adolescent magazines and are aimed on the whole at older children.

The post-1949 works discussed in this study are not selected at random from the range. They are considered important by Chinese critics either because they are prize winners, controversial, frequently republished or the subject of major reviews. Even so, the territory is large and many works are not included. This is especially true of the post-Mao proliferation of books after 1976, which is partly why the scope of this study ends with Mao's death, itself a watershed in China's political, social and literary life. Similarly, the emphasis on fiction is proportionate to the amount of attention it has received in the press relative to other literary forms. Plays, poems and songs are included when they have been specifically reviewed or won prizes. Serial picture books (comics), on the other hand, are included because they were emphasized in the thirties and fifties as the most popular of all the reading material for children and because their development illustrates an important aspect of left-wing policies towards children's literature.

The critical approach and criteria for selection of their leading works by the Chinese themselves have differed from period to period. As Jean Chesneaux maintains, Chinese study history 'as a way of integrating a political thought which is rooted in the present. . . not only is their history filled with crises and sudden shifts, it is read backward, constantly being revised and reinterpreted as these crises and shifts occur'.[13] Survival is one test of a book. Later interpretations have, however, almost always been tested by background research in the newspapers and magazines of the period when the work was originally published. With the exception of the Cultural Revolution period, when almost everything was being questioned, there is evidence of consistent attitudes towards what were considered 'good' books. Indeed, almost all the works and writers pilloried during the Cultural Revolution, or in the preceding rectification campaigns, have been reinstated since the late seventies. Children's literature is cumulative and, throughout most of its history in China, certain texts persist as major literary works. These works and the contextual materials which explain them offer a basis for establishing the canon in the field.

The most striking characteristic of the history of Chinese children's literature is the alignment of certain schools, literary forms and theories with different political factions struggling for power. Literature was one means of establishing and maintaining the legitimacy of social programs. Literary works may, therefore, reflect incompatible ideological positions. It follows that there should be conflicting criteria for judging literary value. While this view is valid at one level of analysis, a further reading suggests that there are basic cultural assumptions, common to all factions, which underpin the judgements and debates on children's literature. The most crucial assumption is that the importance of children's literature lies in its educative function, and that this is located in the social domain. Most critics, whether they are Confucian, liberal or Marxist, regard social and historical context as fundamental. The often vehement debates on children's literature take place within this framework; they question the educational theories and practices and the concepts of childhood which inform children's literature, but never question the primacy of its educational role. In almost all cases literary value in a text is conferred according to its perceived 'educational significance' (*jiaoyu yiyi*) and, as a corollary, its implications for the future directions of Chinese society.

Lu Xun, the 'father' of children's literature and the most influential theorist in the field, reserved 'the very, very, very blackest curses' for all who opposed it, precisely because of its special importance.

No matter who they are, there must be a limit to this eating of children, it must end when they die. And even if the poison of those who oppose the vernacular is as powerful as raging floods and savage beasts, so extremely widespread and long-lived that all of China becomes a pock-marked, bearded (bogey-man), then children everywhere will die in its belly.

All it needs is more murderers of vernacular (literature) to cause total destruction.[14]

Lu Xun's generation of writers in the early twentieth century rejected the entire dead weight of Confucian texts for children. But instead of completely rejecting literature as something unsuitable for children, these far-sighted writers created a new literature specifically for them. From its inception, children's literature in China was both 'a weapon to educate children'[15] and a means of awakening their imagination. It was both militant and full of care. Under the Communists after 1949, published works became increasingly militant and the literary field became a 'battlefield'. By the end of Mao Zedong's days, most existing literature was purged, leaving a few 'revolutionary' works as lone sentinels in a devastated literary landscape. After Mao's death in 1976, the field was reassessed and famous works were rehabilitated. Children's literature was once more called a 'garden'.

This book takes us into both the garden and the battlefield.

Notes

1. Lu Xun, 'Kuangren Riji', *Lu Xun Quanji*, Vol. 1 (Beijing, 1973), p. 291.
2. Mao Zedong, in Liu Yu, 'Jiefangqu Diyizhang Ertongbao', *Ertong Wenxue Yanjiu*, 2 (1959), p. 85.
3. Mao Zedong, 'Talk at a Meeting with Chinese Students and Trainees in Moscow' (17 November 1957), in *English Quotations from Chairman Mao Tsetung* (Peking, 1976), p. 288. The full quote is: 'The world is yours, as well as ours but, in the final analysis, it is yours. You young people, full of vigor and vitality, are in the bloom of life like the sun at eight or nine in the morning. Our hope is placed in you . . . The world belongs to you. China's future belongs to you'.
4. I have located one slim history of Chinese children's literature for the period under study: Jiang Feng, *Zhongguo Ertong Wenxue Jianghua* [*An Introduction to Chinese Children's Literature*], published in Nanjing in 1959. It deals primarily with pre-1949 material. The Chinese in the field recognize the paucity of research, according to statements made to the author during discussions in Sichuan in both 1984 and 1986–87. However, the Children's Literature Writers'

Association, which belongs to the National Writers Association, had plans to publish a history of Chinese children's literature within the next few years (according to an interview with standing member and editor of Sichuan Children's Literature Publishing House, He Qunying, in 1987). In 1998 it is still to be published.

5. Diény, J. P., *Le Monde est à Vous: La Chine et les Livres pour Enfants* (Paris, 1971). There is an excellent study of the books available to children in traditional China with a closing sketch of the new modern children's literature: Hayward-Scott, D., *Chinese Popular Literature and the Child* (Chicago, 1980). There are two English-language bibliographies on Chinese children's literature. The first, mentioned by Diény, is Pellowski, A., *The World of Children's Literature* (New York, London, 1968). It lists only 32 titles. The other, Haviland, V., *Children's Literature: A Guide to Reference Sources* (Washington, 1966) also has a very short section on Chinese children's literature. Margaret Wylie's *Children of China* (Hong Kong, 1962) includes a chapter on children's reading.

6. Diény, J. P., op cit., p. 8.

7. Ibid., p. 8.

8. Ibid., pp. 7–8.

9. Ibid., p. 125.

10. Abrams, M.H., *A Glossary of Literary Terms*, 5th ed. (New York, 1988), p. 20.

11. The Population Census Office Under State Council, Department of the State Statistical Bureau, *The 1982 Population Census of China* (Hong Kong, 1982), p. 64.

12. Chesneaux, J., *China: The People's Republic 1949–1976*, translated by Auster, P. and Davis, L. (Hassocks, 1979), p. xi.

13. Ibid., p. ix-x.

14. Lu Xun, 'Ershisi Xiaotu', *Lu Xun Quanji*, Vol. 11, op. cit., p. 232.

15. Jiang Feng (ed.), 'Qianyan', *Lu Xun Lun Ertong Jiaoyu he Ertong Wenxue* (Shanghai, 1961), p. 1.

1
The Historical Background

In China, modern children's literature began in the early twentieth century. It was written by the first generation of great modern writers such as Lu Xun, Ye Shengtao and Mao Dun. There were, of course, books for children long before this. But these were elementary primers within the Confucian education system, rejected by modern reformers.

This chapter considers the historical background of Confucian children's books up to the end of the early May Fourth period (1926). It outlines the growing challenge in the nineteenth century to the legitimacy of the Confucian canon. This challenge became direct confrontation in the May Fourth period. May Fourth writers for children borrowed ideas and forms from Western literature to attack the dominance of Confucianism which they regarded as inimical to the modernization of China. They believed that only the introduction of modern science and democracy could ensure China's survival as a nation.

At the core of this confrontation lay two very different views on education. Writers such as Lu Xun claimed that Confucian children's texts were rooted in the past and were retrogressive; Confucian texts directed children towards mindless obedience. Advocates of a modern children's literature, on the other hand, sought to inculcate a sense of individual worth and a spirit of scientific enquiry. Progressive thinkers in the early twentieth century considered that the lack of these two qualities explained, in part, the decline of China. These thinkers stressed that education through children's literature should develop the personal capacities of the young.

In this context, it can be said that the Chinese 'discovered' childhood in the early twentieth century. There was widespread interest in Western theories on child psychology and the nature of childhood. The discussions focussed in particular on an evolutionary concept of childhood development and pre-Freudian notions of childhood innocence. These theories served a dual function. First, they undermined Confucian educational practices as 'unscientific'. Second, they underpinned current arguments for new developments in children's education which included the production of 'a garden' of children's literature. Pastoral images of hope and delight reinforced arguments for the emancipation of children from the dark night of Confucian orthodoxy.

Despite the obvious incompatibility between Confucian and May Fourth views on education, they share one striking feature: recognition of the social importance of the educative role of children's books. Confucian children's books clearly sought to perpetuate a living tradition. The success of these texts within the education system offered a partial explanation for the longevity and dominance of Confucian ideology. Twentieth century reformers, therefore, sought to displace them. But the reformist conception of children's literature was still socially determinist in that its stated end was to transform and enrich future Chinese society. Reformists' interest in childhood, albeit genuine, was ultimately shaped more by the emerging forces of nationalism than by disinterested scientific curiosity. Indeed, for a short period the child was the political symbol of China's future.

Traditional Children's Books

Children's books in traditional China were primarily educational. The best known, *The Three Character Classic (Sanzi Jing)*,[1] was a language primer which introduced children to characters, an outline of Chinese history and the social tenets of Confucianism through easily memorized three-character phrases. This book, together with *The One Hundred Family Names (Baijia Xing)*,[2] and *The Thousand Character Classic (Qianzi Wen)*[3] formed a set of elementary Confucian texts for children. They were familiarly known as the *san bai qian* ('three, hundred and thousand') and were learned by heart.

When children had mastered the basics—counting and reading—they continued to follow an approved reading schedule. According to *The Three Character Classic:*

> Those who are learners
> Must have a beginning.
> When *Education for the Young* is finished
> Proceed to the *Four Books*...
> When the *Classic of Filial Piety* is mastered
> And the *Four Books* are known by heart,
> The next step is to the *Six Classics*
> Which may now be studied.[4]

Children's traditional education directed them as early as possible to the *Four Books* which, as the first portion of the Confucian canon, were memorized by all candidates who hoped for success in the public examinations. In meritocratic China, success in these examinations was the gateway to official position, wealth and prestige. In one sense, children's texts were merely necessary stepping stones to the Confucian classics rather than reading matter or 'literature' as we now understand it; indeed, twentieth century critics claimed that children did not understand the texts they recited and were bored to death by them. Nevertheless, these texts were spectacularly successful. They remained within the Confucian canon for centuries because they were well suited to their purpose: the *san bai qian* introduced children to about two thousand characters, the basic number for beginners, and the short, rhythmic lines of *The Three Character Classic* trip off the tongue as easily as nursery rhymes.

Children also had elementary reading material: poetry texts such as *The Thousand Family Poems* (*Qianjia Shi*)[5] and prose story books such as *Daily Stories* (*Riji Gushi*).[6] While books such as these could be called 'children's literature', the Chinese saw them as properly belonging to education; they were texts for 'enlightening the ignorance' (*qimeng*) of the very young. Zhu Xi makes this clear in his comments on *Daily Stories* in *Education for the Young* (*Xiaoxue*):

Education for the young is not just learning by heart. We must begin with language as the basis in nurturing both deep knowledge and a fine application (of that knowledge). *Daily Stories*, whether old or new, must first teach such qualities as filial piety, fraternal love, loyalty, truth, propriety, duty, honour and honesty through stories like Huang Xiang warming his parent's be. . . Only when these (stories) are well known will the basic principles be clear and through long familiarity (the habit of) virtue will become natural.[7]

China produced the world's earliest picture book for children, one century earlier than production of the first picture book for children in the West, *Orbus Pictus* by Comenius (1592–1670). The Chinese book, written in 1542, was an illustrated version of *Daily Stories*, a staple in the Confucian children's canon. Pictorialization was common in both traditional and modern children's books. It enhanced the pleasure of reading and reinforced the educative meaning of the texts.

Approved children's books such as these had three aims: to introduce characters and sentence structure, to impart general knowledge and to transmit traditional Chinese cultural values. The transmission of culture involved more than exposure to literature or factual accounts of Chinese history and philosophy, for the Chinese did not separate knowledge from its application; as Zhu Xi suggests, these books sought to internalize as second nature certain moral attitudes that would produce patterns of behavior which formed the basis of Confucian society. Their acceptance by the child guaranteed survival and continuity of Confucian mores within Chinese culture.

Mastery of the Confucian classics was, however, the prerogative and the hallmark of the educated elite: the literati from whom the mandarins or official class were chosen by examination. The vast majority of Chinese people remained illiterate. They lacked the leisure and wealth required to support the acquisition of a traditional education. Even within the wealthier families, education was principally the domain of the sons. When it existed for daughters, it was directed towards preparing them for marriage, not for public office. Texts for girls, such as *Precepts for Women* (*Nu Jie*) and *Classic for Girls*

(*Nu'er Jing*), set standards for female conduct. Essentially, these texts reiterated and expanded on the maxim contained in the Confucian classic, *The Book of Rites* (*Liji*): 'to be a woman meant to submit'.[8] As Croll claims, books such as these embodied the ideological mechanisms of subordination of women in traditional China. The works rationalized female's acquiescence in their own inferiority and domestic seclusion. The works interacted with other mechanisms of subordination to reduce women to a state of economic dependence, physical subservience and sexual servitude.[9] In short, the Confucian classics which include books for children were the educational pillars of a patriarchal and elite social system.

Children also had access to a vast amount of material which, while not intended specifically for them, seems to have reached them by one means or another. In *Chinese Popular Literature and the Child*, Hayward Scott gives a full account of traditional popular literature available to Chinese children. This includes oral literature such as songs and stories, and popular written literature such as novels.

An historical example of the influence of popular literature on children is found in China's most famous novel, the Qing Dynasty masterpiece called *The Dream of the Red Chamber*. Baoyu, the boy hero, is bored with reading Confucius and Mencius, but enraptured with a pile of books bought for him by his young servant, Tealeaf.
His purchases include:

> Old Inklubber's Stories Old and New
> The Secret History of Flying Swallow
> Sister of Flying Swallow
> The Infamous Loves of Empress Wu
> The Jade Ring Concubine, or
> Peeps in the Inner Palace
> and a heap of playbooks—mostly romantic comedies and the like. . .
>
> Tealeaf uttered a warning: 'Don't take these into the garden. If you do and anyone finds out about them I'll be in real trouble—more than just a bellyful'.[10]

Baoyu ignores the warning and takes a few of the more chaste volumes into the garden where his young cousin finds him. She, too, becomes absorbed: 'she felt the power of the words and their lingering fragrance. Long after she had finished reading, when she had laid down the book and was sitting there rapt and silent, the lines continued to ring on in her head'.[11]

It could be said that the prehistory of modern Chinese children's literature had two branches: material, primarily educational, that was written for children with meticulous care, and material that children enjoyed, but that was not meant specifically for them. Children were seen as immature adults. They were seen to be ignorant (the traditional words for 'early education' and 'elementary texts' contain the character *meng* meaning 'dark, covered, confused, in childish ignorance') and they were to be enlightened through the classics which expounded social and natural 'laws'.

In any society, awareness of the special characteristics of childhood is a necessary precondition for the emergence of a modern children's literature. Aries claims that 'the idea of childhood is not to be confused with affection for children; it corresponds to an awareness of the particular nature of childhood, the particular nature which distinguishes the child from the adult, even the young adult'.[12] Chinese writers on the subject agree that this awareness was lacking in traditional China. Ascertaining the extent to which this is true would require a detailed study, but the proposition is borne out by the description of Baoyu's childhood and adolescence in *The Dream of the Red Chamber*, the masterpiece discussed previously. The description of Baoyu includes his fear of his strict father; his early childhood play with his young female cousin; the rumpus and sexual innuendo in the family school; a wet dream during which he follows the instructions of a fairy, called Disenchantment, in the art of love; sharing these instructions with Aroma, his personal maid; and the erotic literature he read during a period of adolescent discontent. By this time one assumes he is no longer a child. But these descriptions are particular to Baoyu; despite the Chinese love of categorization, there is no mention that these are general attributes of childhood or adolescence. Indeed, the framework of the novel is Buddhist, and Baoyu's life is pre-determined by the operations of karma—he is one of 'a batch of romantic idiots' who are 'sent down into the world to take part in the great illusion of human life'.[13]

Western Impact on Chinese Children's Literature

For more than half a millenium, between the Yuan dynasty (1279–1368) and the early twentieth century, the body of children's texts beginning with the *san bai qian* remained relatively unchanged.[14] Developments and additions were within the general outline set by Neo-Confucians. The pattern was continuity, not change.

From the mid-nineteenth century, however, the thread in Chinese history is change, not continuity. A period of blatant Western influence began with the first Opium War (1840–42) when British forced Chinese to accept opium and to open more treaty ports for trade along the east China coast. The Chinese label this period 'semi-feudal semi-colonial'. However, additions to the body of children's books in the nineteenth century were minimal and only hindsight makes these at all significant; they were precursors to the large-scale introduction of Western children's literature in the twentieth century and a small part of the gathering momentum for change over more than a hundred years which led to the rise of modern China.

Two points suggest that Western influence on children's literature before the twentieth century was negligible. First, from the scant information available (and here we must rely on records of later writers and recorded changes in traditional texts), any additions were kept neatly within the confines of Confucianism and the classical language. Second, the general understanding of children's reading was still traditional in that the literature for them was subsumed by classical education. Western works were introduced as educational tools, for language training in particular, and new ideas were propagated in traditional packages, such as *The Three Character Classic*.

A survey of Western-influenced children's books and translations of Western works available in the nineteenth century clearly shows the dominance of Confucian function and form. The first translation apparently for children was *Aesop's Fables,* published in 1840 in an English-Chinese version for language training. Chen Bochui, writing from memory, claims this was 'the discovery of "the golden key"; the door opened and put us on the path of using Western children's literature in our elementary language texts'.[15] The translations were not intended for children only, but, as in the West, children adopted these fables and they are now entrenched as a familiar part of children's literature. At that time, however, they were primarily educational.

Newly written Chinese works also used traditional forms. For example, the Taiping revolutionaries (1851–64) edited their own version of *The Three Character Classic,* called *The Three Character Classic of the Kingdom of Heavenly Peace* (*Taiping Tianguo Sanzi Jing*). Such variations were not new; what was new was that a movement for the first time incorporated Western ideas, notably from Christianity, in its reform program. Nevertheless, they still used the old rhyming style of *The Three Character Classic* to teach children these new ideas.

The forms and function of Confucian education were still dominant at the turn of the century, but Western content had become more pronounced. Even the great reformer, Liang Qichao, paid tribute to their persistence in the title that he chose to translate Jules Verne's *Two Years of Vacation* at the end of the nineteenth century. This choice of work for translation was particularly appropriate at a time of growing recognition of the need to study science, for Verne's purpose was 'to sum up all the information gathered by modern science in the fields of geography, geology, physics and astronomy and to rewrite. . . the history of the Universe'.[16] But Liang Qichao reshaped the work, calling it—in a curious Confucian twist—*Fifteen Young Heroes: A Gallery of Foreign Models Worthy of Emulation by the Youth of China.*

In 1902, yet another version of *The Three Character Classic* introduced science but kept it firmly within the context of the prevailing patriotic maxim: 'Chinese (i.e. Confucian) learning as essence and Western learning as technique' (*zhongxue wei ti, xixue wei yong*). This version shows a wider horizon than its original. Its beginning places China in the world:

> In the world
> Are five continents;
> East and West
> Two halves of the globe . . .[17]

This version lists countries in the Western 'half' of the world, but in their imperialist role. It tells us that the West has used the cloak of Christianity to invade China.

Despite the minimal Western impact on children's books in the nineteenth century, fundamental changes were occurring in the education system. By the end of the century, Western-style schools had been established by missionaries, and Western learning had been introduced as a subject in the imperial examinations.[18] These examinations were eventually abolished in the early twentieth century. Western learning was gradually eroding the significance of a primarily moral, classical education.

The decline of the traditional education system was to have a profound influence on attitudes towards children's books. In particular, records of writers who lived their childhood at the turn of the century show a marked hostility towards Confucian children's texts. These shifting attitudes are of utmost importance for understanding the evolution of modern Chinese children's literature for, in terms of creators and not creations, this is its true beginning.

China's major modern writer, Lu Xun (1881–1936), found the old texts dead, dark, dull and hopelessly outdated. His brother, Zhou Zuoren (1885–1966), recalled that he *learned* the classics, which he discounted as literature, and *read* widely among the popular novels.

> In the past in China it was thought that children should read only the classics. . . so they had to look for themselves to stave off spiritual starvation.[19]

Ba Jin, who was born almost twenty years later, was still taught in the traditional manner and he records his horror when he found *Lives of Virtuous Women (Lienu Zhuan)* in his sister's room when he was five or six years old. All the women were martyrs![20]

The fullest account of youth's responses to China's changing circumstances is the first section of Guo Moruo's autobiography, *My Childhood (Shaonian Shidai: Wode Tongnian 1892–1909)*, published in 1929. Guo Moruo was probably one of the least important of China's famous writers in the field of children's literature, but he does give a startlingly honest picture of his childhood within the larger social framework.

According to his autobiography, changes in education preceded the emergence of children's literature. The influence of Western imperialism was felt even in his out-of-the-way village in Sichuan, 'but for we children the most telling expression of all these changes was the appearance of new text books'.[21] The abolition of the old examination system in 1903 'inevitably caused changes affecting the social consciousness and came to exercise a direct influence on teaching methods in the family school'.[22] As Guo describes it, previously children had read only the classics and now they had to know something of world affairs. Their teacher, who was progressive, introduced textbooks on subjects like natural science, geography and mathematics. And now, even when the classics were studied, it was not through rote learning but through a comparative and critical analysis of the texts. Thus, drawing on Guo's observations, we could say that the new system of education and the adoption of specialist texts ended the era of the Confucian amateur and ushered in the modern professional. As part of this specialization, traditional 'literary texts' underwent a sort of mitosis, spawning first the formal, information-giving text book of public education, and later the more private, 'literary' book belonging to the written world of modern literature for children.

Education had been a male prerogative, but at this time girls also began attending school. In Guo Moruo's case, this was the family school. Later, the right, in principle at least, of girls having access to literature was never mentioned because it had already been secured by their entry into the school system. The issue in children's literature, as far as audience goes, was to be one of class, not sex: how accessible to the masses should it be.

Guo Moruo's brother attended one of the newly established schools and sent him new city publications at a time when the need for new text books led to unprecedented growth in the already vigorous publishing industry.[23] One novel Guo received, which he calls 'the ancestor of proletarian literature',[24] told of the maltreatment of a Chinese worker-student overseas and kindled Guo's patriotism. His most vivid memory is of a magazine, *The Illustrated Student* (*Qimeng Huabao*), which featured illustrated biographies of Napoleon and Bismarck, both of whom fired his imagination and became his childhood gods. When he read that Bismarck liked dogs, he began to call his own household dogs to follow him whenever he went in or out, fondly imagining himself as 'Bismarck of the East'.[25]

Most remarkable of all is Guo Moruo's description of his adolescence and his adolescent reading. At a time of violent transformation in China, the time of the spiritual awakening of his generation, he too underwent violent personal changes. The first symptoms were at seven or eight years of age. One day, towards the end of Spring, he excused himself from the schoolroom and went to the garden where he saw a young woman seated among the bamboo; he was 'pierced with a sense of beauty and a violent desire to caress the soft, tender, pink hand'.[26] In this incident he saw his first sign of sexual awakening although, to an outside observer, he seemed merely a child. At about eleven years of age, he was so completely overwhelmed by the onset of puberty that nothing contented him. During exercises on a mat with a bamboo pole, he had a delicious sensation followed by an extraordinary lassitude—like a fruit squeezed dry—and he constantly tried to retrieve it. At this time he happened upon books in his brother's collection, erotic books of the same sort that Tealeaf bought for Baoyu in *Dream of the Red Chamber*:

> *Story of the Western Chamber*
> *Beautiful Stories of Western Lake*
> *Reflections of the Moon Among the Flowers*

The first was a forbidden book but he found it so suggestive that his fingers became busy while reading and he 'unwittingly arrives at the third stage of this development'.[27] His sister-in-law told on him (for the books, not the busy fingers, so we must assume that if she did not read them she was at least familiar with the titles) and he received a stern scolding from his mother—to no avail.

His hostility towards his childhood and available reading materials is striking:

> These physiological changes are inevitable and, from their onset, all that can be done is to remove anything which causes excitement. Children's books are obviously important and, looking back, I am afraid that the saintly writings and venerable classics which we daily read in class. . . must bear a heavy responsibility for the early sexual awakening of both myself and my contemporaries.[28]

He claims that bad books do not stop at novels. Even *The Three Character Classic* is unhealthy, according to Guo Moruo, and one passage which was supposed to stimulate boys' zeal for virtue by offering models did, in fact, the opposite and aroused their ardor by drawing attention to sexual differences. The offending passage was:

> Cai Wenji was able to judge from the lute
> Xie Taoyun was able to compose verses;
> They were only girls yet they were quick and clever.
> You boys ought to rouse yourselves.[29]

In this case, Giles' translation of *jing* (meaning, to warn) as 'rouse' is particularly apt. 'Girl' has become a four letter word.

Apart from the factual description of his childhood, Guo Moruo's method of presentation is a product of a later period in Chinese history: the May Fourth Period (1919–36). He was, after all, writing in retrospect. But his own experiences, like those of his generation, were formative in the later recognition of the special characteristics of childhood and the demand for an indigenous children's literature.

Guo Moruo's narrative differs from the depiction of Baoyu's childhood in *Dream of the Red Chamber* in several important ways: acknowledgement of childhood as a concept; complete rejection of the Confucian classics as 'immoral'; and recognition of children's separate needs for their own reading material. These were fundamental in building a modern, vernacular children's literature.

First, Guo Moruo recognizes stages in his childhood development that are not only personal to him, but are also general attributes of childhood and adolescence. While he has, as a touchstone, a vivid, chronological and sensual memory of his own growth, he also claims that these changes are 'physiological' and 'inevitable'. In Baoyu's case, they are personal and particular.

Second, while hostility towards Confucian texts was articulated by his own generation at a later date, Guo, like Zhou Zuoren, Ba Jin (and, indeed, Baoyu), can relate this hostility to his own childhood feelings—be they horror or boredom, spiritual starvation or sexual stimulation. Yet Guo Moruo's generation, unlike Baoyu, extended this hostility to the entire Confucian canon and to traditional teaching methods.

Third, it seems no accident that these boys should accidentally read from the rich store of popular and erotic literature during their adolescence—Zhou Zuoren at fourteen, Guo Moruo with the onset of puberty and, as a fictional example, Baoyu during a period of discontent. They were curious about themselves, they were reaching out, and they wanted to know about the world around them. Baoyu escaped into popular literature. Guo Moruo's contemporaries later claimed in the twenties that children needed their own literature: 'food for the spirit', books which would satisfy both their imagination and their craving for knowledge. In this sense the writers were implicitly referring to older children. When we look at the first children's works translated from the West they were (apart from nursery tales like *Little Red Riding Hood*) for the age group between childhood and youth, which we call adolescence, and the Chinese now call *shaonian*. Stories by Verne, Defoe and Swift are not for little children; they were not written for children at all. They have become children's books because they are gripping stories. As to whether these stories allay adolescent ardor, as Guo Moruo would like, that is a question no one has answered.

Clearly, the understanding of childhood and children's literature, propagated by Guo Moruo's generation in the May Fourth period, was not merely an abstraction relating to an ideal vision of Chinese society. This understanding was rooted firmly in these writers' own early experiences.

May Fourth Children's Literature

The May Fourth period takes its name from a mass political demonstration in Beijing on May 4, 1919. It rallied against the then Beiping (the Nationalist name for Beijing) government which had complied with a term of the Treaty of Versailles after World War I that China cede the province of Shandong, previously held by Germany, to Japan. This initial demonstration was the forerunner of many more rallies, attacking both foreign imperialism and China's weakness. But it was much more. As Goldman puts it,

> It stimulated and galvanized an incipient cultural movement, growing since the late nineteenth century, that was directed at throwing off the weight of China's Confucian tradition and absorbing Western culture. This cultural movement culminated in the early decades of the twentieth century in a literary flowering that was one of the most creative and brilliant episodes in modern Chinese history.[30]

Children's literature is a neglected part of this 'literary flowering' even though, or perhaps because, it was created by the same writers who fashioned a new, adult literature. Lu Xun, Zhou Zuoren, Ye Shengtao, Bing Xin, Zhang Tianyi, Mao Dun, Ba Jin and Lao She make an awesome list. But before children's literature could flower, the older of these writers—as we have seen with Guo Morou—argued for the need for an indigenous children's literature on the basis of changed concepts of childhood, education and reading.

Zhou Zuoren (1885–1967) was an influential figure in modern Chinese literature and a leading spokesperson for humanist literature. He was also the first to point out publicly, as early as 1913, that China, unlike the West, lacked a literature specifically for children and that China and its children suffered because of this lack. He subsequently became China's first major theorist in the field.[31]

Yet whereas both Lu Xun and Zhou Zuoren were both influential theorists and writers, Lu Xun has been deified in China while Zhou Zuoren has been dismissed. For years Zhou suffered the officially-sanctioned dual stigma of accusations that he was both a reactionary and a Japanese collaborator. Consequently, his work has been misrepresented. In post-Mao China, however, some of the stigma has been lifted as scholars have attempted to reassess Zhou Zuoren's contribution to modern Chinese children's literature. This is a crucial step because of his importance in shaping the early contours and directions of the field.

In fact, Lu Xun and Zhou Zuoren shared many common assumptions about children's literature. Both agreed that Confucian classics were dull reading, about as welcome as a sermon on a sunny afternoon. They were also ineffective.

> I owe it almost completely to the reading of novels that I mastered the reading of literary Chinese. The classics were really of no assistance at all.[32]

The brothers also agreed on the necessity for a new, inspiring children's literature and included a fairytale by Hans Christian Andersen in their joint book of translations (1909) as well as collecting regional children's songs from 1911 onwards.

Most important, they shared assumptions of a world of childhood which they identified in evolutionary terms. In Zhou Zuoren's words, '[t]he discovery of childhood (and women!)'

was 'a consequence of discovering the true nature of man'.[33] This 'true nature' came from an understanding of evolution. In 1920, in 'Children's Literature' ('Ertong de Wenxue'), he wrote:

> Formerly, men did not properly understand children, if not treating them as miniature adults to be nurtured by the classics, then ignoring them as ignorant and incomplete small people. Only recently have we known that, although children are somewhat biologically and psychologically different from adults, they are still complete individuals with their own inner and outer life.[34]

From here, Lu Xun and Zhou Zuoren's emphasis on children diverges. Lu Xun commonly analyzes the biological and social role of children in Darwinian terms, their 'outer life'. Zhou Zuoren is interested in their 'inner life'; he explores children's psychology and their growth, or evolution, into adulthood and insists on a separate world of childhood that is long-lasting and independent of other life phases.

> While the twenty or more years of childhood are in one sense a preparation for adulthood they also have their own significance and value. Because life is constant development, we cannot point to any one stage as the real one. I suggest we accept each stage of life—growth, maturity, old age and death—as all (equally) significant. We must reject both the misrepresentation of children as miniature adults and the view that childhood has no independent existence.[35]

It is this insistence on childhood as a stage with its own special characteristics and needs which was, and still is, the rationale for a distinctive children's literature.

Lu Xun gave these new ideas their scientific rationale and articulated them within a larger social vision at the level of the family. In 'How We Should Be Fathers Today' ('Women Xianzai Zenmo Zuo Fuqin') in 1919, he used evolution as the yard-stick to measure the child's survival chances in China. He found that the constraints and submission imposed by the old family system through rigid adherence to tradition led to stultification and extinction. The way of the natural world was one of change, adaptability and reproduction for the continuation of a species into the future, while the way of Chinese society was superstitious, inflexible, attuned to the past and forced children to sacrifice themselves for the older generation. Both physically and morally, Lu Xun claimed, this was unnatural. In his eyes Chinese society went backward, not forward. Children had to be 'liberated' if they were to survive as the future architects of a strong China.

> The emancipation of children is something that is so natural that it should need no discussion but the elder generation has been too poisoned by the old customs and ideas ever to come to its senses. . . . Burdened as a man may be with the weight of tradition, he can yet prop open the gates of darkness with his shoulder to let children through to the bright, wide-open spaces, to lead happy lives henceforth as real human beings.[36]

Lu Xun also looked at Chinese society in his short story that began the literary renaissance, 'A Madman's Diary' ('Kuangren Riji'), in 1918. The madman sees that beneath the veneer of Virtue and Morality lurks a nightmare world of suspicion and fear, 'a place where for four thousand years they have been eating human flesh'.[37] In the preceding essay Chinese society is judged 'unnatural'; in this story Confucian morality is, itself, immoral. The madman cries that 'perhaps there are children who have not eaten human flesh. Save, save the children'.[38] Save them from what? From the savage superstition of Confucian beliefs. From the madness and immorality of Chinese tradition. From retrogression and, ultimately, extinction. Lu Xun's is pleading to allow children to grow to form a society of 'real' people.

The concept which informs these seemingly dissimilar works by Lu Xun is Darwinian. Applied to China, the survival chances of traditional society are, in terms of natural laws, not very promising. But, more than this, his analysis is charged with an emotional symbolism that was rampant in the Maoist era and is still used today: Confucian society is 'man-eating' and the future belongs to children. Within these two poles, books have a part to play. Old society warped the powers of imagination, wonder and curiosity of its people at an early age. According to Darwin, these are faculties which have been of inestimable service to man for his progressive advancement'.[39] It was these very powers which Lu Xun claimed were natural in children and which books, be they about science, mathematics, history or literature, should stimulate and develop.[40] Their part is shown in Figure 1.1 Lu Xun's Schema for Social Evolution.

In Lu Xun's social schema, the enlightened citizen is poised between the Dark and the Light. It is his or her duty to prop open the 'Gates of Darkness' and 'let children through to the bright, wide-open spaces'. To save China, one must first save the children.

Figure 1.1 Lu Xun's Schema for Social Evolution

Darkness	Light
Past Confucian Society	Future Rational Society
Older Generation	Children
Poisonous Superstition	Science
Stultifying Books	Liberating Books
Madness	Happiness
Retrogression	Progress
('a suicidal turning back')	('the path of evolution')

Lu Xun's analysis was developed by other writers in the twenties. Explicitly or implicitly, they completely reject Confucianism, including traditional texts and approaches to child-raising, and insist on scientific attitudes towards children which recognize children's special characteristics and their distinctive needs.

A major Western influence in this regard was John Dewey, who was invited to China in 1919 and lectured in various cities for two years. A central topic of his lectures was children and their education. One of Dewey's first public talks was on the nature of childhood which he considered 'the natural foundation of education'.[41] Dewey's philosophy espoused a child-centered education system which attacked authoritarian, passive and mechanical teaching methods. He thus offered reformers a ready-made recipe for confronting the bulwark of Confucian education:

> The change which is coming into our education is the shifting of the center of gravity. It is a change, a revolution not unlike that introduced by Copernicus when the astronomical center shifted from the earth to the sun. In this case the child becomes the sun about which the appliances of education revolve, he is the center. . .[42]

These notions of a child-centered (ertong zhongxinlun) education and of a 'world of childhood' (ertong benweilun), separate from later stages in life, were to become two of the most controversial issues in the following fifty years of children's literature. Zhou Zuoren was castigated as a representative of the bourgeoisie because he espoused these notions. As Zheng and Fan show, however, these notions were also assumptions in the works of China's leading Marxist writers: Lu Xun, Guo Moruo, and Ye Shengtao, for example.[43] And without these notions there is no rationale for the children's literature which exploded on the urban scene in the twenties and thirties.

There was, as Lu Xun wrote, 'a children's world'.[44] This is explored in more detail in Chapter 2. The influential Beijing newspaper Supplement to Morning Post (Chenbao Fukan), published from 1921 to 1929, contains a fascinating miscellany of articles on Western practice and ideas that explore the many dimensions of this subject: conception, childbirth, breast feeding, bottle feeding, children's development, the family, children's hygiene (including the preservation of teeth and the prevention of infectious diseases), public parks for play, toys, child psychology, children's dreams, kindergarten, education and, of course, children's books. The topics seem both endless and undiscriminating but they are bound by an explicit purpose: to promote understanding of child and hence lay the foundation for a modern Chinese state.

The issue of children was first raised in the context of the home, as in Lu Xun's article of 1919. So it was with children's literature. The words *ertong wenxue*, meaning 'children's literature', were first used in an article on women and children's problems in *New Youth (Xin Qingnian)* in 1918. The term quickly gained acceptance without severing the cord which bound it to other social areas, in particular those connected with the home. Thus it was the influential *Women's Magazine (Funu Zazhi)* that became best-known for its folk tales for children in the twenties, while *Supplement to Morning Post*, a general supplement, was most famous for its 'literary fairy tales', a Chinese language term first used by Zhou Zuoren and which signified these fairytales were intended for a wider audience than children only.[45] Nevertheless, it is often the general magazines which most clearly record changing ideas relating to children, as in the case of *Supplement to Morning Post* where even the organization of the magazine's content shows the growing complexity of topics concerning children, including literature. These topics were first raised in the Home section of the general weekend supplement. Later, children's literature had its own section in a special Home supplement. Later again, the Home supplement was divided into the Women's Supplement and the Children's Supplement, called *Ertong*.

This gradual specialization did not mean that children or their literature were isolated from other areas of Chinese society but that children were increasingly treated as complex and crucial components of China's social organization.

> The home. The home. . . Children are the central figures in a home. . . (In old China they said:) Order the home and then govern the country, govern the country and then the world will be at peace.[46]

This writer goes on to look at the evolution of the home (not the home in terms of social evolution, as with Lu Xun) and claims its basis was in the child's need for maternal support and paternal guidance. He also claims this process was partly disguised in traditional China when the family also functioned as an economic organization, but this structure had disintegrated recently and many home responsibilities had been taken over by the State. Once again his transfiguration is clear: 'the child is the basis of the family and the family is the basis of the State. Therefore, the question of children is not just a children's question but a social question which we must not underestimate'.[47] In this logic, the political significance of children is implied.

Children's literature was a major focus of the new interest in children. Compared to children in other countries, what had Chinese children had to read? The answer was almost nothing, except for boring old books, dry as dust, that bound children with the fetters of a dead language to a moribund culture. The new interest inspired recognition that children needed stimulating, exciting books in the easily accessible vernacular language, books that opened children's minds and their imaginations. The model was Western children's literature and it became official policy to introduce Western works in translation. Although translations were not expected to be faithful to the original until the May Fourth period, they began to trickle across urban China in the 1900s, reaching flood proportions by the twenties. Because of poor records and the staggering number of translations, it is almost impossible to give a precise chronological record of these translations even in the early stages, and we must rely on snippets of information found in various articles.

According to an article in *Literature (Wenxue)* in 1933, the first translation meant specifically for children was of a Western fairytale (was it 'Tom Thumb' or another fairytale? The writer was unclear) and the first editor of children's literature in China was Sun Yuxiu, who 'retold' fairytales from the West.[48] In this account we are not given timings of these developments. However, Chinese writers in the fifties traced a beginning to Lu Xun's translation of Jules Verne's *From the Moon to the Earth* (1903) and *Journey to the Center of the Earth* (1906). They should have mentioned, but did not, that Zhou Zuoren also translated Oscar Wilde's *The Happy Prince* at this time. Despite the haphazard recall, early translations, not necessarily in the vernacular, which later writers remember as important include:

Daniel Defoe, *Robinson Crusoe* (summarized in three chapters)
Fairytales by the Brothers Grimm and Perrault
Jonathan Swift, *The Little Match Girl, The Emperor's New Clothes*
Leo Tolstoy, *Three Questions, The Seed as Big as an Egg*[49]
Oscar Wilde, *The Happy Prince*

If we include Verne's works when we consider this list, we find the selection of children's books for translation was not random. Works chosen for translation were those best known in Western children's literature. No-one could argue convincingly against Tolstoy's literary importance and the formative influence on fairytales of Perrault, the Brothers Grimm, Andersen and Wilde. The works by Defoe and Swift were two of the three most famous in the eighteenth century emergence of the children's book trade in England although, like Verne's stories, they were not originally intended for children.[50] But why not translate the third most famous work, *Pilgrim's Progress*? This suggests some selection criteria, however ill-defined and unstated.

It could be argued that the Chinese would obviously translate the 'best known' works. Yet when we consider what was not translated, it appears that the selection criteria were not what appealed to Western readers but what applied to China's circumstances and rising nationalism. It seems the starting point was society. Translators were interested in Western human and social traditions. Given their experience of Western imperialism, the Chinese were not interested in the West's influential Christian tradition which, we have already seen, was depicted as the cloak of colonialism. Hence, Chinese did not translate the third of the eighteenth-century English best-sellers, *Pilgrim's Progress*, the Christian allegory by Bunyan. Not many of the 'good, godly' Puritan books for children were translated. Verne probably appealed because, as one nineteenth century European critic wrote about Verne's works, 'Someone has been left out'.[51] That Someone was God. This eschewal of Christianity is confirmed in the trend of literature and translations for children which Lu Xun led until his death in 1936: from Society to Socialism, from Verne to Gorky.

Homegrown children's literature, born in the twenties, reflected the preoccupations of the May Fourth period: to modernize and enlighten Chinese society. Some of the earliest published work was a collection of regional children's rhymes which, as part of China's rich, oral tradition, were legitimized through the precedent set by the Grimms and Lang. Ye Shengtao melded fairytale with social realism in the first book of this modern literature, *The Scarecrow* (*Daocaoren*), published in 1921. Bing Xin's famous *Letters to Young Readers* (*Ji Xiao Duzhe,* 1923–26), are more sentimental and tender; they are colored by her golden memories of the idylls of childhood, her romantic view of the 'children's world' (see Chapter 3.)

A work that contains both the realism and the romanticism inherent in children's literature of the time is Xiong Foxi's play, *The God of Children (Tongshen)*. It is about, not specifically for, children. This play was written in 1927, not from idealized sympathy with children, but from pity for the ugly realities of their modern lives. The force, the core of the play, is this ugliness juxtaposed against the May Fourth ideal of childhood: Lu Xun's schema of dark against light (Figure 2.1). Act 1 of the play portrays both the Confucian and the romantic ideals: an old couple and a teacher plead with the God to give them children to continue the rites and pass on their knowledge and culture. This is the Confucian ideal. The God agrees and changes two stars from the night sky into plump, healthy children who come joyfully to earth:

In the skies are clouds and moon,
In the earth are flowers;
Clouds and moon soon disperse,
Flowers quickly fade.
Only our simplicity
Flowers for eternity;
Only our spirit
Progresses for ever. . .[52]

In Act 2, the God finds that the original good intentions of the elderly couple are debased and the children are defiled; gone is the spirit of childhood—the joy, the health, the naivete, the hope, the promise of progress. The children know only how to smoke opium in a dark, sordid room. The God takes the children away because humanity does not deserve them.

Now we will return
Now we will for ever bid farewell to Man.[53]

The play summarizes the views of contemporary reformers on the state of children in Chinese society. Despite the best intentions of parents, children live sullied, sordid lives. As faded flowers, they live within Lu Xun's 'Gates of Darkness'. Undeserved by society, the children in the play are taken away and, of course, without children there is no family, no continuity and, eventually, no China.

Conclusion

Over a short time, the child emerged from the confines of Confucian education—from assumed mental insufficiency—to become a topic of unprecedented literary interest and a key instrument for social reform. These changed attitudes came from deep within the cauldron of ideas that inspired modern Chinese society. They followed logically from changes in education, the formalization of text books and new attitudes to both women and the home.

But there was more than this. Romantically, the child was a symbol of light, hope and progress, of Darwinian 'naturalness' in a society that many Chinese viewed with despair and shame. And perhaps there is a hint of Rousseau, for, in the child, lay the perfect image of the Chinese citizen as yet untainted by the artificial strictures of Confucianism. Pragmatically, then, the child had been placed at the basis of social organization and at the threshold of the future. Hence, China could not move forward as long as the child was bound by false bonds, oppressed by social injustice and neglected through a total misunderstanding of his or her nature. In this light children became the perfect image for Chinese reformers: in children's 'liberation' lay China's salvation.

Children's literature was to be both a symbol and cause of this liberation.

Notes

1. Translated by Giles, H., *San Tzu Ching* (Taipei, 1972). There have been many versions throughout Chinese history; the earliest was by Wang Yinglin (1223–96) in the Song Dynasty.

2. The familiar version was written at the beginning of the Song Dynasty (960–1279 A.D.).

3. The familiar version was edited in the *Nanbei Chao*, 535–43 A.D.

4. Giles, H., *San Tzu Ching*, op. cit., pp. 51–2, 60–1.

5. The name of the editor is controversial, but it is probably Liu Kezhuang (1187–1269).

6. These probably began in the Yuan Dynasty (1279–1368). They are collections of short prose stories mainly taken from history.

7. Zhu Xi (1130–1200), 'Xiaoxue', quoted in Zhang Zhigong, *Chuantong Yuyan Jiaoyu Chutan* (Shanghai, 1962), p. 89.

8. *The Book of Rites*, IX:24, quoted in Croll, E., *Feminism and Socialism in China* (London, 1978), p. 13. *The Book of Rites*, supposedly revised by Confucius (551–479 B.C.), is one of the five Confucian classics.

9. Croll, E., *Feminism and Socialism in China*, op. cit., p. 13.

10. Cao Xueqin, *The Story of the Stone*, Vol. 1, translated by Hawkes, D. (Harmondsworth, 1973), p. 462.

11. Ibid., p. 464.

12. Aries, P., *Centuries of Childhood*, translated by Baldick, B. (Edinburgh, 1962), p. 128.

13. Cao Xueqin, op cit., pp. 53–4.

14. The fullest outline of the development and use of traditional children's texts is by Zhang Zhigong, *Chuantong Yuyan Jiaoyu Chutan*, op cit.

15. Chen Bochui, *Ertong Wenxue Jianlun* (Wuhan, 1959), p. 33.

16. Chesneaux, J., *The Political and Social Ideas of Jules Verne*, translated by Wikeley, T. (London, 1972), p. 23. This is an 1866 outline of Verne's plan by his publisher, Hetzel.

17. Zhang Zhigong, op. cit., p. 21.

18.   Hayward Scott, D., *Chinese Popular Literature and the Child* (Chicago, 1980), p. 110.

19.   Zhou Zuoren, 'Jinghua Lu', in *Zijide Yuandi* (Shanghai, 1923), p. 147.

20.   Lang, O., *Ba Jin and His Writings* (Cambridge, Mass., 1967), p. 16.

21.   Guo Moruo, *Shaonian Shidai: Wode Tongnian,* (Shanghai, 1953), p. 39.

22.   Ibid., pp. 57–8.

23.   'Zhongguo Chubanjie zhi Xianshi Yibie', *Zhongxuesheng,* 41, (January, 1934), p. 1.

24.   Guo Moruo, *Shaonian Shidai: Wode Tongnian,* op. cit., p. 41.

25.   Ibid.

26.   Ibid., p. 51.

27.   Ibid., p. 53.

28.   Ibid.

29.   Ibid., translated in Giles, H., *San Tzu Ching,* op cit., pp. 137–9.

30.   Goldman, M. (ed.), *Modern Chinese Literature in the May Fourth Era* (Cambridge, Mass., and London, 1977), p. 1.

31.   Zhen Guangzhong and Fan Qilong, 'Zhou Zuoren yu Ertong yu Ertong wenxue', *Sichuan Shifan Daxue Xuebao,* Vol. 4, 1986, p. 40. As far as I know, there is no list or collection of Zhou Zuoren's essays on children's literature. From my own readings, the following are his most important works. This does not include his translations.

'Tonghua Yanjiu' (1912)
'Tonghua Lilun' (1913)
'Ertong de Wenxue' (1920) in *Zijide Yuandi* (1923)
'Alisi Manyou Qijing Ji'
'Wangerde Tonghua'
'Gesong Ertong de Wenxue'
'Ertong Ju'
'Ertong de Shu' in *Tan Long Ji* (1927)
'Andesen de "Shi zhi Jiu"'
'Lu Shen de "Yan Xiaoer Yu"'
'Tan "Tongyao Daguan"'
'Du "Gesheng Tongyao Ji"' in *Tanhu Ji* (1927)
'Guanyu Ertong de Shu'
'Du Ertong Shijie Zhouji'
'Chaoxian Tonghuaji Xu' in *Kan Yun Ji* (1932)
'Ertong Gushi Xu' in *Kucha Suibi* (1935)
'Ershi de Huiji' in *Kuzhu Zaji* (1936)
'Shaoxing Erge Shulue Xu' in *Fengyu Tan* (1936)

32.   Zhou Zuoren, 'Xiaoshu de Huiyi', *Zhitang Yiyu Wenbian* (Hong Kong, 1961), p. 9, cited in Wolff, E., *Chou Tso-jen* (New York, 1971), p. 17.

33.   Zhen Guangzhong et al., 'Zhou Zuoren yu Ertong Wenxue', op cit., p. 40.

34.   Zhou Zuoren, 'Ertong de Wenxue', in Huang Zhiqing (ed.), *Zhou Zuoren Lunwenji* (Hong Kong, 1972), p. 44.

35.   Ibid., p. 44.

36.   Lu Xun, 'Women Xianzai Zenme Zuo Fuqin', *Lu Xun Quanji,* op. cit., p. 117.

37.   Lu Xun, 'Kuangren Riji', *Lu Xun Quanji,* op. cit., p. 291.

38.   Ibid.

39. Darwin, C., 'The Descent of Man', in *The Origin of the Species and the Descent of Man* (New York, publication year not recorded), p. 468.

40. Lu Xun, 'Kantu Shizi', *Lu Xun Quanji*, op. cit., p. 43.

41. From the first of a three-lecture series, 'Jiaoyu tianran di jichu' quoted in Keenan, B., *The Dewey Experiment in China: Educational Reform and Political Power in the Early Republic* (Cambridge, Mass. and London, 1977), p. 42.

42. Dewey, J., 'The School and the Life of the Child', in *Dewey on Education*, with an Introduction and Notes by Martin S. Dworkin (New York, 1959), pp. 52–3.

43. Zheng Guangzhong et al., 'Zhou Zuoren yu Ertong Wenxue', op. cit., p. 43.

44. Lu Xun, 'Women Xianzai Zenme Zuo Fuqin', *Lun Xun Quanji*, op. cit., p. 125.

45. Zhao Jingshen, *Tonghua Lunji* (Shanghai, 1929), pp. 1–2.

46. Xu Xingkai, 'Ertong yu Jiating, Ertong Yanjiu zhi Yi', *Chenbao Fukan*, 17 January 1926, p. 7.

47. Ibid.

48. Jiang, 'Guanyu Ertong', *Wenxue*, IV, 1 December 1935, p. 274.

49. For example, Chen Bochui, *Ertong Wenxue Jianlun*, op. cit., p. 34.

50. Darton, F. J. H., *Children's Books in England: Five Centuries of Social Life*, op. cit., p. 8.

51. Chesneaux, J., *The Political and Social Ideas of Jules Verne*, op. cit., p. 68.

52. Xiong Foxi, 'Tongshen II', *Chenbao Fukan*, 20 November 1927, p. 6.

53. Xiong Foxi, 'Tongshen III', *Chenbao Fukan*, 27 November 1927, p. 2.

2

Lu Xun
and the World of Children

Lu Xun, the pen-name of Zhou Shuren (1881–1936), is China's most famous modern writer. This often obscures the fact that, in China, he is also regarded as the most influential figure in the development of Chinese children's literature. This chapter, therefore, narrows the focus to a detailed study of Lu Xun's writings on children and their literature between 1903 and 1936. The purpose is to examine more closely Lu Xun's views on childhood and his contribution to the field of modern Chinese children's literature.

More than any other May Fourth writer, Lu Xun was responsible for establishing 'the child' as a political symbol of China's future. His first vernacular short story, 'A Madman's Diary', ended with the now famous cry: 'save the children'. Lu Xun's concept of children as the future is central to an understanding of both this story and his fiction in general. His conception of children was to become a keynote in the subsequent history of Chinese children's literature. Lu Xun, as we have said, saw himself standing between two worlds, pointing the way for children to move from the Old to the New, from a dark Past to a sunlit Future 'to lead happy lives as real human beings'.

But this brave new world, in the Shakespearean sense, belonged to more than children; it was the direction for the Chinese nation. For Lu Xun, to 'save the children' meant ultimately to 'save' China. The rationale is simple: children are the adults of tomorrow and their environment determines the future of the people. As Lu Xun said, the future belongs to them or, as Mao Zedong said three decades later, foreshortening the same idea, 'the world belongs to them' (*shijie shi nimende*).[1]

Lu Xun insisted that the '"world of children" (*ertong shijie*) is completely different from that of adults'.[2] He rejected traditional upbringing as based on the mistaken notion that children were 'little adults'.[3] Indeed much of his May Fourth writing treats this theme. His typical image of Confucian education is that of a dark prison where the walls cut out the brightness of the real world. The inmates were either swaggering tyrants within their own petty domains, or obedient slaves with bent heads and blank expressions. When they are let out 'they are like small birds freed for a moment from a cage. They cannot fly, hop or sing.'[4]

Along with other May Fourth reformers, Lu Xun argued for the 'emancipation' of children. This was to be achieved through a new and caring education. Education for Lu Xun, was to become more child-centered than previously in China; he advocated a guided awakening rather than forced instruction. His essays on the subject include areas such as teaching, reading, study, home life, food and play.

A new literature for children was to be essential for their emancipation. Although Lu Xun did not write specifically *for* children, he translated selected Western children's stories as models for progressive Chinese writers in the field. In the early May Fourth period (1919–27) these translated works are fairytales. Their central theme is the innocent child at one with nature; in other words, the European notion of the romantic child. In this context, Lu Xun contrasts the prison of orthodoxy with a natural world of childhood delight. Hope resides in China's young.

In the later May Fourth period (1927–36), Lu Xun rejected this romantic notion as idealistic. Instead, he translated examples of Marxist children's stories in which children, not unlike adults, are the oppressed in an unjust, class-ridden society. While children's literature still remained a central interest, his focus shifts from theoretical concepts of childhood to the actual conditions of children in China. He was a key figure, for example, in introducing and critiquing popular literature, such as comic books, for China's illiterate young who formed the vast majority of China's children (Chapter 5). In this period he also took great care in the selection of illustrations for his translated stories.

Lu Xun's view of childhood, therefore, rests on the understanding that it is different from adulthood: it is a separate world that must be respected. Children must be liberated so that they can develop their potential, surpass past generations and enrich future Chinese society.

However, the world of children's literature as Lu Xun conceived it, was never separate from the larger world of China. It touched this larger world at every point, its fluid boundaries changed with social pressures, it was nurtured inside as both seed and successor. Here we have the one recurring theme in the theory of Chinese children's literature: it must never forsake its social role and educational responsibility for these were its life blood. Lu Xun is a founding father and still an essential reference precisely because he locked his views on children and their literature into a wider social vision.

When Lu Xun's view on society changed, so too did his view on suitable books for children. A study of Lu Xun's writings reveals that his perspective moved from a traditional Chinese upbringing, through a belief in science as modernizer, with the young as the means of social reform, to a final commitment to Marxist revolution. This evolution of his thought represents the general trend in Chinese modern history. Mao Zedong was later to write that 'the road [Lu Xun] took was the very road of China's new national culture'.[5]

In this sense, Lu Xun's views on childhood and the role of children's literature emerge as a significant issue in the history of modern China.

Lu Xun and Translations of Western Children's Literature

Lu Xun did not actually write for children; he wrote about children and children's books but, with some notable exceptions, most of his opinions are scattered throughout his stories and essays and do not specifically address the subject of children. He did, however, translate foreign children's books and, from his many translations, those which are now claimed as part of the

Table 2.1 Lu Xun's Translations According to Historical Period

Year	Period	Author	Title	Form	Style
1903	End of the Qing Dynasty	Jules Verne (France)	*From The Earth to the Moon (Yueje Luxing)*	Science Fiction	Translated into the classical language and rearranged into a Chinese format.
1906	End of the Qing Dynasty	Jules Verne	*Journey to the Centre of the Earth (Didi Luxing)*	Science Fiction	Translated into the classical language and rearranged into a Chinese format.
1922	Early May Fourth Period	Vasily Eroshenko (Russia)	*Collection of Eroshenko's Fairy-tales (Eluoxianke Tonghua Ji)*	Fairytale	Translated into vernacular strictly according to the original. Part of China's new vernacular literature.
1922	Early May Fourth Period	Vasily Eroshenko	*Peach-colored Clouds (Taose de Yun)*	Fairytale play	Translated into the Chinese vernacular strictly according to the original.
1927	Later May Fourth Period	Frederick van Eeden (Holland)	*Little Johannes (Xiao Yuehan)*	Fairytale	Translated into the Chinese vernacular strictly according to the original.
1928	Later May Fourth Period	Hermynia zur Muhlen (Hungary)	*Little Peter (Xiao Pide)*	Fairytale	Translated into the Chinese vernacular strictly according to the original.
1935	Later May Fourth Period	L. Panteleev (USSR)	*The Watch (Biao)*	Fairytale	Translated into the Chinese vernacular strictly according to the original.
1935	Later May Fourth Period	Maxim Gorky (USSR)	*Russian Fairytales (Eluosi de Tonghua)*	Fairytale*	Part of the development of revolutionary literature with an emphasis on social classes.

*Called fairytales, really national character sketches.

history of modern Chinese children's literature are shown in Table 2.1.[6]

Two points emerge from this list. First, Lu Xun intended none of these translations to be for Chinese children. Only *The Watch* was originally intended for children aged over ten, as well as teachers, parents, writers and other interested people, but even in this case Lu Xun wrote in the preface that he was unable to use the simple language which would suit them. Even so, the translated works represent the direction in which progressive children's literature was to develop. In 1936 Chen Bochui searched for Verne's *Two Years on Vacation* to retranslate for Chinese children and in 1956 more of Verne's books were translated into Chinese as part of an upsurge of interest in science fiction for the young. Translations of Eroshenko's fairytales influenced Chinese fairytale writers and embodied the romantic idea of childhood current in the early May Fourth period. *Little Johannes* by van Eeden, where Johannes leaves the fairytale world of childhood for the sterner, real world of humanity, marks a turning point in the social implications of the fairytale. The stories by zur Muhlen and Panteleev were models for socially committed, Marxist children's literature in the thirties as part of the Communist commitment to a Russian-style revolution in China. Gorky's *Russian Fairytales* are not fairytales at all but short sketches of different facets of the Russian character and were certainly not meant for children. However, Maxim Gorky himself was the major spokesman on a new Soviet children's literature after the 1917 revolution and, in China, his work was held up as the Marxist model for children's literature between the mid-thirties and 1960.

The second observation from this list (Table 2.1) relates to the selection of these works. The most obvious restriction was the availability of works in the two foreign languages he knew, Japanese and German, as Lu Xun usually translated through translations. Sometimes he simultaneously used translations in both these languages. He acquired these books in different ways: accidentally finding one in a bookstore, for example, or ordering another from Germany after reading a review in a German literary magazine. Nevertheless, he read widely and did not translate indiscriminately from European literature. He chose works as examples of progressive Western thought to inform Chinese writers and educators rather than for Chinese children to read. But the main selection criterion seems to have been the social implications of each book, for according to his statement in each preface, a translation was always linked to his own analysis of the needs of Chinese society at that time.

Lu Xun believed that translations played an important part in the liberation of people's minds from the yoke of Confucianism, by shattering the shell of China's cultural isolation and offering stimulation, challenge and new truths in the most pleasantly digestible form of all: literature. The controversies, virulent factional fighting, adulation and even murder which is so much part of modern literature in China, has exactly the same general cause as the fighting between the various political parties and groups: extract the egos and personal histories of the main protagonists and the arguments center on how to save China and what sort of ideology can legitimately build and govern a new society. The world of children and their literature, which includes these eight translations by Lu Xun, was part of the same argument and was not so very different from the world of adults. Immediately, therefore, these works are pointers to the road ahead for China. They move beyond 'the world of children' to the future world of people, which he so often said belonged to children: 'the future is the era of our sons and grandsons'.[7]

These translations belong to three distinct periods in Chinese history, three distinctive literary styles and they span Lu Xun's entire literary career. In the following sections these translations are analyzed within the framework of a chronological survey of Lu Xun's works which are relevant to children's literature. These sections are organized according to the three periods: End of the Qing Dynasty, Early May Fourth Period and Later May Fourth Period.

Lu Xun's Early Translations in the Qing Dynasty

In 1903, at the age of twenty-two, Lu Xun embarked on his literary career with two translations from Jules Verne's collection of science fiction, *Extraordinary Voyages* (*Voyages Extraordinaires*).[8] The translations were of *From the Earth to the Moon* and *Journey to the Center of the Earth*.

He borrowed from Verne to popularize science through fiction; only in fictional dress can it 'seep into the brain and not become boring'.[9] At a time when he was pondering the roots of China's backwardness and ideal types of human nature, science offered an exciting road into Western culture. He recognised an obvious lack of interest in science in traditional Chinese culture which for him explained China's lack of progress. To Lu Xun this was the crucial difference between advanced Western societies and primitive China:

> Our national fiction is full of works dealing with the sentimental, historical, satirical and bizarre. Only science fiction is as rare as a unicorn's horn. This is one reason for the backwardness of our knowledge. Therefore, if we want to fill this gap in today's world of translations, and lead the Chinese people to progress, then we must start with science fiction.[10]

Where better to start than with Verne, one of the most popular storywriters in the nineteenth century and the pioneer of science fiction (as distinct from science fantasy) in the West? As observed to Verne in the introduction of the 1959 edition of *Journal to the Center of the Earth*:

> Verne's great contribution to literature was his realization that the actualities of science could be as exciting and romantic as the magic of Sinbad in *Arabian Nights*. The strength of his stories was that even when his head was in the clouds, his feet were firmly on the ground. . .
>
> There can never be another Jules Verne for he was born at a unique moment in time. He grew up when the steam engine was changing the material world and the discoveries of science were changing the world of the mind. That revolution is now far behind us; we take it for granted that the future will be different from the present, forgetting that for the greater part of human history, a man's way of life did not differ from his grandfather's—or his grandson's. Verne himself is one of the reasons this is no longer true; he was the first writer to welcome change and to proclaim

that scientific discovery could be one of the most wonderful of all adventures.[11]

Lu Xun, too, grew up when the steam engine was changing the face of China, when Western technology was changing worlds far beyond China's shores, with Japan as the most successful example of strong modern nationhood in Asia, and when Western science was just beginning to shift Chinese minds. Just as the West was forcing China from its geographical isolation, so too, Lu Xun strove to force the prevailing Chinese mindset out of centuries of cultural insularity and Confucian aversion to change. Science brought with it a new philosophy of nature and humanity and it was this, rather than technological expertise, which Lu Xun proclaimed in the opening paragraph of the preface to his translation of *From the Earth to the Moon*.

> In ancient times, before the awakening of men's minds, Nature ruled supreme and even high mountains and rolling seas were enough to form an obstacle. Then men learned how to hew and splice wood and conceived of transport; oars and sails became daily more advanced. Only when you look far away across the seas to the meeting of water and sky then, like the quivering spirit and trembling body, it dies into nothingness. Then steam drove steel, warships sped under sail and, as man expanded his domination, so Nature's power declined and the five continents joined under one roof, civilization was handed on to create the world of today.[12]

Lu Xun, like Verne, questions the relationship of humankind to the natural universe. Instead of patterning the human world on a heavenly hierarchy, he sees the history of humankind as a gradual technological evolution which confronts the fearful force and dangers of nature and brings continents, civilizations and people into contact in 'the world of today'. Evolution and the historical necessity for change were to be the foundation of Lu Xun's world view; translations were to bring other civilizations under the same roof into contact with China.

Within this evolutionary world view, a person's stature depends on the part played in the progress of civilization. There are far-sighted, daring individuals (his Nietzchean concept of the supermen like Byron) 'who are strong, uncompromising, sincere, truthful and scornful of convention. Their powerful utterances brought about a national rebirth, making their countries great in the world'[13] just like Verne's heroes in these two early stories. Lu Xun continues in the preface to *From the Earth to the Moon*:

> Mankind is a species which hopes to progress and so a part of them reach out for glory and, never satisfied, build up great hopes, use the mind to break through the forces of Nature and conquer space, coolly going the way of the gods with no obstacles. . . (Jules Verne) writes about those who develop this hope.[14]

If scientific knowledge and the search for truth were prerequisites for social progress, so too was the liberation of the full dynamic potential of the individual. Professor Hartwigg, in *Journey to the Center of the Earth*, is a fictional example of one of these daring and powerful intellects who fear no obstacle. He descends, with two other men, into the earth's interior to investigate the theory of the central fire and is terribly indignant to learn that their raft voyage on the Central Interior Sea has wasted their time:

> 'The elements themselves conspire to overwhelm me with mortification. Air, fire and water combine their united efforts to oppose my passage. Well, they will see what the earnest will of a determined man can do. I will not yield, I will not retreat one inch; and we shall see who shall triumph in this great contest— man or nature.'[15]

Similarly, the story line in *From the Earth to the Moon* follows the overcoming of all obstacles—gun powder, location, design, metal for the cannon, money and so forth—once the bored and declining membership of civil war veterans in the Baltimore Gun Club, Maryland, decide to shoot a missile to the moon. Lu Xun's own poetic comments at the end of each chapter in his translation emphasize the heroic stature and vision of these men (and I say 'men' because he wrote in the preface that this story was outstanding even though it contained not a single woman![16]) At the end of chapter five, when problems of location and finance have been solved, Lu Xun added:

> Truly, this is:
> Chirp, chirp, the cicada,
> Is content to know only Spring and Autumn!
> Only a great sage,
> Can go on a carefree journey.[17]

Thus, Lu Xun is primarily interested in science as enlightenment, and in the implications of science for society at large. Progress, the continual advancement of the frontiers of knowledge, is equated to social betterment. Only after stating his view of society and the world, does Lu Xun move to the importance of fiction in popularizing science, as Verne did in *Extraordinary Voyages*. As Chesneaux pointed out, *From the Earth to the Moon* is 'basically nothing more than a long series of popular lectures on lunar astronomy'.[18] To make the story more palatable for Chinese readers, Lu Xun mixed in some classical Chinese to save space and 'where the wording was dull or not suited to the experience of my fellow countrymen, I made a few changes and deletions'.[19] One of the changes was to rearrange the Japanese translation, which kept Verne's original twenty-eight chapters, into fourteen chapters with double headings. Moreover, he ended each chapter with the time-honored devices of the traditional Chinese story-teller and of popular fiction: a short moral summary in poetic form and variations of the ending, such as 'if you want to know whether the projectile made it to the moon or fell back to earth, wait until the next chapter'. Compared to the strict translations he produced later in the May Fourth period, here in his first translation Lu Xun was introducing ideas rather than foreign literary structures, styles or the use of the vernacular.

Journey to the Center of the Earth is a flawless example of Verne's art in which a well-researched scientific background is an intrinsic part of the storyline. Every discovery is carefully classified and discussed in the light of contemporary scientific controversy, and all scientific instruments are explained. But basically the story is a fictional illustration of evolution, and therefore close to Lu Xun's heart; as the three men descended deeper into the bowels of the earth they retreated down the evolutionary time scale. First, there are rock formations and fossils; later, two fearsome antediluvian reptiles, the great fish lizard and the sea crocodile, fight to death in the subterranean central sea; man-like creatures herd mastodons in a primeval forest. The three explorers follow an initial clue, tracing the footsteps of an earlier Icelandic explorer who was muzzled by the Church: the authority of tradition is set up as diametrically opposed to scientific truth. In this translation Lu Xun has still presented the story in classical Chinese under chapters with two headings, but has not added the moral comment or the 'if you want to know what happened next. . .' formula.

Most critics footnote Lu Xun's early interest in science by mentioning these two translations of science fiction. But what sort of science is presented here to Chinese readers? The young Lu Xun, as revealed in the preface, was as full of optimism in science and the future as are these two early stories by Verne. Verne's later stories are more pessimistic, more aware of social realities with a new theme of the perversion and immoral use of scientific knowledge. As Jean Chesneaux points out further in his study, *The Political and Social Ideas of Jules Verne*, the ultimate claim on Verne was the idea of progress and, for Verne, this means 'the modification of the relationship between men and nature, much more than a change in the relationships between man and man or in the structure of human societies'.[20] Moreover, for Verne, progress implied Western domination.[21] Progress also claimed Lu Xun, but he used evolution to argue for changes in human relationships and social structures in China. From Lu Xun's own writings, we can infer that it was Huxley's *Evolution and Ethics*, which influenced him more than Darwin's *On the Origin of Species*. The human and social dimension of progress obsessed him because he recognized a philosophy in evolution that would counter Western domination and strengthen China.

Lu Xun's central importance to his nation was to help pioneer a new philosophy in China and to assimilate that philosophy to Chinese needs with a considered recognition of its social consequences. As Koestler states, this also happened in the West, albeit more slowly:

> Those men who created the upheaval which we now call the 'Scientific Revolution' called it by a quite different name: the 'New Philosophy'. The revolution in technology which their discoveries triggered off was an unexpected by-product; their aim was not the conquest of Nature but the understanding of Nature. Yet their cosmic quest destroyed the medieval vision of an immutable social order in a walled-in universe together with its fixed hierarchy of moral values, and transformed the European landscape, society, culture, habits and general outlook, as thoroughly as if a new species had arisen on this planet.[22]

Western critics miss this fundamental point when they claim that Lu Xun 'was to remain essentially a critic of the old society, not a builder of the new one'[23] or that he had no 'cure' for China's ills.[24] Without this new philosophy that Lu Xun promoted, there would be no new literature, no concept of human equality and no new society. Without the concept of evolution, there could be no later acceptance of Marx's evolutionary view of social progress. Without the dream and hope, there would be no thrust for change and revolution. China would have remained within the walls of a medieval universe.

During the early period of translating science fiction, Lu Xun did not recognize the need for a children's literature or a children's world. Verne did not write for children and Lu Xun certainly did not translate these stories for children. Nevertheless, the most important elements in Lu Xun's world view before 1907—evolution, progress, liberation of the individual and education through fiction—were to form the foundation of his later views on children and their literature. Children, not science, were the owners of the future; because their minds were not yet walled-in and poisoned by old ideas, they could be liberated by changes in education and by a new literature.

In 1906, the year his translation of *Journey to the Center of the Earth* was published, Lu Xun became disillusioned with science as the means of modernizing China. He left his work in medicine for literature and returned home to China from study in Japan. He believed that real sickness was in people's hearts and minds. Lu Xun later wrote that in his youth he dreamed many a beautiful dream, but in Japan, 'discussions of a dream future had to cease' for there was no answer from the living.[25] China still needed dreams—not dreams of the future but rather of the immediate present',[26] he wrote in 1925—and he shifted his creative genius from describing the distant horizon to knocking down the 'walled-in universe' of China's immediate present. Walls, in Lu Xun's mature writing, were a symbol of isolation and darkness. For example:

- The image of people suffocating in 'an iron house without windows' in the preface to his first collection of short stories, *Call to Arms (Nahan)*;
- Children imprisoned behind 'gates of darkness' in 'How We Should Be Fathers Today';
- 'In China there are walls everywhere but they are invisible, like "ghost walls", so that you knock into them all the time';[27] and
- 'I do not know how others may feel but I, personally, have always felt as though there was a high wall here in our midst, separating each of us from the other so that communication becomes impossible.'[28]

Lu Xun wrote his first short story in the hope of destroying the iron house,[29] in awakening Chinese from their long Confucian sleep to the possibilities of a real life without 'ghost walls'. He was spurred by a dream in the present and hope for the future.

Lu Xun and Children's Literature in the Early May Fourth Period

The concept of 'a world of children' was integral to Lu Xun's mature world view in the early May Fourth period (1919–26). This concept is most succinctly, if somewhat simply, explained in 1927: 'The childish can grow and mature; and as long as they do not become decrepit and corrupt, all will be well.'[30] The dichotomy lay in a 'natural' upbringing which allowed children to grow towards independence and maturity, and a Confucian upbringing which forced children into an 'unnatural' mould of unquestioning submission and intellectual stagnation. Children were the seeds of society and the direction of their growth depended on careful cultivation.

Lu Xun's short stories were devoted to tearing down the decrepit walls of traditional Confucianism. Where they describe children, with 'A Madman's Diary' and 'My Old Home' ('Guxiang') as the best-known examples, they concentrate on the corruption of childhood inherent in the old system of education and the leeching of all childish joy, curiosity and wonder.

'A Madman's Diary' is a bitter expose of the entire history of Chinese civilization and its corrupting influence on children. A pictorial version of the madman's vision would plunge us into a hellish nightmare of fear and distorted faces: 'green-faced, long-toothed'[31] and eyes cast down or gleaming murderously. Beneath men's virtuous masks 'their teeth are white and glistening: they are all man-eaters.'[32] The introduction, in constipated literary Chinese, is followed by the first entry, a crazy vision of enlightenment which brings with it fear in language which is by contrast, vivid, colloquial and concise.

I

Tonight the moon is very bright.
I have not seen it for over thirty years, so today when I saw it I felt in unusually high spirits. I begin to realize that during the past thirty-odd years I have been in the dark; but now I must be extremely careful. Otherwise why should that dog at the Zhao house have looked at me twice?
I have reason for my fear.[33]

In the next entry, there is no moon at all and the madman sees the strange, strange eyes of people, even children. He ponders on the reason.

. . . But then what of the children? At that time they were not yet born, so why should they eye me so strangely today, as if they were afraid of me, as if they wanted to murder me? This really frightens me, it is so bewildering and upsetting.

I know. They must have learned this from their parents![34]

Everyone—a dog, his neighbours, a woman on the street and even his elder brother—wants to eat people. The madman looked up history in ancient times and, over every page, found the words 'Virtue and Morality' and, in between the lines, 'Eat people'. He is thought to be mad and all shun him. In entry VIII, he meets a young man and asks if it is right to eat human beings but, in the end, the man grows pale and says it is wrong to talk of such things.

I leaped up and opened my eyes, but the man had vanished. I was soaked with perspiration. He was much younger than my elder brother, but even so he was in it. He must have been taught by his parents. And I am afraid he has already taught his son: that is why even the children look at me so fiercely.

IX

Wanting to eat men, at the same time afraid of being eaten themselves, they all look at each other with the deepest suspicion. . .

How comfortable life would be for them if they could rid themselves of such obsessions and go to work, walk, eat and sleep at ease. . .[35]

He realizes that he is said to be mad so that, when he is eaten, people will be pleased. He calls out twice:

'You should change at once, change from the bottom of your hearts! You must know that in the future there will be no place for man-eaters in the world. . .'

XI

The sun does not shine, the door is not opened, every day two meals. . .

XII

I can't bear to think of it.

I have only just realized that I have been living all these years in a place where for four thousand years they have been eating human flesh. My brother had just taken over the charge of the house when our sister died, and he may well have used her flesh in our rice and dishes, making us eat it unwittingly.

It is possible that I ate several pieces of my sister's flesh unwittingly, and now it is my turn. . .

How can a man like myself, after four thousand years of man-eating history—even though I knew nothing about it at first—ever hope to face real men?

XIII

Perhaps there are still children who have not eaten men?
Save the children. . .[36]

In this mad world of fear and darkness there is only one cry of hope and it is, significantly, the story's last words: 'Save the children'.

I have dwelt at length with 'A Madman's Diary' because I believe that most Western critics underestimate the strength and cultural resonance of this ending, seeing it as 'sentimental', wisdom restricted to a simple 'message',[37] or idealization of youth. William Lyell puts it most kindly:

> Since he [Lu Xun] did not want to be assimilated into the society around him, it followed as a corollary that he should idealize youth. For Lu Xun, 'growing up' was necessarily bad. It meant assimilation into a social structure which he saw as evil: maturing was equivalent to being corrupted.[38]

Such readings fail to recognize that children and childhood work at two levels in this story: at the literal level as victims to be eaten and, by the end of the story, as a symbol of the Chinese nation. Lu Xun is idealizing not youth, but the possibilities of youth given a different upbringing; 'growing up' is not necessarily bad, but bad in the China of his time; maturity means a healthy growth and is, in a sense, the opposite of being corrupted. Lu Xun did not want to freeze children, and by implication China, in an eternal world of childhood, fearful of growing up like Peter Pan. Rather he sought to develop the human potential of certain childhood qualities. The children in this story are negative examples; they are as inhuman as the adults because of a centuries-old chain of learning passed from generation to generation. Lu Xun's essays on children's education, we shall find, focus on the need to break this chain and to free children from mindless bondage. Just as his translations of children's literature were meant for adults, so too these essays were addressed to parents themselves. His writings were didactic in that the liberation of children depended on enlightening their parents and educators.

Of his short stories, the one with the most positive view of childhood and his hopes for children in the future is 'My Old Home' (1921). After twenty years Lu Xun returned to his old home and was saddened by the decay. The one happy memory is his childhood friendship with Runtu, the son of a part-time laborer who worked for his family. Runtu introduced him as a child to an exciting world:

> I had never known that all these strange things existed: at the seashore there were shells all colors of the rainbow; watermelons were exposed to such danger, yet all I had known of them before was that they were sold in the greengrocer's.
>
> On our shore, when the tide comes in, there are lots of jumping fish, each with two legs like a frog. . .
>
> Runtu's mind was a treasure-house of such strange lore, all of it outside the ken of my former friends. They were ignorant of all these things and, while Runtu lived by the sea, they like me could see only the four corners of the sky above the high courtyard wall.[39]

When he meets Runtu again as an adult, Runtu is not as Lu Xun remembered and they find it difficult to talk:

> He stood there, mixed joy and sadness showing on his face. His lips moved, but not a sound did he utter. Finally assuming a respectful attitude, he said clearly:
> 'Master! . . .'
> I felt a shiver run through me; for I knew then what a lamentably thick wall had grown up between us. Yet I could not say anything.[40]

Runtu's son, Honger, and Lu Xun's nephew, however, become fast friends as the older generation had done many years before. Leaving his old home,

> I lay down, listening to the water rippling beneath the boat, and knew that I was going my way. I thought: although there is such a barrier between Runtu and myself, the children still have much in common. I hope they will not be like us, that they will not allow a barrier to grow up between them. But again I would not like them, because they want to be akin, all to have a treadmill existence like mine, nor to suffer like Runtu until they become stupefied, nor yet, like others, to devote all their energies to dissipation. They should have a new life, a life we have never experienced.[41]

Once again, the 'walls' of hierarchy cut out 'the treasure house' of the real world that he glimpses through Runtu. Once again, the symbolic confrontation is between walls and darkness and color, light and freedom. The dream of a new life for children is still there.

> As I dozed, a stretch of jade-green seashore spread itself before my eyes, and above a round golden moon hung in a deep blue sky. I thought: hope cannot be said to exist, nor can it be said not to exist. It is just like roads across the earth. For actually the earth had no roads to begin with, but when many men pass one way, a road is made.[42]

If Lu Xun's early fiction raises the problem of childhood in China, then his essays in this period move beyond this and offer a rationale, a new direction, for a changed upbringing. In 1918 he wrote that the future of China could be seen not only in young children of the day but in younger fathers, a point of view he had already presented in 'A Madman's Diary'. He continues:

> The Austrian misogynist, Otto Weininger, divided women into two categories: mothers and prostitutes. Similarly, men can be classed as fathers and profligates. The fathers again can be divided into two groups: the fathers of children and the fathers of 'men'. Since all the former can do is to beget children, not bring them up, they still have something in common with profligates. The latter not only beget children but also try to educate them, in order that they may be real mean in the future.
>
> At the end of the Qing dynasty, when a normal college was first set up in a certain province, an old gentleman was horrified. 'Why should one have to learn to be a teacher?' he demanded indignantly. 'At this rate, there will soon be schools teaching men to be fathers!'
>
> This old gentleman thought that the only thing required of a father was to beget children, and since everyone knows instinctively how to do this, there is no need to learn it. But the fact is that China today needs schools for fathers, and this old gentleman should be enrolled in the lowest class.
>
> For in China we have many fathers of children, but in the future we want only fathers of 'men'.[43]

Children becoming 'real men' is seen to depend on the education they receive at school and at home:

> In the conditions of childhood, we see the fate of the future. We new people talk about love, talk about the nuclear family, talk about independence, talk about happiness, but it is very rare for anyone to raise the problems of home education, school education and social reform on behalf of our sons and daughters.[44]

Again, the responsibility for children's behavior is firmly placed on adult shoulders. If children fight over food, for example, then this is the influence of older people in the home; children's nature and behavior is molded by the environment and they 'learn by example' (*haizi xuele yangle*).[45] Thus, education, as Lu Xun defines it, was not restricted to a school system or textbooks but involved every aspect of a child's upbringing in a specific social setting; a prerequisite for a changed education was, therefore, a changed environment or, at the least, a changed view of society. The scope and influence that Lu Xun attributed to education, including the importance of models, was the element of continuity within Chinese culture. The revolutionary features were its content and social aim.

Both aspects—the importance and the purpose—of education, are clearly set out in a 1919 essay on the duties of parents: 'How We Should Be Fathers Today'. Here argument was based on evolution and the fact that the young must supersede the old in the continuation of a species. The premise, which preceded the argument, already implied social change and the independence of youth. Lu Xun introduced it as a natural law:

> The situation in the living world is
> 1. the necessity to preserve life;
> 2. the necessity to continue that life;
> 3. the necessity to develop that life (this is evolution).
>
> This is the way of all living things and must also be the way of fathers.[46]

Supporting this law with biological examples, he explains that if this is the way of Nature in the survival of a species then any society which flouts it is unnatural and doomed to extinction.

Within this biological schema, food preserves life and sexual reproduction continues a species. Why continue life? Because evolution never stands still and is apparently never regressionary. 'Therefore, life which comes after will have more meaning, be nearer completeness and so be more valuable and precious than that which went before; former life must be sacrificed to that'.[47] This evolutionary idealism was immediately qualified by the extent to which any society recognizes it. 'The pity is that China's old world view is almost the complete opposite of this law. The basic unit should be the young but they, conversely, make it the old; the emphasis should be on the future but they, conversely, place it in the past.'[48] Traditional models asked sons to sacrifice themselves for their parents and used examples from the past instead of looking to the future. Traditional Chinese society was, therefore, unnatural and retrogressive and led first to stagnation and then to extinction.

Lu Xun's new world view had profound moral implications for Chinese parents because it thrust into the future rather than conserving the past. Old virtues like filial piety subjugated the young to the old and had no moral value, while 'self love', its opposite, was the basis of life-preservation and a will to survive. According to Lu Xun, if fathers thought of the future then they should pass on neither physical illnesses nor spiritual deformities. Their duties are threefold: after birth, which preserves life, and food, which maintains it, fathers must educate their children to develop into stronger, healthier, wiser and happier people than themselves, thereby surpassing the previous generation and the past. Enlightened men, therefore, move beyond a 'natural self love' to an unselfish love which sacrifices themselves for later, new men.

Lu Xun's schema was explicit. Parents must first understand children and their world so as not to hinder children's development. He wrote:

> Formerly, Europeans mistakenly saw childhood as preparation for adulthood; the Chinese mistake is to see children as 'little adults'. We have only recently recognized, because of the research of many scholars, that the world of children (*ertong shijie*) is completely different from that of adults. If we do not begin with this understanding and always act crudely, we will greatly hinder children's development.[49]

Second, parents must guide, not order, children. The world changes and children must be adaptable to different circumstances with the ideal qualities of strength, morality, independence and flexibility. And, third, parents must liberate children. Sons and daughters both belong, and do not belong, to their parents. Because they belong, parents have a duty to educate them, but because their destiny is eventual separation, parents must also liberate them. In short, 'parents, then, in respect of their children, must nurture them in good health, wholeheartedly educate them and completely liberate them'.[50]

Lu Xun then discusses parents' fears about liberating their children and recognizes that many have social causes so that 'the only basic way out is to improve society'.[51] The duties of fathers involve nothing less than a total shift in the philosophy, content, moral implications and methods of education.

> To sum up, enlightened parents must be completely responsible, unselfish and willing to make sacrifices, none of which are easy things to do, especially in China. For the old to liberate the young, enlightened Chinese must wipe out the old debts, on the one hand, and open up a new road, on the other. As I said in the beginning, 'we are burdened with a heavy responsibility to prop up the gates of darkness with our shoulders and let children through to the bright, wide-open spaces to lead happy lives, henceforth, as real human beings.[52]

This 'new road' was 'the road of evolution' (*jinhua lu*).

Perhaps we now better understand the philosophical foundation of 'A Madman's Diary'. The madman sees the horrible truth in the tradition of two stories of the same name by Gogol and Tolstoy. In Lu Xun's story, the distorted faces, strange eyes, fear, imprisonment and darkness belong to an artificially created society of four thousand years which has rejected a fundamental law of nature. Conversely, the possibilities of childhood with Runtu in 'My Old Home' are curiosity, joy and immersion in the natural world (birds: wild pheasants, woodcocks, wood-pigeons, 'blue-jacks'; animals: badgers, hedgehogs and *zha*; shells all colors of the rainbow; fish by the seaside),[53] while the traditionally educated young Lu Xun and his friends saw 'only the four corners of the sky above the high courtyard wall'.[54]

It was this polarity between the 'unnatural' and the 'natural', as Lu Xun defined them, which informed his ideas on a new literature for children. In his book of childhood reminiscences,

Dawn Flowers Plucked at Dusk (*Chaohua Xishi*, 1927), the classical children's books, such as *The Illustrated Twenty-four Examples of Filial Piety* (*Eshisi Xiaotu*), *The Thousand Character Classic* and *The Hundred Names*, are presented as boring, fearful books that children do not understand; fun things are gardens, fairs and festivals and delightful, illustrated books such as *The Mirror of Flowers* (*Hua Jing*), a seventeenth-century manual for gardeners, and *The Book of Hills and Seas* (*Shanhai Jing*), which contained many early myths and legends 'with pictures and man-faced beasts, nine-headed snakes, three-footed birds, men with wings and headless monsters who used their teats as eyes'.[55] The short essay, 'From Hundred-plant Garden to Three-flavor Study' ('Cong Baicaoyuan dao Sanwei Shuwu'), describes the prison sentence of a traditional upbringing; the young Lu Xun moves from a garden paradise behind his house where all sorts of things happen, especially beside an old mud well, to his teacher's study where the children sit tediously reciting the old classics. He can not even ask questions like 'What is this insect *guaizai*, Sir?' without risking his teacher's anger. The title, indicating the shift from garden to study, richly suggests the claustrophobia.

In Lu Xun's view, a new children's literature should develop a child's imagination, curiosity and early exploration of natural phenomena. He wrote much later, in 1934,

> Children must be respected. They often imagine the world, beyond the moon and stars, what it is like under the earth, the use of flowers and herbs, the language of insects; they imagine flying into the sky and burrowing into an ant's nest. . . hence the books we give children are of the utmost importance and of the utmost difficulty to write.[56]

It is interesting that each of these aspects of childish imagination are dealt with in five of his translations, now said to belong to children's literature: the works by Verne, Eroshenko and van Eeden. Lu Xun claimed that old picture books, which were often republished for children, were shoddy and unsuitable because the artists simply lacked the concrete knowledge of something as large as the universe or as small as a cricket. This so-called education was the education of fools and 'when children grow up they will become real fools just like us'.[57] They needed all sorts of books, not just literature, in the easily accessible vernacular language: travelogues, science, mathematics, physics, history, biology and comic books which satisfied their curiosity and gave them useful knowledge. 'You must be like the bee and taste many flowers to make honey, but if you only sip in one spot what you produce will be very limited and dry.'[58]

It was during this 'Nature Period' that Lu Xun translated the works of the two fairytale writers, Eroshenko and van Eeden. The works are not traditional fairytales, such as *Cinderella*, but 'literary fairytales' which adopt this genre to say something important about contemporary society. Indeed, fairytales, with their lack of division between the worlds of men and animals, were particularly apt for any writer who believed in the theory of evolution and contact with the natural world. This point was not missed by Chinese conservatives who made the fairytale the focus of their attack on the new children's literature. Hence, like Verne's science fiction, the works by Eroshenko and van Eeden not only are positive examples of foreign literature but also espouse a new world view.

Vasily Eroshenko, a blind Russian poet, was well-known in Beijing. In late 1921 he was deported from Japan and came to China where he lived for a while with Lu Xun and his brother. In 1921 and 1922, Lu Xun translated a collection of his fairytales and his play, *Peach-colored Clouds. Morning Post* published some of these translations and reported on his life and lectures. Lu Xun wrote that he had heard of Eroshenko only after Eroshenko was banished from Japan and this inspired Lu Xun's translations 'to propagate the bitter cry of the cruelly oppressed and to awaken the hatred and anger of the Chinese people towards the powerful and not to stretch out my hand from some "temple of art", plucking forth a precious, foreign flower to plant in our Chinese garden of art'.[59] Although these translations were not meant for children (Eroshenko thought that *Peach-colored*

Clouds would suit Chinese youth), they represent, for Lu Xun, the heart of childhood:

> (The author) calls for a universal love between all men, without the sorrow of love, and I have unfolded his childlike, beautiful and sincerely-felt dream. Perhaps this dream is a veil to cover the author's own sorrow? If so, then I will dream through a dream but I do not want the author to ever wish to leave this dream of childlike beauty but to continue to beckon men towards it and see a real rainbow. . .[60]

Lu Xun often mentions dreams. In a 1918 poem, many dreams deceive him in the darkness, calling out, but he cannot see the colors and does not know who speaks. . . 'Ignorant in the darkness, feverish, a headache. Come, come! A dream I can understand'.[61] Perhaps this dream is not Lu Xun's but he equates it with childhood and dreams through it.

Most of these translations, including the play, were chosen by Eroshenko. Lu Xun himself chose only four tales: 'The Narrow Cage' (Xia de Long), 'Beside the Pond' (Chibian), 'Eagle-heart' (Diao de Xin) and 'A Spring Evening Dream' (Chunye de Meng). All four strive for a new humanity, a rebirth.

'A Spring Evening Dream', first published in *Morning Post* in October 1921, describes an idyllic, mirror-like lake in the distant mountains. The story tells how once a nature painter stayed there before he returned to the east, believing his own studio to be more beautiful and his own paintings of women to be more lovely. A disappointed lover also came to the lake but left for the west to drown his soul's sorrow in drink. In Spring, the lake comes to life and the creatures, intoxicated with beauty, dream their Spring evening dream. One evening a wealthy, thirteen year-old girl comes to the lake, carrying a firefly cage, and meets a poor, fourteen-year-old boy on his way to catch goldfish. They argue and go their own way. The girl takes a firefly, the boy a goldfish, and each takes their catch home. A mountain spirit sets the creatures free but the price is the shining scales of the goldfish and the firefly's wings of light. Again, the children come to the lake, meet and fight. The girl sees a mountain spirit with the firefly's wings and tries to catch it; the boy sees a lotus-flower spirit with a hat of golden scales and tries to pluck the flower. Both fall into the water, cry for help and are saved by the King of the lake. The spirits who had stolen these creatures blame the children. The girl explains that she loves beauty and the boy says he loves creatures and wanted to care for the goldfish. The King shows them that lovers of beauty harm it through possessiveness. The children then wake up beside the lake and, reconciled as friends, are together. Meanwhile, the goldfish and firefly are still asleep, dreaming. It is, Lu Xun said, really 'a Spring evening dream of a Spring evening dream'; the author's ideas, modeled on an idyllic view of nature, are peaceful, not dangerous.[62] The dream is that the two children, unlike the painter and lover, will rid themselves of destructiveness, possessiveness and petty fighting and live happily. Its message of hope and of faith in children resonates clearly with Lu Xun's world view.

'Beside the Pond' is not so idyllic. It is about the futile but heroic strivings of two butterflies. Born during the day, the butterflies believe when dusk comes that the sun has vanished and so they fly east and west searching for the sun to bring it back so all things may live. The other creatures are frightened by such subversive activity. The owl, the head official with an office in a pine tree, sends out fellow creatures of darkness to capture the rebel butterflies before they expand their numbers. In the morning, a group of primary school students finds a drowned golden butterfly and their teacher uses this as a warning to the students never to venture into deep water. Another group of middle-school students finds a dead silver butterfly beside the pond and their teacher, who is destined to go up in the world, warns children that it died searching out new lands: 'Therefore, the most important thing for any man in the world is to be happy with his position in life and satisfied with his possessions'.[63]

The students ask about those who have neither position nor possessions but the teacher repeats what he has already told them, adding that this is the primary aim of education. But, ends Eroshenko, 'not a single person knew that these two butterflies died because they could not bear the darkness in the world before their eyes and that they wanted to restore the sun and save the world'.[64] The questioning love of the butterflies and students in their pursuit of the light contrasts with the sleepy owl, his henchmen and the dogmatic teachers who seek to maintain the existing order.

'Eagle-heart' advocates revolution. Again, searching for light and freedom are crucial. In this story, two children of a hunter are taught how to live by eagles, the kings of birds, who bring them up as young eagles and teach them their song:

> Love the sun,
> Fly up to the sun!
> Never fly down,
> Never look down. . .
> Below is the dark, narrow cage,
> Below is the cemetery of slaves[65]

The children are so strong, aspiring and brave that when, after five years, they return to live in the 'narrow cage' with men, the villagers call them 'eagle-heart' brothers. Meanwhile two young eagles that have been brought up by men are killed by the eagles for forgetting their aspirations and real nature. The two eagle-heart brothers later lead a revolution that results in their execution, but mothers teach their children about the two brothers and someone, somewhere, sings their song. People who save the world must have the heart of an eagle, ends Eroshenko. Here the call to revolution is unambiguous and heralds Lu Xun's later translations.

Eroshenko's fairytales are 'dreams of child-like beauty. . . which beckon men toward them', just as Verne's inspiring heroes forge social progress. Like Lu Xun's, Eroshenko's tales in this period advocate a different education based on the beauty, strength and strivings in the natural world, so that people may move from the dark and narrow cage of contemporary society to rich and free lives lit by the sun. Youth and beauty are intermingled in these dreams of a better future.

Yet Lu Xun always had doubts about his dreams. In 1923, he wrote that dreaming, like lying, was magnificent in a time of suffering.[66] By the mid-twenties he was losing his faith in fairytale worlds and in children as the harbingers of a better world. The young, he said in 1925, have all 'grown old'.

> Hope, hope—I took this shield of hope to withstand the invasion of the dark night in the emptiness, although behind this shield there was still dark night and emptiness. But even so I slowly wasted my youth.
> I knew, of course, that my youth had perished. But I thought that the youth outside still existed: stars and moonlight, dead, fallen butterflies, flowers in the darkness, the ill-omened call of the owl, the weeping with blood of the nightingale, the indecision of laughter, the dance of love. . . Although it might be a youth of sadness and uncertainty, it was still youth.
> But why is it now so lonely? Is it because even the youth outside me has perished, and the young people of the world have all grown old?
> . . . The young people of the world are very placid.[67]

Nevertheless, in 1927, in a defense of the vernacular language, he writes: 'our young people must turn China into an articulate country. Speak out boldly, advance fearlessly, with no thought of personal gain, brushing aside the ancients, and expressing your true thoughts. . . Only then shall we be able to live in the world with all other nations.'[68] While he still believed in the revolutionary potential of youth, he had doubts that the development of childhood qualities and kinship with Nature was sufficient to save China. In his next fairytale, the search for the sun becomes an illusion, because the sun is not a life-giving force but only a monstrous and lethal man-made lamp. By 1927, in a political period known as the White Terror, he had moved from Science and Nature, through a re-education of children to a class analysis, on Marxist lines, of Chinese society. At the same time, he stopped writing short stories.

During the transitional year of 1926, he translated a Dutch children's book simply because he loved it,[69] a book that had first moved him in an earlier, crucial stage when he left medicine for literature. This was Dr Frederik van Eeden's *Little Johannes*. It is about the human, not social, condition. A necessary part of growing up, according to Lu Xun, involves the 'tearing of childhood dreams into fragments' because growing up, happily or unhappily, entails a search for knowledge: this is 'the contradiction in human nature and the sorrow and joy intertwined in disaster and fortune.'[70] But Johannes attains wisdom and self-understanding, a mixture of joy and sorrow, because he never forgets his dreams of youth. Van Eeden's original is a fairytale for children in simple language but Lu Xun sees it as an adult fairytale which, moreover, surpasses most others in its wisdom and sensitivity. Literary critic Andrew Lang places it in the modern tradition of the fairytale in the West which, by the eighteenth century, was a literary genre, a vehicle for both satire and moralities; in it, 'the man's fancy consciously plays with the data and forms of the child's imagination'.[71] The fairytale element is the concrete vehicle through which to express the journey of a man's soul: blithe and happy with Windekind, child of the sun and moon, the hopeful quest for knowledge with the gnome-like Wistik, doubt and despair with his teacher of science, grave and awesome in the face of death. 'Events in it,' wrote Lu Xun, 'merge reality and fantasy'.[72] Or as the author himself begins, 'Much in this may seem a fairy story but it all really happened. . .'.[73]

Little Johannes spends a happy childhood playing in the large garden behind an old house. He lives with his friend, Windekind, and the flowers and birds: crickets, elves, ants and cockchafers all share their world with him, and Johannes learns that all animals have their lore and legends. The cockchafer, whose enemy is the bat, chases the light which is really an ordinary lamp, that kills him. Johannes learns the language of butterflies and birds and the faces of flowers. But he is always asking questions: why is the world like it is, why must things die, do miracles ever happen? He asks Windekind: 'Is the Great Light, God?' And Windekind answers:

God? . . . I know, Johannes, what you are thinking of when you speak that word—of the chair by your bedside where you knelt to say your prayers last evening—of the green serge curtains in front of the church window, which you gaze at by the hour on Sunday mornings—of the capital letters in your little Bible—of the Church-bag with its long pole—of the stupid singing and the stuffy atmosphere. All that you mean by the word, Johannes, is a monstrous false image. In place of the sun, a huge petroleum lamp, to which thousands and thousands of flies are helplessly and hopelessly stuck fast.[74]

And so Windekind teaches him to pray; a tremulous, silent communication with the world. For both van Eeden and Lu Xun, childhood happiness belongs in gardens and nature, while rooms and book ideologies are 'stuffy, stupid. . . a monstrous false image'. Lu Xun wrote that 'in childhood, men follow Windekind and are friends with creation'.[75]

Johannes then meets Wistik who searches for truth in books and, in particular, the one book which explains all mysteries. Windekind tries to tell him that 'the book' only exists like a shadow and can never be grasped but Johannes persists and Windekind disappears. His search for 'the book', for answers, continues throughout the story. He is deceived by fair-haired Robinetta, a girl with a robin, with whom he falls in love. He meets Pluizer, the plucker and spoiler, who leads Johannes to study and question, denying him compassion. Pluizer shows him death, worms in a coffin, the decay of beauty at the ball and even his own death and, in his despair, Johannes even forgets his love for Robinetta. To Pluizer, ideas of a Great Light are 'mere visions and dreams! Men alone exist—and I myself'.[76] Johannes then studies medicine with the Doctor, who beguiles him with yet another false image: the grand idea of science and the advancement of mankind to which all vulgar, smaller feelings must give way. They dissect everything, even his friend the rabbit, and Robinetta.

Johannes learned and listened, diligently and patiently—day after day, month after month. He had very little hope, but he understood that he must go on now as far as possible. He thought it strange that the longer he sought the light, the darker it grew around him.[77]

But when Johannes' father dies and Pluizer takes the knife to dissect him for science, Johannes fights until a blood-red mist comes before his eyes. Gentle and grave, Death tells him that he loves men and only through death will he find the book.

Johannes' heart is light. He flies with Windekind and sees on the shore a boat with Death at one end and Windekind at the other. Then he sees a figure who first made him weep for men in the garden and he must choose between Death and Windekind or the grave man.

> 'There where men are and their misery, there lies my way... I shall guide you there and not the false light which you have followed.' Then Johannes slowly took his eyes off Windekind's vanishing form, and put up his hands to the Grave Man. And led by him, he turned and faced the cold night wind, and made his toilsome way to the great dismal town where men are, and their misery.[78]

As Lu Xun wrote, 'only when Johannes looks into his own soul (and turns towards the town)... does he realize that the book cannot be found among men but from two places only: one is Windekind, but he has already lost his earlier merging with Nature; the other is Heine—Death, the stage before a reemerging with Nature. And when he looks closely, they are both on the one boat...'.[79]

Dreams, hopes, despair and uncertainties lived with Lu Xun, as they did with Johannes. At this time, Lu Xun wrote to his wife that 'my ideas are really not easy to comprehend all at once because there are many contradictions therein... of humanitarianism and individualism. Thus, sometimes I suddenly love people or suddenly hate them'.[80] But he was honest enough with himself to be convinced over time that there were no easy answers and no grand ideas, like science, Wistik's book or a childlike merging with nature, to explain or solve the human predicament. And, like Johannes, he went on in the darkness.

Lu Xun and Children's Literature in the Later May Fourth Period

In 1927, the White Terror, when the Nationalists purged the Communists from their ranks, pushed Lu Xun towards a more radical alternative for China.[81] He saw young students inform on others and he could no longer believe that the young were the hope for the future, or, indeed, that they would grow up better than their parents: 'Facts are facts; the bloody drama has begun and the actors are youth, and self-satisfied youth at that'.[82] He turned increasingly to a Marxist view of society and the necessity for a class revolution. This involved a dramatic shift in the kinds of books he translated from Western children's literature. His later two translations, *Little Peter* (1929) and *The Watch* (1935), do not describe the idyllic nature of childhood, beckoning men towards a dream, but the actual cruel, hungry existence led by children of the poor. Society is no longer seen in the fairytales' dichotomies of old and young, 'unnatural' and 'natural', but in class-based dichotomies of rich and poor, capitalist and worker.

Little Peter is a series of six fairytales by Hungarian writer, Hermynia zur Meuhlen, 'a genuine socialist author'.[83] Little Peter—lying in bed with a broken ankle and bored, lonely and frightened while his mother works in a factory—is shown the world through the life stories of everyday objects in his room: a piece of coal, a matchbox, a bottle, a hat, an iron kettle and a snowdrop all take on separate personalities and speak to him. It is this magical transformation which lightens Peter's gloom, dispels his fears and brings him friendship. Most importantly, it teaches him that, if only people were not so stupid, they could change society and lead lives less miserable than the lives of he and his mother. Realizing that Marxist terminology, like 'capitalists' and 'the system', are incomprehensible to a child, the objects that tell their stories translate these concepts into living images which Peter takes to heart.

The coal describes the lives of the rich and poor in the mines; the matchbox tells how a young forest tree killed a cruel landlord, but that single acts of heroism cannot change a social system; the bottle explains how hell, like the factory in which he was born, where children look like old men, is really man-made and full of well-dressed capitalists, not black devils with horns; the hat tells how the dyes that make such lovely colors actually poison people; the kettle contrasts his luxurious, early life in a rich household (and his relationship with a snooty, silver teapot) to his life in a servant's house where people are cold, starving and sick; and the snowdrop on a red plate prophesizes that selfish Winter, with his servants of frost, ice and snow, must eventually give way to Spring. 'It is a real pity that it cannot be like this in the human world',[84] says the hat. Spring flowers in people's minds, responds the bottle, and the kettle tells them all of a book which prophesizes that the many poor will unite against the rich. 'In the world of men', says the matchbox, 'eternal Spring will come. But they must fight for it!'[85] Peter is delighted, for in that world, his mother would not live a life of daily drudgery in a factory. Nor would his own life be so bleak. And the snowdrop sings, as if Spring is already in the air.

Illustration 2.1

from *Little Peter*

Like *Little Johannes*, *Little Peter* was written originally for children, the children of workers. But, Lu Xun wrote in the preface, its audience changed when transplanted into Chinese soil. 'The primary reason is that workers' children are uneducated and unable to recognize either the characters or format of these essays so it has absolutely nothing to do with them, never mind the fact that they have no money to buy books and no leisure to read them.'[86] Even educated children in China would find the background and objects unfamiliar. Moreover, this sort of fairytale was little-known in China: the author 'who advocates everyone's right to exist (Essay 2), that everything must be achieved through struggle (the end of Essay 6) and so on, uses the guise of the fairytale to cloak stains of blood and sweat. In China, especially, there are few such fairytales and no thorough, solid theoretical works to support them.'[87] Hence, once again Lu Xun targeted adults: those who have not lost their innocence, who have not forgotten the working masses, although they themselves may not work, or just those interested in world literature to let them know 'that in the world of modern, proletarian literature there is this sort of author and this sort of work'.[88]

The fairytale, 'a form of literature primevaly old, but with infinite capacity to renew its youth',[89] is transplanted into China as part of proletarian literature and as a vehicle for revolution. It advocates class struggle and explains why this is necessary. The Springtime in *Little Peter* anticipates a classless society in post-revolution China. This dress, the guise of 'blood and sweat', was a precursor of the best-known revolutionary works for children in the thirties, including those by one of China's most famous children's authors, Zhang Tianyi.

Lu Xun's most influential translation was, however, *The Watch* by Soviet author, Leonard Ivanovich Panteleev (1935). Along with *Little Johannes*, it gave him most trouble to translate:[90]

> . . . my illness of the last few days is probably due to the pace at which I have been translating a fairytale, more than forty thousand

characters in ten days, and it seems my present physique cannot support this. But the fairytale is finished. It is by Panteleev, who was born a vagabond, and it is very interesting. . .[91]

It is not, in fact, a fairytale, but a realistic story about the life of an orphan boy on the streets and his gradual psychological changes and confidence inspired by being sent to a children's home. With a less intrusive ideology than that of *Little Peter*, *The Watch* clearly conveys that the life of children depends on the wider, social environment; the world of children is really the same as 'the world of men'.

The story opens with Petika, who thinks he is about eleven years old, roaming the market place. He is famished, and unable to resist the warm smell wafting from a cake stall, steals a cake, sniffs it, and stuffs it in his pocket. He is caught and sent once again to prison for the night. There he meets an old drunk who, not realizing Petika is also a prisoner, offers him a glittering gold watch for his freedom. The watch becomes the seductive symbol, if only he can pawn it, of the avenue to a new life.

> First, I'll buy a loaf of white bread. A very large loaf of white bread. And butter. I will eat it spread on the bread and after that I'll have a cup of cocoa. Then I will buy a sausage. Also cigarettes of the finest quality. And clothes: trousers, shirt. . .[92]

But Petika is not released from prison the next morning and is instead escorted, because of his poverty and youth, to a juvenile home. While his police guard is having a drink, Petika seizes the opportunity to escape and runs like the wind until he finds he has lost the watch and, crying, returns to search for it. He finds the watch but is recaptured and so he continues with the policeman to the juvenile home that seems to Petika just like a prison. First he has a bath with the watch stuffed in his mouth, then dinner where he eats, eats and eats. Petika's thoughts are ruled by two things: to retrieve the watch that he had buried in the garden, only to find that all the wood for winter was dumped over it, and to escape. All this time the old drunk is pursuing him to retrieve his watch. One night Petika escapes through the window and finds his watch, but is driven back inside by the watchdog. So life goes on, through a long, long autumn and winter, during which time Petika makes friends, goes to class, reads books and finally, for his diligence in shifting the woodpile (albeit for his own secret purpose), is made treasurer. He is busy, happy and trusted. Whereas earlier his life was dictated by finding the watch, when it is safely in his pocket again he realizes he has nowhere to run. He feels ashamed of stealing, without knowing why. Much later he meets his friend, Natasha, pawning the watch chain in the market place. She insists it belongs to her father, and Petika realizes he stole the watch from Natasha's own father. Stunned, he returns the watch, runs out of the market place and finishes his errand for the juvenile home (Illustrations 2.2 to 2.5).

The Watch is an excellent children's story. At one level, it is full of adventure—stealing, imprisonment, escape and fights. Yet it is not an overtly 'political' or 'edifying' book of the sort that Petika, himself, hated.[93] Moreover, Lu Xun, who always expected a high standard of illustration, included twenty-two line drawings by Bruno Fuk, taken from the German edition, to illustrate Petika's adventures.

Panteleev's story, at another level, is a social story. Petika's actions and thoughts are governed by his attitude toward the watch: stealing, obsession with escape after retrieving the watch, learning patience, shame, and finally return of the watch. In 1936 the story was cited as a model for children's literature in China because it 'shows that vagabonds are not heaven-sent lowly creatures but are created by the social environment so if we want to get rid of these undesirable social products. . . we must come up with concrete means of changing society'.[94]

Lu Xun, in the preface, also emphasizes the social relevance of this story. While he intended it to be for adults, he also introduced it as part of children's literature in which it followed the 'realistic' fairytales in Ye Shengtao's 1923 collection, *The Scarecrow,* offering an alternative to classical stories republished for Chinese children. He includes the introduction to the Japanese edition as being relevant to China in the thirties:

Illustration 2.2

'Stealing in the Market', from *The Watch*

Illustration 2.3

'An Outstretched Hand in Prison', from *The Watch*

Illustration 2.4

'Arguing with a Policeman', from *The Watch*

Illustration 2.5

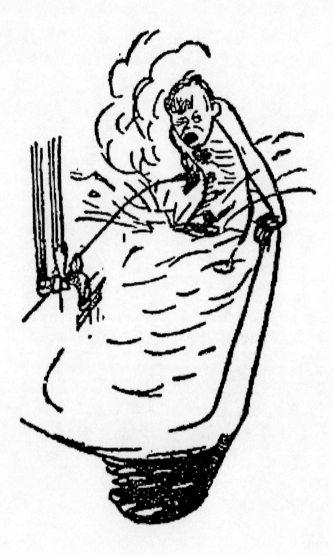

'The First Bath in Five Years!', from *The Watch*

> To sum up, although old fairytales have old-fashioned sensitivity, feelings, plots and life-styles, they have absolutely nothing of today's new children who use new eyes and new ears to look at the worlds of animals, plants and men.
>
> So I decided to definitely give these new children a new work so that they could always blossom and grow in an ever-changing new world.[95]

All Lu Xun's translations for children offer children and their educators a new way of conceiving a children's world. Behind the stories lies the dream, the elusive hope, of 'an eternal Springtime for mankind' and that children will grow, like Petika, into 'real' men.

If Soviet literature commanded the attention of major, leftist writers in China of the thirties, then Maxim Gorky (1868–1936) was its outstanding representative. In Russian literature,

> Gorky's voice suddenly resounded like a clarion, calling to a new courage and faith in life. His favorite heroes were the outcasts whose freedom from social or any other ties gave them a pride and self-assertiveness of their own. Some of his early characters sound like Nietzscheans from the gutter. These he may have over-idealized, or used as mouth-pieces for his own philosophy of life, yet his very rhetoric served as a stimulus and a tonic. Having embraced the cause of the working class, Gorky soon became its literary spokesman.[96]

Gorky's clarion call was eagerly heeded in China. In 1912, in a letter to Sun Yatsen, he saw Russians and Chinese united in a common struggle 'for a victory of ideals... (against) enemies who plan to destroy the sunlight so that they may comfortably go about their dark and greedy work'.[97] His message sounds very much like Lu Xun's. When Lu Xun translated Gorky's *Russian Fairytales* in 1935 he did not introduce the author in the preface, because Gorky was so well-known in China. The sixteen tales, 'although called "fairytales", really describe, from all angles, the many facets of the character of Russian people, and were definitely not written for children'.[98]

Nevertheless, Gorky's writings on children and their literature were devoured hungrily by Chinese revolutionary writers so that, by the fifties, Gorky and Lu Xun were the oracles for China's new children's literature. Indeed, the literature of accusation of both authors masks a gentle and humane attitude to children's books, and both writers gave their works careful thought. The themes that Gorky suggested were suitable for 'a new kind of literature for children' (a view first published in 1933 and translated into Chinese in 1936) espoused an evolutionary world view:

> . . . the earth, air, water, plants, animals, how man appeared on earth, how man learned to think, how man learned to make fire, how man learned to make his labour and life easier, the significance to man of his discovery and use of iron and other metals etc., about the marvelous advances in the work of science, thoughts and deeds, regarding techniques of the future, why and how people made up tales and legends, what religion is and why it was invented, how science made giants of men, the history of engines from the steam-driven to the diesel, and two natures i.e. from Nature's power over Man to Man's power over Nature', in that order.[99]

Again, this is very much like Lu Xun's themes, beginning with his translations of Verne, but with a Marxist additive which emphasizes the historical importance of labour and the struggle of the working masses. Gorky, like Lu Xun, also invested children with great importance, writing that 'today, perhaps more than ever before, children are the best and most necessary things on earth'.[100] They both also admired a combative spirit in children: Lu Xun said of his own son that he would 'dare to speak, dare to laugh, dare to curse and dare to fight',[101] while Gorky, in a letter to Anton Chekhov, wrote more personally of his own son:

> There is talk of your impending marriage. . . It's a good thing to be married if the woman is not made of wood and is not a radical. But the best thing about marriage is the children. Incidentally, my little son is a bag of tricks. . . it is comical but somewhat

unpleasant to hear the two-year-old rascal shouting at his mother at the top of his voice: 'Go away, you anathema'. . .[102]

Lastly, literature and education played the same role in Gorky's 'On Themes':

> The problem of themes in books for children is, of course, a problem of the line of social education to be followed with respect to children.
>
> In our country education is tantamount to revolutionizing, that is to say, liberating the child's minds from modes of thinking laid down by its father's and ancestors' past, ridding it of delusions rooted in centuries of a conservative way of life—one built on the class struggle and the individual's striving to defend himself and to assert individualism and nationalism and 'eternal' forms and laws of social behavior.[103]

Of the two writers, Gorky is, perhaps, the more positive, more certain of Marx's 'genius' and 'great teachings'.[104] Lu Xun never joined the Chinese Communist Party. Both men, however, laid the foundation for a new children's literature in their own countries.

Marxist children's literature of the type Lu Xun introduced, with its emphasis on social realism as a form of critical exposure, effectively ended the romantic exploration of childhood consciousness with its 'world of children'. Instead, the world of children was portrayed as that of poor victims in the present, and anticipated a just, ordered social system in the Marxist vision of the socialist future. Thus, in *Little Peter* the fairytale element offers the vision while Peter's life is the reality. *The Watch,* however, anticipates the vision in two contrasting environments: one, the hungry thieving life of a vagabond, and the other, the caring, well-fed warmth and friendship in the juvenile home. Indeed, hungry, homeless children on the streets of Shanghai is the everyday theme in revolutionary children's stories in the mid-thirties. Sometimes the children die, but more often the end is happy: food and a larger purpose when they join the revolution. This symbolism of darkness and light described life before and after Liberation in children's books written after

1949. Here, revolutionary struggle would redeem Chinese society.

Lu Xun died in 1936 on the eve of the war with Japan, but at the end of the twentieth century he is still the acknowledged reference for children's literature in China. In 1936 a young writer, Chen Bochui, one of China's most prominent figures in children's literature from the thirties to the eighties, met him in a Shanghai bookstore. The young writer was searching for Verne's *Two Years on Vacation* to retranslate for children when, unexpectedly, a voice suggested that perhaps it was not very well known. 'My heart skipped a beat and I couldn't help calling out: "Mr Lu Xun"!'[105] Lu Xun suggested that there was no use in translating it and, after further questioning, that he did not know if there was anything worth translating from Japan, England and America. Lu Xun had also read Chen Bochui's children's stories. Although this young writer had read Lu Xun's two socialist translations, it was not until 1946 that Chen Bochui realized the social direction of these books and that science fiction, irrelevant in wartime, was still relevant in a postwar construction period just as Gorky had demanded in 'On Themes'. In short, Chen recognized that Lu Xun was right, although he could not know the future direction of children's literature. Twenty years after Lu Xun's death, Chen Bochui was to say:

> Each time I read those pages in Lu Xun. . . essays, on children's education and children's literature, so full of militant strength, so rich in guidance, I gain a deeper and deeper understanding which often spurs me on in my work and provides me with a compass on the 'road' of children's literature.[106]

Conclusion

The nature of childhood and of children's literature are both major issues and causes in Lu Xun's mature work. But they are not the central issue. The obsession at the heart of all Lu Xun's writings is how to 'save' China.

Lu Xun's interest in childhood and children's literature always focussed on their implications for the direction of social change in China. He did not explore the psychological implications of the Western notion of the child's particular nature, as Zhou Zuoren and others did. He did not examine the concept of developmental stages in children's intellectual, emotional and sexual lives. Neither did he deal with the types of literature suitable for children at different developmental stages. His concern was not with the individual child but with children as part of his nation, China.

Lu Xun accepted the notion of a 'world of children' as a scientific fact. On this basis he argued for changes in education and development of a vernacular children's literature as strategies for effecting social change.

What seems a tenuous link between today's stories for children and the shape of tomorrow's society is cemented by the importance Chinese attribute to education and to literature as part of education. Lu Xun is firmly within this Chinese tradition. Confucian, May Fourth or Marxist: the element of continuity in these philosophies lies in the belief that education, not innate defects or natural potential, determine a person's character and beliefs and, therefore, one's social behavior. This helps us 'to comprehend the extraordinary faith and optimism the Chinese place on the educational system for the solution of the most vital social issues of the day: Alter people's conduct with educational means and thereby solve the problems'.[107]

Lu Xun wanted to change the content of education in order to discard the 'untrue' and 'perverted' beliefs inherent in Confucianism. He wanted to introduce science and imaginative literature so that children, whose youth made them particularly malleable, would grow into 'real' people and would build a new and viable society. This is the basis for Lu Xun's bitter hatred of the traditional Confucian texts, his insistence that children must be 'liberated' from the old morality, his demand for a modern educative literature and, last, his introduction of Western literature through translation as positive examples of progressive foreign values.

Lu Xun's emphasis on the social importance of children's literature prevailed in Mao's China. He was convinced that its importance lay in its determining influence on future society.

Hence he argued that children's literature played a major role in any long term strategy for social change. However, his views on the content of suitable children's literature itself, as evidenced by the works he translated, shifted according to the particular strategy he embraced at the time: Darwinian science, romantic idealism and Marxist revolution.

Mao Zedong claimed that Lu Xun took 'the very same road as China's new national culture'. Lu Xun's views on childhood and children's literature therefore offer fresh perspectives on the political forces competing for hegemony in modern China. It is well known that Lu Xun powerfully influenced modern Chinese literature; it is little known that he is also one of the founding fathers of Chinese children's literature.

Notes

1. Mao Tse-tung, 'Talk at a Meeting with Chinese Students and Trainees in Moscow', op. cit., p. 288.
2. Lu Xun, 'Women Xianzai Zenme Zuo Fuqin', op. cit., p. 125.
3. Ibid.
4. Lu Xun, 'Shanghai Ertong', Lu Xun Quanji, Vol. 5, op. cit., p. 161, translated by Yang Xianyi and Yang, Gladys, 'Shanghai Children', in Lu Xun: Selected Works, Vol. III (Beijing 1959), pp. 335–6.
5. Mao Zedong, 'On New Democracy' (1940), Selected Works of Mao Tse-tung, Vol. II (Peking, 1975), p. 372.
6. Jiang Feng (ed.), Lu Xun Lun Ertong Jiaoyu yu Ertong Wenxue (Shanghai, 1961), pp. 82–4.
7. Lu Xun, 'Wushiqi Xiandai de Tushazhe', Lu Xun Quanji, Vol. 2, p. 70.
8. William Lyell notes that Lu Xun translated at this time a work which was perhaps Verne's Les Anglais au Pole Nord, but no publisher was found and the manuscript was lost. See Lyell, W., Lu Hsun's Vision of Reality, op. cit., p. 65, note 32.
9. Ibid., p. 11.
10. Ibid.
11. Verne, J., Introduction, Journey to the Center of the Earth (New York, 1959), pp. v, vii and viii.
12. Lu Xun, Preface, 'Yuejie Luxing', Lu Xun Quanji, Vol. 11, p. 9.
13. Lu Xun, 'Moluo shi li shuo', Lu Xun Quanji, Vol. 1, translated in Leo Ou-fan Lee, 'Genesis of a Writer', in Goldman, M. (ed.), Modern Chinese Literature in the May Fourth Era, op. cit., p. 181.
14. Lu Xun, 'Preface, Yuejie Luxing', Lu Xun Quanji, op. cit., p. 9.
15. Verne, J., Journey to the Center of the Earth, op. cit., p. 183.
16. Lu Xun, Preface, 'Yuejie Luxing', op. cit., p. 10.
17. Lu Xun, 'Yuejie Luxing', op. cit., p. 49.
18. Chesneaux, J., The Political and Social Ideas of Jules Verne, op. cit., p. 29.

19. Lu Xun, Preface, 'Yuejie Luxing', op. cit., p. 11.
20. Chesneaux, J., *The Political and Social Ideas of Jules Verne*, op. cit., pp. 36, 64.
21. Ibid., p. 64.
22. Koestler, A., *The Sleepwalkers: A History of Man's Changing Vision of the Universe* (New York, 1963), p. 13.
23. Lyell, W., *Lu Hsun's Vision of Reality*, op. cit., p. 62.
24. Hsia, C.T., *A History of Modern Chinese Fiction* (New Haven and London, 1961), p. 46.
25. Lu Xun, Preface, 'Nahan', *Lu Xun Quanji*, Vol. 1, p. 272, translated in Yang Hsien-i and Gladys Yang, *Selected Stories of Lu Xun*, (Peking, 1972), p. 3.
26. Lyell, W., *Lu Hsun's Vision of Reality*, op. cit., p. 246.
27. Lu Xun, '"Pengbi" Zhiyu', *Lu Xun Quanji*, Vol. 3, p. 122.
28. Lu Xun, 'Ewen Yiben "A Q Zhengzhuan" Xuji Zuozhe Zishu Zhuanlue', *Lu Xun Quanji*, Vol. 7, p. 445, translated in Lyell, W., *Lu Xun's Vision of Reality*, op. cit., p. 238.
29. Lu Xun, Preface, 'Nahan', *Lu Xun Quanji*, Vol. 1, p. 274, translated in Yang Hsien-i and Gladys Yang, *Selected Stories of Lu Hsun*, op. cit., p. 5.
30. Lu Xun, 'Wusheng de Zhongguo', *Lu Xun Quanji*, Vol. 4, p. 27, translated in Yang, Gladys (ed.), *Silent China*, (London, Oxford, New York, 1973), p. 167.
31. Lu Xun, 'Kuangren Riji', *Lu Xun Quanji*, Vol. 1, p. 280, translated in Yang Hsien-i and Yang, Gladys, *Selected Stories of Lu Hsun*, op. cit., p. 10.
32. Ibid.
33. Ibid., p. 278, translation pp. 7–8.
34. Ibid., p. 279, translation pp. 7–8.
35. Ibid., pp. 286–7, translation pp. 14–15.
36. Ibid., pp. 290–1, translation pp. 17–18.
37. See Hsia, C.T., *A History of Modern Chinese Fiction*, op. cit., pp. 52–3: 'He displays throughout his writing career an indulgent attitude toward the young and the poor, especially the young, which is the more insidious form of sentimentality. . . his general attitude is clinched by the phrase in 'The Madman's Diary', 'Save the children'. See also Fokkema, D.W., 'Lu Xun: The Impact of Russian Literature', in Goldman, M. (ed.), *Modern Chinese Literature in the May Fourth Era*, op. cit., p. 97: 'Lu Xun's heroes cannot and need not have a political programme. Their wisdom will be restricted to "saving the children". . . a simple and sane philosophy. . .'.
38. Lyell, W., *Lu Hsun's Vision of Reality*, op. cit., p. 305.
39. Lu Xun, 'Guxiang', *Lu Xun Quanji*, Vol. 1, pp. 348–9, translated in Yang Hsien-i and Yang, Gladys, *Selected Stories of Lu Hsun*, op. cit., p. 57.
40. Ibid., p. 353, translation p. 60.
41. Ibid., p. 357, translation p. 63.
42. Ibid., pp. 357–8, translation p. 64.
43. Lu Xun, 'Suigan Lu, 25' (1918), *Lu Xun Quanji*, Vol. 2, pp. 15–16, translated in Lyell, W., *Lu Xun's Vision of Reality*, op. cit., p. 23.
44. Lu Xun, 'Shanghai de Ertong', in Jiang Feng, (ed.), *Lu Xun Lun Ertong Jiaoyu Yu Ertong Wenxue*, op. cit., pp. 13–14.
45. Lu Xun, 'Manma', in Jiang Feng, op. cit., p. 37.
46. Lu Xun, 'Women Xianzai Zenme Zuo Fuqin', op. cit., p. 118.
47. Ibid., pp. 119–20.
48. Ibid., p. 120.

49.   Ibid., p. 125.

50.   Ibid., p. 124.

51.   Ibid., p. 128.

52.   Ibid., p. 130.

53.   Lu Xun, 'Guxiang', op. cit., pp. 347-8, translated in, Yang Hsien-i and Yang, Gladys, *Selected Stories of Lu Hsun*, op. cit., p. 57.

54.   Ibid., p. 349; translation p. 57.

55.   Lu Xun, 'A Zhang yu Shanghai Jing', *Lu Xun Quanji*, Vol. 2, p. 357, translated in Yang Hsien-i and Yang, Gladys, *Dawn Blossoms Plucked at Dusk* (Peking, 1976), p. 23.

56.   Lu Xun, 'Kantu Shizi' (1934), *Lu Xun Quanji*, Vol. 6, p. 43.

57.   Ibid.

58.   Lu Xun, 'Shuxin: Shi Yanli Min', in Jiang Feng, *Lu Xun Lun Ertong Jiaoyu Yu Ertong Wenxue*, op. cit., p. 41.

59.   Lu Xun, 'Zayi' in Jiang Feng, *Lu Xun Lun Ertong Jiaoyu Yu Ertong Wenxue*, op. cit., p. 54.

60.   Lu Xun, Preface, 'Ailuoxianke Tonghua Ji', *Lu Xun Quanji*, Vol. 12. p. 290.

61.   Lu Xun, 'Meng', *Lu Xun Quanji*, Vol. 7, p. 395.

62.   Lu Xun, Postscript of 'Chunye de Meng', *Chenbao Fukan*, 22 October 1921, p. 1.

63.   Lu Xun, 'Chibian', *Lu Xun Quanji*, Vol. 12, p. 337.

64.   Ibid.

65.   Lu Xun, 'Diaode Xin', *Lu Xun Quanji*, Vol. 12, p. 340.

66.   Lu Xun, 'Xiwang', translated in Yang Hsien-i and Gladys Yang, *Silent China*, op. cit., p. 68.

67.   Ibid., p. 122.

68.   Lu Xun, 'Wusheng de Zhongguo', op. cit., p. 27, translated in Yang Hsien-i and Gladys Yang, *Silent China*, op. cit., p. 167.

69.   Lu Xun, Preface, 'Xiao Yuehan', *Lu Xun Quanji*, Vol. 14, pp. 5–14, translated in Lang, A., *Literary Fairytales*, (London, 1895), p. 9.

70.   Ibid., p. 8.

71.   Lang, A., *Literary Fairytales*, op. cit., p. vi.

72.   Lu Xun, Preface, *Xiao Yuehan*, op. cit., p. 7.

73.   Van Eeden, F., *Little Johannes*, op. cit., p. 1.

74.   Ibid., pp. 74–5.

75.   Lu Xun, Preface, *Xiao Yuehan*, op. cit., p. 8.

76.   Van Eeden, F., *Little Johannes*, op. cit., p. 159.

77.   Ibid., p. 180.

78.   Ibid., pp. 221–2.

79.   Lu Xun, Preface, *Xiao Yuehan*, op. cit., pp. 8–9.

80.   Mills, H.C., 'Lu Xun: Literature and Revolution—From Mara to Marx', in Goldman, M., (ed.), *Modern Chinese Literature in the May Fourth Period*, op. cit., p. 206.

81.   For an account of the circumstances that influenced Lu Xun's turn to the left see ibid., pp. 191–220.

82.   Ibid., p. 210.

83.   Lu Xun, Preface, 'Xiao Bide', *Lu Xun Quanji*, Vol. 14, p. 238.

84.   Ibid., p. 289.

85.   Ibid., p. 292.

86.   Ibid., p. 238.

87.   Ibid., pp. 238–9.

88.   Ibid., pp. 239–40.

89.   Lang, A., *Literary Fairytales*, op. cit., p. v.

90.   Xu Guangping, 'Guanyu Lu Xun de Shenghuo', in Jiang Feng (ed.), *Lu Xun Lun Ertong Jiaoyu yu Ertong Wenxue*, op. cit., p. 75.

91.   Ibid., p. 80.

92.   Lu Xun, 'Biao', *Lu Xun Quanji*, op. cit., p. 308.

93.   Ibid., p. 376.

94.   Ying Can, 'Ertong Nian de Ertong Wenxue, *Zhongxuesheng*, 62 (February, 1936), p. 189.

95.   Lu Xun, Preface, 'Biao', *Lu Xun Quanji*, op. cit., p. 297.

96.   Lavrin, J. (ed.), *Russian Stories: Pushkin to Gorky* (London, 1946), pp. 19–20.

97.   Mao Dun, 'Gaoerji he Zhongguo Wenxue' (1946), *Mao Dun Wenji*, Vol. 10 (Hong Kong, 1966), p. 112.

98.   Lu Xun, Preface, 'Eluosi de Tonghua', *Lu Xun Quanji*, Vol. 14, p. 425.

99.   Gorky M., 'On Themes', in *On Literature* (Seattle, 1973), pp. 220–4.

100.   Gorky, M., 'To H.G. Wells' (1916), in *On Literature*, op. cit., p. 368.

101.   Xu Guanping, 'Yinwei de Jinian', in Jiang Feng (ed.), *Lu Xun Lun Ertong Jiaoyu yu Ertong Wenxue*, op. cit., p. 77.

102.   Gorky, M., 'To Anton Chekhov' (1900), in *On Literature*, op. cit., p. 361.

103.   Gorky, M., 'On Themes', op. cit., p. 214.

104.   Ibid., pp. 215–16.

105.   Chen Bochui, 'Huiyi yu Celi', in *Zuojia yu Ertong Wenxue* (Tianjin, 1957), p. 91.

106.   Ibid., p. 93.

107.   Munroe, D., *The Concept of Man in Contemporary China* (Ann Arbor, 1977), p. viii.

3

A New Children's Literature

Children's literature flourished in the May Fourth period (1919–36). By the eve of the Anti-Japanese War in 1937, this new literature was commercially prosperous and well-established in China's major coastal cities. Children now had both a new literature and the old literature that was traditionally available to them.

The new children's literature is part of May Fourth literature in general. It shares many authors and was subject to the same political influences. Very early in this period these writers were apparently united against Confucianism. In the 1920s, however, they formed groupings loosely based on ideological positions concerning the role of the modern literature they were producing. By the late twenties many of the major writers had identified with a Marxist solution to China's problems and insisted that literature be aligned to this position. Democratic reformist writers countered by arguing for an 'apolitical' modern literature.

This chapter concentrates on developments within the new children's literature. Throughout the 1920s there were debates on the content of suitable children's books and the social role of the new children's literature. By the late twenties, these debates had centered on fairytales. Confucianists stridently opposed fairytales as ideologically subversive. Non-Marxist writers regarded the fairytales, ancient or modern, as belonging to the proper pastoral world of childhood. They accepted Hans Christian Andersen but rejected zur Muehlen. Revolutionary writers adapted the form of the fairytale to educate children about the realities of Chinese society. They replaced the pastoral world with what they considered was the real world. They accepted zur Muehlen but rejected Andersen as irrelevant to contemporary Chinese society.

Despite the complexity of the field, these divergent views within the new children's literature are evident in the first two major works produced for children: Ye Shengtao's fairytales (beginning in 1921) and Bing Xin's letters (1923–26). Both are regarded by Chinese as early children's classics.

Analysis of these texts reveals the fundamental point on which they differ: their views of childhood. Ye Shengtao's first collection of fairytales explores and questions notions of childhood within the context of the harsh realities of Chinese society. That is, he depicts the 'outer' world of children, the society in which they live. This type of literature became increasingly politically aligned, especially from 1927, and developed into revolutionary children's literature (see Chapter 4). Lu Xun was the major theorist of this school. Bing Xin's collection of letters, on the other hand, accepts and explores Western notions of childhood innocence. That is, she describes the 'inner' world of children, the world of their imagination. This type of literature developed into 'non-aligned' urban and commercialized children's literature. It belongs to the romantic trend in the May Fourth period. Lu Xun's brother, Zhou Zuoren, is the major spokesperson for this school of children's literature.

According to most Western commentators, romanticism is the dominant feature of all May Fourth literature. This chapter on May Fourth children's literature questions certain assumptions about the nature of that romanticism. Romanticism in this period is supposedly characterized by a concern with self-discovery, sentiment (*qing*) and a return to nature. It is said to be emotional, not rational.[1] However, in this history of children's literature I suggest that 'nature' and 'self-discovery' were indissolubly linked to contemporary notions of childhood. These notions, in turn, were part of a logically and pragmatically conceived schema for social change. By dismissing such instrumental concerns as 'sentimental', Western commentators have missed both the sociopolitical rationale for the 'discovery' of the child in the May Fourth period and the importance that writers attached to the development of the new children's literature as a means of social change.

Chinese writers did not ignore the social significance of the various views of childhood. For writers such as Lu Xun and Ye Shengtao, 'old' children's books isolated children in the past; the 'romantic' school isolated them in a world of pastoral delights. Both views were difficult to sustain in a China facing invasion and civil war.

Revolutionary writers therefore insisted that children's literature revert to its Confucian and original May Fourth role: part of a children's education that must be primarily concerned with the realities of Chinese society and its future directions. As this view is the prevailing trend in Chinese children's literature until the post-Mao period, this chapter includes the Marxist critique of children's literature in the later May Fourth period.

Ye Shengtao's Fairytales

For children, the literary revolution of the May Fourth period signified a new concept of childhood, a new social role and a new literature. While Lu Xun carved out the central arguments, it was the younger writer, Ye Shengtao, who produced the first fruit: fairytales. As one of China's foremost modern writers, he helped shape modern Chinese literature for both adults and children. As the noted critic, Prusek, stated, his work embodied a 'new sensibility'. Therefore,

> Ye Shengtao's work, like the work of Lu Xun, offers a suitable opportunity for tracing more precisely what the literary revolution really signified and what new features not present in the old literature characterize the products of the literary revolution.[2]

Ye Shengtao began writing fairytales in 1921 and published these as a collection, *The Scarecrow* (*Daocao Ren*), in 1923. This was the first book in China's new children's literature. Lu Xun lamented, '[i]t pioneered a native path for the fairytale in China. Who would have thought that (in the ten or so years) after this there is not only no change but not even anyone following

,

him'.[3] Ye Shengtao is assured of a permanent place in the history of Chinese children's literature as the first author, as a major editor of children's magazines and books, and as the pioneer of the fairytale, a genre which stood at the center of the debates on children's literature over the next half century.

Like many children's writers, Ye Shengtao began his career as a teacher. In a review of his life that appeared in *The Juvenile Student* (*Zhongxue Sheng*) in 1931, he wrote that after his graduation in 1911, he became a primary school teacher for accidental reasons: in those days 'there were not many social critics and magazine editors around and so there was not all the present fuss and bother [about the problem of A Future]'. Ten years later he was elevated to the position of a middle-school teacher because, as he wrote, 'and this is very tricky, some magazines had published a few of my short stories. People thought that if I could write short stories, then I must be good at literary composition; and if I was good at literary composition then I could naturally teach it and so, with little apparent suitability, I became a teacher of the national language'.[4] Until the outbreak of the war with Japan, when he moved inland to Sichuan, Ye Shengtao continued to teach in middle-schools and universities but he considered his main work to be editing for large publishing houses, first in Beijing and then in Shanghai. His long career, which includes a vice-ministerial position in the Ministry of Education after 1949, testifies to a committed working interest in children and a particular concern with their education.

Ye Shengtao wrote about the world he lived in and it is not surprising, therefore, that children should play a prominent part in even his adult fiction. He wrote in 1951:

> In retrospect, I seem never to have written about anything of which I had only vague or hazy knowledge. In other words, I cannot write anything by merely imagining it, though I do not banish the element of fancy. I lived in cities, towns and villages, and I wrote what I had observed there. As a teacher, I knew something about life in educational circles and I wrote about that. In a rather elementary and superficial way I watched the gradual

development of the Chinese Revolution and I wrote about that too.[5]

Thus, some of the best of his early fiction deals with teachers and school children. As Hsia has observed of these works, they show 'a playful tenderness and a serious pedagogic concern, as well as an astonishing command of the juvenile mind'.[6] His fiction for children, however, does not necessarily describe children but analyzes society *for* them through the medium of the fairytale. Like Lu Xun, Ye Shengtao does not separate the worlds of adults and children but sees them as integral parts of a social whole, whether it be the future dream or the present reality.

Neither is Ye Shengtao's juvenile fiction essentially different in intention from his adult fiction. It is still part of education but in the widest sense of the word; it is a literature of high purpose and part of the thrust towards liberation and a society of 'real men' in Lu Xun's social schema. Along with other writers in the Society for the Study of Literature founded in 1921, he wrote 'literature for life'. He told children in 1931 that observation of the world, not flowery elegance, was the most important qualification for a writer:

> . . . the basic requirement for writing fiction is a pair of penetrating and observant eyes and my eyes are not penetrating enough. . . Of course, it is not necessary to train one's eyes just for the sake of writing fiction but trained eyes do, in reality, nourish life'.[7]

Prusek's 'new sensibility' was, for Ye Shengtao, a new way of looking at life and writing about it; it was literature for a 'new' life. The significant point of departure in his children's stories is his use of the fairytale, a revitalized and controversial genre of the May Fourth period so well-suited to the argument for imaginative, vernacular literature, injected with realism.

His fairytale writing spanned the inter-war period (1921 to 1936). As this was a period of traumatic upheaval in society, politics and literature, his work reveals considerable changes in outlook over this time. To borrow his words, his eyes saw different things at different points in time.

The Scarecrow (1923)

As a totality, the fairytales in *The Scarecrow* place the romantic image of the child—the vision of their ideal world—in the actual context of contemporary Chinese society. They swing between the light and the dark, the dream and the reality, that was essential to the May Fourth social analysis and the argument for social change.

The first fairytale, 'The Little White Boat' ('Xiao Bai Chuan', first published in 1921), explores the romantic assumption. It begins with an idyllic description of a river.

> A small stream is a home for all sorts of lovely things. They grow small red flowers, slightly smiling, but sometimes they dance and that is a delight to see. Droplets of pearly dew on green grass, like fairies' clothes, dazzle men's eyes. The surface of the stream was covered with leaves of duck-weed from which towered some cassia-yellow flowers just like tropical beds of lotus—you could say it was a lotus-bed in fairy land. . .
>
> On the right bank of the stream was moored a very small white boat. It was a very lovely boat, its whole body was white and even the rudder, oars, cover and sails were completely white; it looked like a long and narrow shuttle. This boat would not carry fat people. If a fat person went to step inside, the boat would tilt over and throw them into the water. Neither would it carry old people. If an old person sat inside, with grey-black skin and a web of wrinkles on his brow, and tried to blend with the white and beautiful, then it would certainly make the old die for shame. This small boat would carry only exquisite and beautiful children.
>
> Just then two children walked towards the edge of the stream. One was a boy, dressed in white with a face rosy as an apple. The other was a girl, dressed in light blue like the sky, and with a rosy face even more delicate.[8]

The setting is immediately recognizable as the idyllic world of pastoral bliss. Even the children are ideal; they have no names and stand as symbols, not real children. They board the boat, sing to the fishes and paddle along the river until a storm blows up and they lose their way. They come to a place with persimmons, a rabbit and a wise old man who offers to send them home if they can answer three questions:

> 'The first question is: Why do birds sing?'
> 'They sing for those who love them', she immediately answered.
> . . . 'The second question is: Why do flowers have fragrance?'
> 'Fragrance is good, and flowers are the symbol of goodness', the boy hurriedly said.
> . . . 'The third question is: Why did the little white boat let you ride in it?'
> She held up her right hand just as if she were in the classroom and knew the answer: 'Because we are pure—only then will the little white boat harmonize with us and carry us'.
> The man smiled broadly, 'I will take you home!'[9]

This then is a lyrical song to the innocence and purity of the child. Jiang Feng claimed:

> . . . when Ye Shengtao began writing fairytales he cherished the pure innocence of childish hearts and he loved children. He therefore thought to shape them through wonderful fairytales and let them always retain that spirit of innocence. So he strove to write of the beauty of Nature so children would love it; he strove to describe children's innocent imagination and lead them into an ideal world.[10]

'The Little White Boat' is far removed from dark and difficult reality in its mystical merging with Nature; it is like William Blake's *Songs of Innocence* without the depth of *Songs of Experience*. Here, Ye Shengtao has followed both Lu Xun (1919) and Zhou Zuoren (1920) in their insistence on a special world of children. The work was published in the same year that Zhou Zuoren and Bing Xin began a 'World of Children' section in the *Morning Post* and that Eroshenko came to Beijing. Indeed, the description—the river, a boy and girl, the lyricism and idealism—is similar to Eroshenko's fairytale, 'A Spring Evening Dream', which Lu Xun translated in October, 1921. It is difficult to escape the conclusion that both the romantic idea of children and the nature of the fairytale were topics for discussion in The Society for the Study of Literature, particularly when two Society members, Ye Shengtao and Zhou Zuoren, were writing about both at this time. And yet another member, Bing Xin, adopted the same romantic idea as a foundation of her fiction writings.

Two more tales (both included in a small, 1956 collection of Ye Shengtao's fairytales)[11] further explore two of the symbols of childhood—goodness and love—first raised in 'The Little White Boat'.

'The Seed' ('Yike Zhongzi'), written five days after 'The Little White Boat', looks at the fate of a flower, as a symbol of goodness, when it is planted at the various levels of Chinese society. It qualifies the ideal with the question: where will the seed sprout, grow and blossom?

> Once upon a time there was a seed. It was as big as a walnut and its green skin was very lovely. No-one who saw it could help loving it. It was said that if planted in soil, it would put forth a jade-green shoot and, of course, its flower would be even more beautiful. No rose, peony or chrysanthemum could compare with it. And no orchid, cassia or tuberose would be able to match its fragrance. No-one had ever planted this seed, however, so no-one had ever seen its beautiful flowers or smelt its fragrance.[12]

The king took it as a symbol of his power; a rich man bought it as a symbol of his cultivated taste; a shopkeeper planted it as a sign that he would soon be rich; and a soldier picked it up, superstitiously sure that he would now be promoted. Each in turn could not sprout it and, believing it dead, threw it away. Finally, it landed in a green wheatfield.

> There was a young peasant working in the wheat field, his skin like burnished copper. Muscles stood out on his arms; he was like a sculptured giant.[13]

He planted, tilled and watered it with the rest of the field and soon:

. . . on its tip a bud appeared: at first it was as big as a walnut, then it grew and grew until it was the size of a tangerine, an apple, a grapefruit and finally a watermelon. Then it blossomed. The petals were red, layer upon layer of them, while there was a mass of golden, yellow stamens. A strange rich fragrance spread from the flower. The fragrance clung to all who came near and never vanished.[14]

The seed, which gives both the flower and the fragrance, only blooms for the humble young peasant, 'a sculptured giant'; he and the villagers have their reward. The people, be they king or peasant, are not real individuals but representatives of a class, and virtue belongs only to the poor peasant, his unselfish heart and uncomplaining toil. The implementation of the ideal in China is, therefore, immediately linked to a certain class.

Illustration 3.1

from 'The Seed'

While 'The Seed' looks at flowers and fragrance, 'The Thrush' ('Huamei Niao'), written in March 1922, answers the old man's first question to children in 'The Little White Boat': Why do birds sing? The answer qualified love as an ideal in Chinese society. The thrush lived in a palatial golden cage where he was tenderly cared for by Elder Brother who loved him and loved to hear him sing. But he could not hear the beauty and feeling in his own song; he just sang for Elder Brother and his friends, for those who loved him. One day the cage door was left open and the thrush flew away and, like the bird in Wilde's 'The Happy Prince', he saw scenes of misery: a rickshaw boy, bent and sweating as he pulled his passengers; cooks sweating in a kitchen so the rich could eat the choicest food; and a frightened young girl forcing herself to sing to a lute. With each new scene the thrush ponders on the meaning of this injustice and then opens his beak and sings a sad, sad song. And so he learns the essence and meaning of his art.

> The world is full of unhappy things, in cities, mountains, small rooms and tall buildings. The thrush saw this and was filled with intense sorrow. Then he sang a sad song, he sang for himself, to ease his own feelings at all this misery. Never again did he sing for only one person or only one class of people.
>
> But the worn-out workers in the factory, the tired peasant toiling in the fields, the red-eyed spinning girl, the rickshaw puller who ran until his legs gave . . . they all heard the thrush sing and felt comfort in their hearts, forgetting the misery they had met; they all raised their faces and said softly, with a small smile: 'What a lovely song, what a lovely little thrush!'[15]

The writer, like the thrush, has left the golden cage of Confucian concepts and social hierarchy, and looked with new eyes at the wide world beyond. He saw injustice and misery, and the essence of his art is to tell others and to bring comfort.

What, then, has happened to the initial romantic assumption? This is the pre-Freudian Western image of childhood, imported into China, with its notions of innocence, purity and love and with its deeper roots in 'lest ye be as a little child, ye shall not enter the kingdom of Heaven. . .'. Prusek has pointed out how 'European romanticism found a kindred spirit and mood among Chinese revolutionary youth'.[16] But like the seed, it was qualified when planted in Chinese soil. In children's literature, there is an acknowledged debt to Hans Christian Andersen and Oscar Wilde. When Ye Shengtao was asked if Wilde (and

Eroshenko) had influenced the simplicity and poetry in his stories, he replied:

> I can't say there was a direct influence and I did not think of them when I was writing. But, thinking it over, I can't say there was no influence at all. It's like the spices in a kitchen, you may mix in only one sort but there are many sides to the aroma.[17]

This observation fits with his early reading; he picked up any book and read, not systematically but as time permitted. The book may have been written in Japanese or English, but, as he did not really understand these languages, he turned to translations that were sometimes badly done.[18] Nevertheless, Andersen was, and still is, the prime example of the modern fairytale writer among Chinese writers (Wilde and Eroshenko having been conveniently buried with time). 'The Thrush' has a particular parallel in Andersen's 'The Emperor and the Nightingale': the cage, a luxurious prison, and the song, a spontaneous offering to the world which brings comfort in the end. Ye Shengtao adds a class analysis. Andersen's fairytale takes us back to Blake (and Rousseau before him) for, with Blake, we have one of 'the first coordinated utterances of the Romantic Imaginative and Spiritually Sensitive Child'.

> 'How can the bird that is born for joy,
> Sit in a cage and sing'.
> 'The bird that is born for joy' is the child of Blake's *Songs of Innocence;* his 'cage', the late eighteenth century England of the *Songs of Experience.*[19]

So far there is an obvious similarity. But Blake's whole Vision with the child as a symbol, confronted 'the fundamentals of English rationalism: the 'Idiot Reasoner'. . . Bacon, Newton and Locke'.[20] In China, on the other hand, one of the earliest and most important Western contributions was that very 'Idiot Reasoner': scientific analysis. Reason and romanticism joined hands to reanalyze Chinese society and redefine Chinese Man, and confronted Confucian superstition as the antithesis of Science. In Chinese soil in the early years of the May Fourth period, the child is a symbol of growth, progress and a future, not a symbol of untrammeled imagination and sensitivity. Innocence and purity, devoid of their Christian overtones, are not positive spiritual virtues so much as a state as yet unrestricted by Confucian convention—that is, they are qualities defined by their negation. Thus, when Ye Shengtao uses his eyes and his 'new sensibility' in 'The Thrush', he describes Chinese society and not Chinese children. We could say he rewrote Blake's poem thus:

> How can the bird that is born for sorrow,
> Sit in a cage and sing?

'The bird that is born for *sorrow*' not joy, is the writer with wide-open eyes; 'the cage' is Lu Xun's walls—outmoded Confucian concepts of art, man and society—which must be destroyed for survival. In the last analysis, Romanticism serves a social vision and not a spiritual rebirth in our Christian tradition.

The last fairytale in the collection, 'The Scarecrow' (June, 1922), describes Chinese society without any reference to the dream. It is the exact opposite of 'The Little White Boat'; here, images of despair flash through the black background of night. The writer looks through the eyes of a scarecrow, who, unlike the thrush, is powerless to move or act.

> The countryside and what happens in the fields by day have been described by poets in beautiful poems and painted by artists in delightful pictures. At night, poets after drinking become a little tipsy, their exquisite musical instruments in their arms. None of them has time to go to the fields then. Is there anybody who can tell what the fields are like and what happens there at night? Yes, there is the scarecrow.[21]

The scarecrow lives through a night which brings despair or death to three women and their children: white caterpillars eat the new rice shoots of a poor peasant woman already broken by diphtheria and the deaths of her husband and son; a tired fisherwoman with a dying child does not have enough food to give him; and a desperately unhappy woman, who has been 'sold like a cow or a pig' to pay her husband's gambling debts and must leave her child behind, drowns herself in the river. The scarecrow 'hated himself for being rooted to the ground, like a tree, unable to move a step. Surely it was a sin not to save the woman from death. His sin hurt him more than his own death. 'Let day break quickly! Let the peasants get up quickly! Let the birds fly quickly to spread the alarm! Let the wind blow away her desire for death!' As he breathed this silent prayer, all around was dark and not a sound could be heard.'[22] Like the Happy Prince, he sees a world of injustice. But unlike the Happy Prince he can do nothing: there is not the luxury of charity, individual escape or a bird as a messenger of good as in Wilde's imagery. Indeed, how can there be a 'world of childhood' when in the scarecrow's world children have difficulty staying alive?

Thus the collection of fairytales in *The Scarecrow* moves between light and happiness on the one hand and utter darkness and death on the other. From liberation to the real restrictions in Chinese society—between the Vision and the Reality lies the Abyss.

Illustration 3.2

from 'The Scarecrow'

It should be said that the available Chinese critiques of *The Scarecrow* are fundamentally different from my interpretation of the volume as an integral whole. For example, Jiang Feng, in *An*

Outline of Children's Literature (1959), claims that these fairytales document Ye Shengtao's own transition from idealism, 'the world of dreams', to melancholy 'common to many of the petty bourgeois writers at that time',[23] and he points to 'The Little White Boat' as particular proof. This is the common opinion in Chinese critiques.

While each tale can stand on its own, the shared symbols and the organization of the collection itself, *written within seven months,* invites my view of this collection as a full exploration of 'the world of childhood' in a Chinese setting. This is strengthened by Ye Shengtao's two collections of short stories written at the same time: *Barrier* (*Gemo*, 1922) and *Conflagration* (*Huozai*, 1923). They share scenes with certain fairytales in *The Scarecrow*: a longer version of a girl wearily forcing herself to sing to a lute in 'Barrier' is used later in 'The Thrush', for example, and the picture of peasant life in 'The Morning Walk' ('Xiaoxing' in *Conflagration*) looks forward to 'The Scarecrow'—including an insect plague and a poor man who drowns himself due to family persecution. Indeed, the essential difference between 'The Morning Walk' and 'The Scarecrow' is that the narrator/author is replaced by that fairytale element, the inanimate scarecrow. We have already isolated this as the significant new feature in his children's stories. Yet 'The Morning Walk', which anticipates 'The Scarecrow' in structure (such as 'miniature shots of peasant life'),[24] incident and mood, was written on November 6, 1921, just nine days before 'The Little White Boat'. Therefore, it would seem that Ye Shengtao did not undergo any simple chronological transition from idealism to melancholy within seven months. Rather, he seems to have explored a complicated set of themes at this time. One central theme in his literature for both adults and children was the complexities of the 'world of children' in China.

The Scarecrow is a pioneering work in the history of modern Chinese literature, not just Chinese children's literature. Although it was written for children, it is about childhood. It explores the early roots of European romanticism through a core symbol, the child, so essential to Rousseau's 'Natural Man', Blake's 'Vision', Coleridge's 'Imagination' and Andersen's

'Innocence'.[25] In *The Scarecrow* the symbol is almost immediately transmuted and qualified through the prism of a traditional Confucian concern, social man, and a new Chinese nationalism, the future of their society. The first fruit in children's literature has a distinctly Chinese flavor.

The Ancient Stone Hero (1931)

Ye Shengtao's second collection of fairytales, *The Ancient Stone Hero* (*Gudai Shixiang de Yingxiong*), shows a considerable change in outlook from *The Scarecrow*. He describes his own dissatisfaction with his previous writing in 1930:

> Why is it that I have recently written less and less and not written anything at all this year? There is an easily understood metaphor which is very fitting when I think about it.
>
> A man buys a new camera and, straight away, sets the focus, presses the button and turns the film. Soon the roll of film is finished and so he inserts a new one, resets the focus, presses the button and turns the film again. At that time any scene is a worthy subject: a little girl, just smiling beside the window, has an aura of innocence and so he snaps her; an old mother, smoking a waterpipe, has an old-fashioned flavor and he snaps her; he travels outside and sees a tall tree, flowing water, a peasant and a shepherd boy and, feeling strongly moved, he cannot pass it by and so he snaps that too. . . This is all very satisfying.
>
> But later, although he has achieved a certain standard, he eventually puts the camera away?. . . (Why?) The conditions he hopes to photograph are more than before, the meaning must be deeper, the framework more suitable, light and dark more clearly defined, and so on and so on, and if the quality cannot meet these conditions it is better to put the lens away. At this time, he naturally looks on photography as uninteresting. I wrote a lot in the past because of my enthusiasm and to reach a stage now where I seriously put the lens away is a natural progression.[26]

Ye Shengtao, himself, confirms Prusek's analysis of his early writings as 'film-like sequences of shots from real life not related to any subject' but 'simply a form of presentation of a certain atmosphere, a certain situation, or a set of human relationships'.[27] The artist is a cameraman. The common link between scenes in the early fairytales is a symbol—the boat, the seed, the thrush, the scarecrow.

The cause of Ye Shengtao's change in outlook undoubtedly lay in the disillusion, shared by many writers, over the split between the Nationalists and the Communists in 1927. Ye Shengtao describes the feeling in a partly autobiographical novel about a school teacher, Ni Huanzhi. While the fairytales in *The Ancient Stone Hero* still focus on society, light and dark is seen as a confrontation between rich and poor, the framework is of growing class revolution and not social reform. The 'film-like sequences of shots' are no longer linked by a central symbol but are driven by the inexorable logic (and necessity) of a Marxist revolution, derived from outside the particular artistic process. Whereas before, the symbol of the dream confronted the shots of reality, there is now an attempt to bridge the gap through revolutionary action.

'The Ancient Stone Hero', which gives the second collection its title, was written in 1930 and published in the first issue of *The Juvenile Student* in January, 1931. The editorial commented that 'Mr Ye Shengtao's fairytales. . . are rich in satire'.[28] In this story, to commemorate an ancient hero, the people request a sculptor to make a statue of him. The sculptor agrees and gradually creates a mental image of the statue, complete in detail to the last hair, so that it will seem like the living hero and not a dead stone statue. It is made according to this image and placed, on a tall pedestal of small stones, in the center of the city. Anyone who came there first saw it 'just as the first sight in Paris is the Eiffel Tower'.[29] And anyone who passed beneath it had to stand still and respectfully kowtow before they moved on. The statue, therefore, grew arrogant, believing he occupied a privileged high position and felt contemptuous of his fellow stones beneath him. The pedestal stones tried to remind him of their original common state in stone but he would not listen, saying they would only become equal when the sky and earth became equal. A small stone answered:

Even now you are not really separate from us. We are still a whole block, we have only changed appearance. You look, from the top of your head to our lowest level, don't we stand together? Moreover, because we are changed into our present form, your position is not at all stable. You stand on our bodies, we need only shake once and you will not stand so loftily. . . [30]

The argument continued and the statue is frightened and tried to make up a little but when he eventually fell down one night, both he and the pedestal are reduced to small and big stones lying on the ground. They are a nuisance and the citizens use them to build a northbound road. The stones are pleased:

'We really are equal.'
'We are not illusory at all.'
'We have united to build a real road which men may happily walk upon.'[31]

This fairytale was later included in language textbooks and Ye Shengtao, in 1956, summarized its meaning for the many teachers and children who had written to him about it.

At that time, I thought the primary meaning was in the editing. Big or small stones when united in a block to build a true road that men may tread, have the most meaningful life for stones. Before the road was built, when the big stone was a statue of a hero and the small stones formed a pedestal beneath, there was not any great meaning. As for the arrogance of the big stone after he is carved into a statue of a hero, thinking himself different to the masses and looking down on people: I only wrote it like this to show the 'psychology' of the big stone at that time. . . The description of how the small stones felt when they saw the arrogance of the big stone was also completely according to their 'psychology' at that time.[32]

Illustration 3.3

from 'The Ancient Stone Hero'

The social implications of this fairytale are clear. It toppled the high and mighty from their pedestal and reduced men to their common humanity so that—'the primary meaning'—they may happily walk upon a 'real road'. Fundamentally, its meaning is the same as Lu Xun's *Old Tales Retold* (*Gushi Xinbian,* 1922–35) which rewrote the legendary heroes as ordinary people; 'having less respect for the ancients than for my contemporaries I have not been able to avoid facetiousness. . . At least I have not made the ancients out as more dead than they are'.[33] Dead ancients, dead statues: this fairytale is within the May Fourth sensibility. Ye Shengtao's tale adds a new dimension, however, in its logical progression from an original common state in the uncarved block to the illusion of hierarchy in the positioning of the statue atop the pedestal stones and, finally, to a resolution in a leveling of all the stones, with its return to equality and unity. This is given extra force by Ye Shengtao's reversal of the roles of dream and reality; the dream is now the 'real road', contemporary class hierarchy is based on an illusion.

'The Emperor's New Clothes' ('Huangdi de Xinyi') in this collection also destroys an illusion, the illusion of power. It is based on Hans Christian Andersen's story of the same name.

In the original there is an Emperor whose sole care is beautiful clothes: 'Just as they say of a king, 'He is in council', one always said of him, 'The Emperor is in the wardrobe'.[34] He is cheated by two tailors who declare they weave the finest fabric and make the most beautiful clothes which possess a magical quality that makes them invisible to anyone who is unfit for office or very stupid. Fearful of their own position, Emperor, ministers and people all take part in the pretence that the Emperor is wearing clothes until, one day, he leads a procession:

> 'But he has nothing on!' a little child cried out at last.
> 'Just hear what the innocent says!' said the father; and one whispered to another what the child had said. 'Here is a little child that says he has nothing on.'
> 'But he has nothing on!' said the whole people at length. And the Emperor shivered for it seemed that they were right; but he thought within himself, 'I must go through with the procession'.
> And so he carried himself still more proudly, and the chamberlains held on more tightly than ever, and carried the train which did not exist at all.[35]

Ye Shengtao continues the story in his version: 'What happened afterwards? Andersen did not say. Really there were many, many things'.[36]

The illusion shattered, people look at their Emperor and see him as he really is; just a man, but particularly skinny, black, hairy and with bones 'like a hen'. They laugh to each other, and the Emperor, hearing them, persists angrily with the illusion and orders the immediate execution of anyone daring to criticize his clothes. During the Sacrifice to Heaven, alone, three hundred people are killed like pigs. Two casualties are the Emperor's favorite concubine and most loyal minister. His tyranny grows; he passes a law that forbids the people to talk or laugh in his presence and so, whenever he goes out, the streets are always empty. One day, however, he hears a child crying and a woman singing and orders his soldiers to break down the doors and

Illustration 3.4

from 'The Emperor's New Clothes'

arrest anyone who utters a sound. But a strange thing happens. The people surge from their homes, surround the Emperor, touch him, pull him and pummel him, shouting: 'Take off your illusory clothes! Take off your illusory clothes!' (Illustration 3.4).[37]

The soldiers come out of the houses and, seeing the Emperor sitting on the ground looking just like a monkey, burst into laughter. Soon everyone is laughing and the Emperor falls into a dead faint!

Despite the similar plot, the two fairytales are markedly different in their primary meaning. The point of Andersen's tale is that a child has more wisdom than an Emperor or the wisest minister. It is innocence which destroys the illusion. Innocence, spontaneity and love, the supposedly natural qualities of childhood, are central to Andersen's fairytales:

Andersen, imbuing his tales with an invincible belief in a better future, communes with the soul of children, harmonizes himself with their deep nature, allies himself with their deep mission. He upholds, with them and through them, the ideal forces which save humanity from perishing.[38]

This is, indeed, similar to the early May Fourth view of childhood but the notion was fading by the thirties. Innocence plays little part and has no power in Ye Shengtao's version. Power belongs to the people. He uses Anderson's tale for a different purpose; like the writer, people use their eyes and look at the Emperor and discover he is only a man, after all. It is not just the Emperor's new clothes which are an illusion but the social position of the Emperor himself, with his paraphernalia, his 'clothing', of power. Naked, he is reduced (like the stone statue) to his true state as an ordinary man—except he is uglier than most. And it is a united people, not a single child, who eventually force the Emperor from his pedestal.

The fairytales in Ye Shengtao's second collection are imbued with a new force which takes them beyond the literary revolution and into revolutionary literature. There is a conviction that people must unite and fight for their equality; social leveling is the beginning of the 'real road' which leads to happiness and laughter for the Chinese people.

'The Experiences of a Locomotive' and 'Animal Talk' (1936)

Ye Shengtao published his last two fairytales in 1936: 'The Experiences of a Locomotive' ('Huochetou de Jingli') and 'Animal Talk' ('Niaoyan Shuyu'). Both were published in a new magazine, *New Adolescents* (*Xin Shaonian*), of which Ye Shengtao was an editor. Both take on the urgency and patriotic spirit of children's literature on the eve of the Japanese occupation in China. And both have a background of war.

Illustration 3.5

from 'The Experiences of a Locomotive'

In 'The Experiences of a Locomotive', a locomotive was built in an English factory and sent to China to serve the people, *all* the people and not just one as locomotives sometimes did. That was slavery and meant that others could not reach their destination. The train became familiar with his route, the scenery and his passengers. One day, a crowd of several thousand students boarded the train because of a national emergency but a contingent of police ordered them to disembark and a group of foreign-dressed men tried to negotiate with them. But the students stood firm: 'We will not get off the train. We will never get off the train until we reach our destination!'[39] The locomotive was impressed with their staunch hearts and grew so angry that he could not leave the station but, suddenly, his wheels began to turn and he was on his way.

The iron rails slipped by under my wheels. Fields, rivers, villages and forests spun past in the dusk. The wind twirled snowflakes as if it were filling the void with dust. I ran, ran at full speed, using

my great strength to carry this aroused and selfless group of
students and their fiery, fearless hearts, forward, forward. . .[40]

It was their 'fiery, fearless hearts' that overcame all
difficulties; when stranded by the engine-driver in a snowy
wasteland, the students themselves started the engine, and when
the rails were torn up, they themselves mended them in the icy
night. 'Gradually the sky lightened. The snow stopped. In the
faint blue morning light, on a dazzling silver world',[41] the
locomotive could see them working tirelessly and he was filled
with admiration and a wish to always serve them. The students
seemed to answer with their song:

> Who piles up obstacles on our road of progress, peak after peak?
> Who piles up obstacles on our road of progress, peak after peak?
> No-one sighs for the hardships we meet on the road,
> Sighs are useless. Useless!
> We, we will, will light the explosives under the ground,
> And take aim! Pow! Pow! Pow!
> See the peaks on the mountain range, the sky topples, the earth
> shakes!
> Blow up the mountain peak,
> Open up the mighty road!
> Staunch hearts,
> United as one!
> We, we are the pioneers of a new road!
> We, we are the pioneers of a new road!
> Pow! Pow! Pow! Haha! Haha! Pow![42]

In 'Animal Talk', the same militant activism has replaced the
passive and lonely misery in *The Scarecrow*. When a mouse and
a sparrow—two lowly creatures—go out to discover how
humanity uses words, they find only two instances of principled
usage, like the honesty of 'one is one, two is two'.[43] The first
time is when a large crowd of people shout: 'We have hands, we
want work. We have stomachs, we want food'.[44] The second
time is when they hear a speech by a tall, bearded, angry-eyed
commander of an ill-equipped army:

The enemy has now come to our land. They want to kill us, shoot us, ferocious bandits simply cannot compare with them. We have only one road and that is a strong defense.[45]

Illustration 3.6

from 'Animal Talk'

In these fairytales on the eve of war, the urgent, patriotic virtues are unity, selflessness and dedication. They became part of war literature and reach back to *The Ancient Stone Hero* in 1931. Ye Shengtao uses the fairytale element, a talking train or a sociologist sparrow, to give a fresh perspective on social inequalities. These tales are situated in the real world, not fairyland.

Hence, their real beginning is in *The Scarecrow* which 'pioneered a native path for the fairytale in China': the path of social criticism and a dream for China. Ye Shengtao's fairytales consistently champion the cause of the poor and oppressed, and beckon them towards a new life. A real life. Like Lu Xun's work, Ye Shengtao's tales are the fruit of a 'new sensibility' that searched for a new society to replace the older order that the masses so passionately hated and wished to shatter like the ancient stone hero. Like Lu Xun, Ye Shengtao pits the imagery of life and light against the old world of death and darkness. At the core of his art was the conviction that all people are equal and the eventual realization that they must fight to secure that equality. Like Lu Xun, in the end he called for a class revolution. If as Mao claimed 'the road Lu Xun took was the very road of China's new national culture', then Ye Shengtao and his fairytales trod the very same road.

Bing Xin's *Letters to Young Readers*

Bing Xin's *Letters to Young Readers* is considered to be the earliest work written for children. Chen Xiu claimed that, while Ye Shengtao's work exploited the fairytale as 'a special form belonging to children's literature', his aim was to use fairytales as a vehicle 'to reflect the real ugliness of contemporary society'.

> [Thus, the first work] written genuinely for children and, moreover, about their life must be Bing Xin's *Letters to Young Readers*.[46]

Bing Xin is the pen-name of Xie Wanying (born 1902). Her *Letters to Young Readers* (*Ji Xiao Duzhe*, 1923–26), serialized in 'The World of Children' section of the *Morning Post* supplement, was the second major publication in China's new children's literature. At this time she was already a famous poet and short story writer, publishing her first story in 1919, at the age of seventeen, and her best works in 1923: two collections of poetry, *Myriad Stars* (*Fanxing*) and *Spring Waters* (*Chunshui*) and a collection of short stories, *Superman* (*Chaoren*). According to Zhang Tianyi,

> [T]hese works were read by almost everyone interested in art and by practically all female students. The author's emphasis is on polished writing, inserting a few droplets from the old literature, but this is not at all repugnant just as feet, liberated from their ancient bindings and wearing high heels, are still attractive. These works manifest the author's femininity and make you savor a

gentle, delicate, warm and mild love; she does her utmost to imbue her writings with these flavors but, because of this, they are narrow thematically. They do not move outside poetry, maternal love, human love, innocence and humanitarianism... The style and method of her *Letters*... are the same.[47]

The dominant note in Bing Xin's 'new artistic sensibility' was uniquely feminine. Whereas Ye Shengtao's fairytales are about society and social classes, and swung in the thirties to a militant male pitch, Bing Xin's fiction is mostly about women and children and softly tuned to keynotes of tenderness, love and nostalgia. In her best stories, she pinpoints that psychological moment when a major character is aware that life has irretrievably changed; a boy leaving home ('One Year Away From Home', 'Lijia de Yinian'), the death of a beloved sister ('Zhuanghong's Elder Sister', 'Zhuanghong de Zizi') or, as late as 1936, a lonely career woman meeting a happily married man who had proposed to her ten years earlier ('The West Wind' 'Xifeng'). With this awareness of change comes a sense of loss and disillusion which colors her stories just as the introduction of a minor third colors a tune. Marcela Bouskova identifies this central emotional tone as 'pathos'.[48]

Figure 3.1 Emotional Structure in Bin Xin's Stories

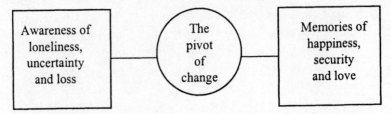

Structurally, there is always a balance and contrast arising from the same character's memories of earlier happiness and security, often in childhood, which are reinforced by Bing Xin's own particular concept of 'love' (Figure 3.1).

It is Bing Xin's idealization of love that weights the scale towards memories and happiness. This love is not class comradeship or loyalty, but feminine and maternal. The noted writer, Shen Congwen, claimed it was not a sensual love,

> but a sort of motherly compassion, a sort of child-like purity, which forms the moral basis, the desire for peace, in her writings. Its description in her *Superman* collection harbors a gentle sorrow. But the author's peaceful life gives her a strength which avoids tragedy and sings a very warm and very soft song.[49]

Her emphasis on 'love' as the moral foundation of her work, therefore has a paradoxical function in the text: it both accentuates and mitigates the sense of loss and pathos which pervades her work. It brings balance and harmony.

The important point for our discussion is that the golden memories of happiness and love belong to the world of children in Bing Xin's set of emotional values. In a period that sought to understand the special nature of childhood, she articulated and celebrated it. She idealized children into the only true symbols of love. For her,

> Except for the universe,
> Only children are always lovable
> Talking to them needs no calculation,
> But you need to show respect.
> Raising their heads to joke,
> Lowering their heads to play with water.
> Whether you ponder deeply,
> Or sing so slightly,
> They are good;
> On a donkey's back
> Beneath a monastery gate,
> They suddenly turn their heads to look,
> Always alive,
> Laughing.

'The Lovable', in Keaide, 1921[50]

This short poem, with its free form, uneven lines and lack of rhyme so different from classical poetry, actually swayed the editors of *Morning Post* that Bing Xin's poetry, for which she is now famous, was 'poetic'. Her first poem from *Myriad Stars*, written under the influence of Tagore, elicited a phone call from one editor (her cousin) asking: 'What is it?' Embarrassed, she answered, 'Just something belonging to miscellaneous writings. . .' and it was published under 'New Art' for want of a classification. When 'The Lovable' was published under 'Miscellaneous Thoughts', with the editorial comment that it belonged to poetry, it gave her sufficient confidence to further experiment with poetry and fiction.[51] She grew along with the new literature.

The main themes of Bing Xin's fiction—idealization of love and celebration of childhood—are nowhere more obvious than in her *Letters* where she reminisces about her own life. Most of the letters were written from America.

> In the Autumn of 1923 I went to America. At that time my interest was not in fiction but in letters. Because I wanted to write in this style and I had an audience, I could fairly easily turn my wishes into reality. At the same time, letters are very free and, in one section, can relate many fragmented but interesting things. The result was that, during my three years in America, I wrote twenty-nine letters to young readers. I originally thought to use the language of children, the language of innocence, but the more I wrote the more removed I became from this intention. This is an inescapable fault. But, due to my experience of three years outside China and my feelings during an illness, I was able to write freely and I felt happy.[52]

The chronological framework, which forms the superficial thread in *Letters*, is her trip to America, her three-year sojourn there, and her return home. Within this framework, she fills her letters home to China with poetry, anecdotes and discussion of disparate topics, those 'fragmented but interesting things' which give her passages of lyrical description a full-bodied flavor and a contact with reality. Her physical presence in a certain place leads to its description, her own feelings and loosely associated ideas. Leaving China, she quotes a poem by Wordsworth on how he felt about England when he traveled abroad, for example (Letter 8). Feeling sick on a wet day, she tells children, 'I write most easily when I am sick, quiet, and it is raining' (Letter 26).

She tells them about the view from her hospital window, her trips to Boston and Massachusetts, the forests and wide roads in America. She relates amusing incidents, such as teaching a child the Chinese characters for 'sky' and 'earth'. The child remarked that the Chinese language was very funny to begin with such big things; their language began with writing little things like 'cat' and 'mouse'. At a time when the West was a model for China, with many students studying abroad, she offered children glimpses of a Western country and another way of life and made it live for them vicariously through her.

Figure 3.2 Emotional Structure in Bing Xin's *Letters to Young Readers*

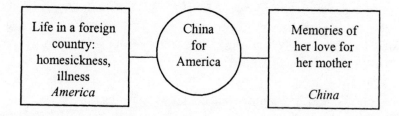

But these first-hand glimpses of another world are surrounded by the mist of Bing Xin's own reminiscences and feelings (Figure 3.2). The theme is not so much America itself as the distance and difference of America to counterpoint and review her own childhood. Time and again, she returns to it. The central thread is not *going* to America but *leaving* her mother, her family and China (in that order). Despite the fragmented structure of the content of *Letters*, the emotional structure could be schematized more precisely as emphasizing her love for her mother and for China.

The balance is tipped in favor of China and childhood both because of the passionate emphasis she gives them and because she actually returns to her mother and China in the very last letter. In Letter 1 she tells children that she, too, used to be a child and is still very often like one. She is already homesick at the thought of leaving home even though her brother suggests that, since the world is round and she will be on the other side, they can pierce it with a hollow bamboo pole and see each other whenever they like. Perhaps she will grow fatter! She leaves home as if in a dream and on her return, in Letter 28, she writes to her mother: 'Beloved mother!. . .

> My heart is drowning and alight with a mother's love. After three years away I have not changed and I am still my mother's girl as I was three years ago, I am still the precious girl my mother held many, many years ago. . . Mother! People in a dream are only people in a dream and, apart from you, who could be the eternal haven of my soul?'[53]

Letter 29, which chronicles her return, begins in ecstasy and tears of happiness: 'I am home!' Indeed, these letters to children were appropriately dedicated, in 1927, to her mother: 'She was the first and last person I ever loved and, whenever I pick up my pen her frowning or smiling face always wells up before my eyes.'[54]

She wrote in the preface that the book had 'child-like happiness and innocent tears',[55] although there are probably more tears, even tears of happiness. One of many examples relates to a worrying incident that happened when she was young and a small grey mouse stole under her chair to pick up crumbs. She tried to cover it up with a book but the dog came in and caught it. She felt guilty and cried and laughed at the same time. Then her mother asked her about the mother mouse waiting for her baby. Later, she told an adult about this but it was treated as such a trifling incident that she only dared to repeat it now, to children (Letter 2). Part of her idealization of childhood is the romantic belief that children, in their natural innocence and sensitivity, possess an *a priori* wisdom that decreases with age. Much of her strength as a writer *for* and *about* children lies not so much in an evocation of their joys as in a sympathetic rendering of their fears and sorrows that seem so petty to an adult, but flood their entire being. This strength comes from her own vivid memories of childhood.

What saves these apostrophes to mother-love from a sickly slide into sentimentality is that they are usually based on a concrete happening and firmly rooted in her own early experience. Letter 7 begins with life on a boat at sea where the waves rock her back to childhood and, in the second section, describes living beside Lake Wabah. She then asks herself which she likes better, the sea or the lake?

> It is as if the sea is my mother and the lake my friend. I was intimate with the sea in my childhood and am intimate with the lake now. The sea is deep, vast and limitless, without a word, her love is mysterious and great. I yearn most to recapture that love. The lake is red-leaved, green-stemmed and has many colors. Her love is warm and lovely. I quietly return this love. This may be too abstract but I don't know how else to describe it.[56]

This short passage is a focal point in one of her longer letters but, primarily a poet, she first creates a context of concrete imagery and then, with a deft pen, relates this to an idea. The image becomes a metaphor.

Bing Xin's art comes more from subjective experience than from social analysis. If her relationship with her mother influenced her idea of love, it was also her early environment that molded her feeling for Nature. She paints in words to highlight the mood and color of a place, rather than its clear lines and layout.

> From very small, I was a lonely child, living beside the sea in Mount East (in Fuzhou)... When I was three or four and just understanding things, every year, every month, all I saw was: the purple mountains, the limitless sea, the blue clothes of the navy and their gray-white boats. All I heard was: the mountain wind, the ocean waves, the resonant voices and the sound of the trumpet in the clear morning and deep night. The monotony of my life made me develop intellectually and tread a path which was not normal for young girls.[57]

Just as here the description of her life supports the fact of her loneliness, so too the famous descriptions of natural scenery in her letters are always harmonized with her own feelings. Bing Xin merges with Nature in such a way that a scene, herself and a mood are at one. A critic's comment on her first book of poetry could equally apply to *Letters*: '[H]er words have a new clarity, her memories have the sweetness of honey.'[58] The essential lyricism in her writing, which was not at first recognized even in poetic form until 1921, is the element that lifts such an unlikely genre as letters into the realm of pioneering works for children in modern China.

There is also a subconscious aspect of Bing Xin's writing. Her relationship to Nature and to her mother is passionately penned and has no hint of maturing sexuality or wider social responsibility. It is almost as if she, like many of her fictional characters, did not want to grow up. This is especially clear in her many descriptions of the sea, which she usually genders female and which often denotes her mother. 'Mother. You are the vast sea and I am only the foam on the wave, prancing for a moment.'[59] Bing Xin's ideal is to merge into that 'vast and limitless' sea of love just as she used to feel part of her mother in childhood. She remembered one occasion when 'at that time, the universe did not exist, only my mother and I, and finally I did not exist, only my mother; because originally I was part of her.'[60] Bing Xin said that Christianity and Tagore influenced her idea of love, but it would probably also be true to say that they helped make a child's love for its mother into a cosmic principle; her ideal world is a womb written as large as the universe with none of the insecurities and loneliness of the real world. A longing for an uncut umbilical cord. Her mother is a haven for her soul to which she wants to return and this is not surprising when we consider the gap between her secure, warm world of childhood and her move, in adolescence and womanhood, to the turmoil and ferment of Beijing in the twenties and her move again, aged twenty-one, to progressive America. Bing Xin was not timid as her travels confirm, but childhood perhaps represents an emotional escape from the changes she continued to confront.

In documenting the 'new artistic sensibility' of the May Fourth period, it could be said that, where Lu Xun educated fathers to a new social role, Bing Xin celebrated an eternal bond between mother and child. Where Lu Xun saw childhood as part of the natural continuum of life, she idealized it to the point of isolation. Where Lu Xun and Ye Shengtao adopted the romantic qualities of childhood as symbols of the future, growth and hope, she used the same qualities to point to the past, with regret, and the tragedy of growth. Where Lu Xun and Ye Shengtao confronted the black night of old China with a sunlit future, she fought the grayness of present reality with a golden past. Where they looked forward, she looked back.

Many critics are ambivalent about Bing Xin's work. They point to the popularity of her work but criticize its sentimentality and narrow social concern. Prusek called her 'a doll in an ivory tower'.[61] Bing Xin fares badly whenever judged according to the dictates of social realism and the demands of a revolutionary society, which is to say that her work is judged for what it is not, rather than what it is. The most noted quality in her writings is its feminine style and, from this standpoint, Bing Xin depicted a psychological reality that was unique amongst contemporary writers. As in the work of Jane Austen, it is not the breadth of her social picture, but the depth of a familiar area. In a period when intellectuals consciously sought to reject the old traditions and create a new and better society, she translated a regret for the old and a bewilderment, particularly for women, about an uncertain future. Certainly, the changes for young, cosmopolitan women in China in this transitional period were probably greater than those for men and she yearns for peacefulness and security. Change, peace and a longing for security are all keynotes in Bing Xin's art. Even subconsciously she was a feminine writer.

It is not too fanciful to claim that she authentically captured a certain mood in Chinese society, encapsulating, with a lingering delight, the romantic yearnings of a new generation and a nostalgia for the old order which was still a vital force, yet to produce, for example, the later masterpieces of the great, traditional painter, Huang Binhong. She captured this mood through the new literature. She has a mastery over the vernacular and unobtrusive structure in her best stories, she was one of the pioneers in children's literature and, most importantly, she created a new poetic style. But she could not adjust to the temper of a different time, the changing social demands on literature, without denying the springs of her own art. She does not follow a general development in children's literature but remains enmeshed in a definite period. Her work fully, and ingenuously, embodies the romantic ideal of childhood from an unashamedly feminine stance. Her work highlights the absence of critiques on the female, the feminine, and feminine perspectives on the 'new sensibility' of the May Fourth period, the new literature and children's literature at a time of tumultuous change for China.

Children's Literature in the Inter-war Period 1921 to 1937

From its beginnings in Ye Shengtao's fairytales and Bing Xin's letters, children's literature in China blossomed in the inter-war period. In the cities, especially Shanghai, children's literature was well established as part of the commercial publishing world and as part of the process of modern education by 1936. Children had their own magazines and books as proof of the recognition of 'a world of children' with its specialized literary needs. Many famous authors wrote for children and their literature was reviewed and discussed in the major literary journals of the period.

In 1920 Lu Xun's brother, Zhou Zuoren (1885–1966), accomplished a crucial task for developing the field: the classification of childhood into various stages with correspondingly suitable types of literature. In an early essay on children's literature, he argued that man's life cycle spans three main periods, childhood, maturity and old age, with childhood taking up the first twenty years. This, in turn, is divided into babyhood (1–3 years), early childhood (3–6 years), later childhood (6–10 years), adolescence (10–15 years) and youth (15–20 years). Children's literature is for those between three and fifteen years; Zhou links their age, interests, level of schooling and reading (reorganized in Table 3.1).[62] The four categories today conform to various stages within the Chinese school system: kindergarten; lower and upper primary school; and lower middle school.

The controversial issue in the inter-war period was the content of children's literature. Writers and critics were divided

Table 3.1 Zhou Zuoren's Classification of Childhood Stages and Suitable Literature for Each Stage

Age and Schooling	Stage of Development	Reading Matter
Early Childhood (3–6 years) Kindergarten	Learn primarily through sensation and copying. Learn to connect ideas. Little difference between reality and fantasy.	1. Poetry (old or new) with emphasis on sound and rhythm, e.g. nursery rhymes. 2. Simple fables. 3. Fairytales, especially Western translations. 4. Happy, not cruel stories.
Later Childhood (6–10 years) Lower primary school	Development of memory and observation. Real experiences and limits on fantasy. More articulate and imaginative.	1. Poetry, form and content important. Nursery rhymes and traditional poetry. Need new poems. 2. Fairytales, e.g. Andersen or traditional stories like those in *Journey to the West* (*Xiyouji*). 3. Nature stories, akin to fables, on plants and animals. Must rely on translations.
Adolescence (10–15 years) Upper primary and lower middle school	Early adolescence much like later childhood. Growing awareness and knowledge of social morality etc.	1. Poetry, simple, classical and ballads. 2. Legends. While Zhou Zuoren did not consider national heroes suitable, they became an important part of children's literature. 3. Realistic stories, e.g. *Robinson Crusoe, Don Quixote, The Scholars* (*Rulin Waishi*) and *The Travels of Lao Can* (*Lao Can Youji*). 4. Fables, e.g. Greek myths, stories from Chinese classics and Buddhism. 5. Drama, little available. May adapt legends or use translations.

on ideological grounds. Conservatives disapproved of the new children's literature because it was deliberately subversive of traditional Chinese values. May Fourth reformers, such as Lu Xun and Zhou Zuoren, completely rejected the Confucian children's classics. However, the reformers themselves were divided on the political alignment of some children's books. Zhou Zuoren, for example, was strongly critical of any intrusion of adult controversies regarding politics and ideology into children's books, believing that the imaginative, happy stories without overt didacticism, such as those by Andersen, were 'closer to a children's world'.[63] Unlike Lu Xun and Ye Shengtao, Zhou Zuoren forgot that the new literature was itself a vehicle for new ideas and social change, and, over the years, it forged closer links with revolutionary ideologies (through stories like *Little Peter*) and political movements. Lu Xun's view of the world of children as ultimately dependent on the larger world of men was to be the prevailing one in children's literature.

At the heart of this controversy over political content was the fairytale, a genre introduced from Europe. Townsend defined the term as it is used in the West:

> Fairytales, ancient or modern, are about magic, set in the indefinite past and incorporating traditional themes and materials; they are about giants, dwarves, witches, talking animals, and a variety of other creatures, as well as good and bad fairies, princes, poor widows, and youngest sons. Folktales are the traditional tales of the people. They are often fairytales but do not have to be; 'folk' indicates the origin; 'fairy' the nature of the story.[64]

Zhou Zuoren was particularly influential in introducing into China the fairytale as a genre and explaining to Chinese people its history in the West. 'Fairytale', the English term, he explained, came from the fairies in the most primitive stories but, strictly speaking, this sort of fairy is found only in England! The Chinese word, *tonghua*, is more suitable because its literal meaning is 'child's story' and, believing that children's development follows the evolutionary path of humankind, childish imagination is similar to 'the literature of primitive societies' which first created fairytales.[65] While China has traditionally had this sort of story, the term was actually introduced from Japan, where it was first used in the eighteenth century for children's stories.[66]

Chinese interest in fairytales was, in fact, part of a wider literary interest in the whole submerged oral tradition, including myths, legends and folk tales, which was raised from its lowly status in the Confucian literary hierarchy and reinterpreted by May Fourth writers within an evolutionary framework.

Diehard Confucianists hated fairytales, claiming that the lack of distinction between the worlds of animals and men warped children's proper social behavior and perverted the pattern of development devized by Confucius who said to one disciple: 'One cannot herd with birds and beasts. If I am not to be a man among other men, then what am I to be?'[67] In short, these conservative writers did not accept the implications for humanity that followed from the concept of evolution. They believed that 'talking birds and animals', the quaint term they used for fairytales in the twenties and thirties, 'certainly made for unclear thoughts, perverted behavior and no differences between animals and men'.[68] The norms in Confucian education were precisely those which placed men above animals in traditional children's texts and are summarized in the most important book of all, *The Three Character Classic*: 'if a man does not learn, he is not equal to the brutes'. Because such obscene perversions came from the very nature of the fairytale, the provincial head of Hunan forbade their distribution and requested the Ministry of Education to similarly censor them throughout the land. The fairytale sparked a national debate in 1931. Lu Xun countered the conservative criticisms:

> Children's minds are not the same as those of high Confucian officials in that they can progress instead of eternally standing stock still in the same place and still believing, even when they have grown long, long beards, that they can ride a giant to fairyland and become Emperor. This is because they will later understand a little science and realize that so-called giants and fairyland do not exist in this world (1931).[69]

Zhao Jingshen translated many Western fairytales, in particular those of Oscar Wilde, and wrote a rather long book, *A Collection of Discussions on Fairytales (Tonghua Lunji)*, published in 1927. He was influenced by Zhou Zuoren's views. He wrote that one of the urgent tasks was to decide which fairytales were suitable for children and decided on 'educational' fairytales (Figure 3.3).[70]

Figure 3.3 Educational Fairytales for Children: Zhao Jingshen

According to Zhao Jingshen and Zhou Zuoren, these were fairytales selected from both the folk and modern traditions; suitable Western examples were stories by the Brothers Grimm and Hans Christian Andersen, respectively. They rejected frightening stories from the folk tradition and the modern, politically aligned fairytale. In both cases unwelcome adult imagery (from either the superstitious past or the revolutionary present) intruded into children's pastoral world. In short, they were committed to the romantic notion of childhood; they were committed to democratic reforms and not to a Marxist revolution.

According to this figure, Lu Xun's translations and Ye Shengtao's fairytales all belong outside 'educational' fairytales for they go beyond the form to espouse a new morality and world view derived from adults. Zhao Jingshen, for example, considered that only the first half of Ye Shengtao's *The Scarecrow* was suitable for children while the second half, with its bleak social picture, was more suitable for adults.[71] Nevertheless, Lu Xun and Ye Shengtao's adaptation of the form to a specific Marxist content from 1927 onwards was to be the main type of fairytale in modern children's literature. In Lu Xun's view, children's education was much more important than the content of a particular tale:

> As many people have asked whether they are suitable for boys and girls, I shall mention my view in passing. Some say that to teach children these legends will only make them superstitious and do much harm; but others argue that these fairytales are suited to childish natures and will interest without injuring them. It seems to me that the whole question hinges on the state of education in this country. If children can receive a good education, they will study science and know the truth and not be superstitious. In that case no harm will be done. But if young folk can have no better education and make no further mental progress, they will always believe the legends they heard when children, and this may be bad for them.[72]

By the thirties, there were four main schools, each with its separate political implications, in children's literature in China. There were: books belonging to the classical Confucian tradition, either in their original, literary form or translated into the new vernacular; books belonging to the popular, colloquial tradition; a flourishing trade in modern, commercialized literature; and revolutionary children's literature, which was the bridge between early May Fourth literature, war literature and the literature of the new People's Republic. This fourth school is discussed in detail in the next chapter. The first three schools are surveyed below.

The Continuation of the Confucian Tradition

The Confucian tradition was the stated enemy of the new literature for children. However, children's literature is cumulative, not constantly replaced, and Confucian texts held their own, despite the savage criticism they received from the May Fourth intellectuals. In 1934 there was explicit government support for them in 'The New Life Movement', which reintroduced the old values and Confucian ideology to support the Nationalist government under Jiang Jieshi (Chiang Kai-shek). Politically, it was a rather sterile, if not escapist, move: Confucianism had been stripped of its outer life with the removal of the imperial system and the examination system, and had been robbed of its core internal values by the inroads of Western science and materialism. Lu Xun was especially caustic about old stories republished, often in the vernacular (or semi-vernacular), for children: 'these stories were created not only before children's parents were born, but even before their grandparents were born, so you can imagine how 'useful' and 'interesting' they are.'[73]

But these stories were extraordinarily popular. We cannot expect a book like *The Three Character Classic* to suddenly give up its best-seller status of half a millenium. Numerous reports suggest that the old trilogy, *san bai qian*, was still the foundation stone of education in the private family schools and used as supplementary reading material in the new foreign-style schools.

Nor was the Confucian tradition a dead hangover from the past; the continual rewriting and re-publication of old texts still went on. Thus, the popular *Chinese Stories (Zhonghua Gushi)*[74] was in the tradition of the old *Daily Stories (Riji Gushi)*; this was a collection, in twelve volumes, of well-known examples of Confucian models for children, each with a separate illustration. These included tales of the more gruesome aspects of filial piety, such as the son who cut out part of his own liver as medicine for his sick father or the dutiful daughter who avenged her father's murder. Moreover, they were in the classical language—a mortal sin for the modernizers. Yet between 1915 and 1940 the first volume of *Chinese Stories* was reprinted thirty-six times. The conclusion is inescapable: there was demand for this literature; parents bought these works and children read them.

Traditional Popular Literature

This included, first, the famous vernacular novels—or excerpts from them—which seem to have always been favorites with children aged over ten. The works had already been approved by the early May Fourth writers, probably because they were written in the vernacular and were part of China's rich store of oral literature. In 1932, Mao Dun claimed that eleven- and twelve-year-old children searched out this literature (just as Zhou Zuoren and Guo Morou had, one generation earlier) because, apart from 'over-Westernized' foreign translations, there was little available for this age group. 'Moreover, children (still) secretly borrow all sorts of forbidden books (literally, 'poisonous things')—there is no way of stopping this.'[75]

Second, this literature included the genuine folk oral tradition, traditionally despised in China but made respectable in the May Fourth period. The majority of translations in children's magazines were still Western fairytales and, with these as models, work began in the twenties on collections of China's own folklore and folksongs. By 1936, according to one critic, this constituted the largest part of children's literature.[76]

At first the editorial spirit was 'scientific': to record the oral tradition, like the Grimm brothers in the West a century earlier. A collection of folk songs and children's songs from Beijing (where most of the work was done) shows that, whether pungent, witty, cruel or lilting, the works described things as they were, often in an earthy vernacular: Pockmarked boys, pretty girls who get most soup when they stand in line, brides of ten years or more and 'if a boy steals pins and thread, a pimple will grow in his eye for others to see'.[77] Here, in full, are two very simple songs:

> Big Belly,
> Opened a pawn stall,
> No money at all,
> He sold his trousers.[78]

Marry a man, marry a man,
Wear gold, wear silver;
Marry a husband, marry a husband,
Wear clothes, and eat food.[79]

Like English nursery rhymes, these lyrics are fun and obviously teach rhythm and words before the meaning (or lack of it) is understood. As well the lyrics pass on customs, superstition and humor.

However, radical writers in the thirties were committed to social change and, while conceding the popular wisdom in folk tales and songs, objected to the old customs and superstitions embedded in them. 'The characteristic of the era', lamented one critic, 'is a race against time. We are so terribly backward.'[80] And he suggested updating legends and tales, as the Americans did when they rewrote *Robin Hood* as *Bows Against the Barons*.

Indeed, many critics in the thirties disapproved of traditional tales and Western fairytales—full of brave princes who defeat evil monsters thereby gaining high position and marrying beautiful virgins—because they were irrelevant to contemporary social issues. Another stringent critic advocated a Russian model: *The Watch* (*Biao*) by Panteleev and translated by Lu Xun in 1935.[81] This critic insisted on relevant social literature and not irrelevant old tales.

Qu Qiubai (1889–1935), China's first important Marxist literary theoretician, recognized the popularity of traditional forms, unlike the reformist literature of the May Fourth period which was too Westernized in its form to be readily accepted by the masses. In 1931 and 1932, he proposed a marriage between the familiar old forms of popular literature and the revolutionary content of May Fourth literature in order to popularize revolution through a popular medium. This was later known as 'new wine in old bottles'.

Modern Commercial Literature

According to Qu Qiubai, this was a phenomenon of the cosmopolitan coastal cities where the publishing industry made use of mass production techniques.[82] In children's literature, this was the most flourishing and diverse category. It was partly the arguments and feuds over children's literature, with their separate philosophical and sociopolitical implications, that stimulated such diversity and growth in a very new field. Zhonghua Shuju seems to have published more conservative works while Kaiming Shudian brought out works in the new literature, such as Ye Shengtao's fairytales, for example. In Shanghai especially, children's books were cosmopolitan, sophisticated and varied.

In the thirties, Shanghai was the publishing center of China. Since the term 'children's literature' was first introduced in 1918, this field had become a lucrative business with spectacular growth in publications from the city's numerous publishing houses. Beginning in 1928, many publishing houses put out anthologies of works (often translations) for children: subjects included the history of humankind (Shangwu Yinshuguan), world children's literature (Kaiming Shudian), astronomy (Xiandai Shuju) and science literature by the Soviet author, Ilyin. Books and magazines often advertised these anthologies. Publications from Zhonghua Shuju in 1935 advertised its collection of Chinese fairytales, with a short blurb, a list of thirty titles and the following invitation:

> Don't waste time, don't go and play,
> All sit and see what our fairytales say!
> ... THE MORE YOU READ, THE MORE YOU KNOW.[83]

While these anthologies were aimed at eleven- and twelve-year-olds, another growing market was in magazines that covered all age-groups. A 1935 survey counted twelve of these magazines in Shanghai alone and this figure does not include those magazines specifically for older children, such as *Zhongxuesheng* (*The Juvenile Student*), for which Ye Shengtao was co-editor and contributor. The magazine review article which carried this survey noted that a major part of these magazines featured literature. While noting the magazines' variety, the reviewer raised the familiar thirties' criticisms: the science articles are too dry, the language is neither classical nor vernacular and is often lifeless, and there is an overemphasis on fairytales which are the same old-hat translations, such as fairytales by the Brothers Grimm or *The Waterbabies*. The author summarized his findings with an extended culinary-style critique of the three major children's magazines. *Little Friends* (*Xiao Pengyou*) and *The Children's Magazine* (*Ertong Zazhi*) offer children a bowl of thin vegetable and beancurd soup; children dip in their chopsticks and fish out a stalk of vegetable but that is hardly satisfying. *The World of Children* (*Ertong Shijie*) is worse, just a slightly larger bowl of hotchpotch with a mindless continuation of the editorial policies in vogue 'before the Japanese attacked Manchuria in 1931'. The fault lay not so much with the ingredients as with the cooks in the kitchen.

> Our young customers have a fine appetite. A vegetable beancurd soup will fill their bellies, but it will not have the flavor of a rich dish of vegetables which wafts before their noses and suits their digestion when they eat it.[84]

Children's literature was originally created because it was thought that children needed 'food for the spirit'. Literary gourmets looked at the menu in the thirties and found that the social stock was watered down, the cooks were unskilled, the recipe was mindless repetition and the diet did not suit a Chinese palate. Still, they had come a long way since the accusation of 'starvation' in traditional China.

Translations for children, like magazines, were also criticized for a mindless continuation of earlier trends; a review of pre-war literature in the thirties, remarked that, except in a few instances, the Chinese had already translated the best and now anything Western was thrown before children, even if unsuitable and out of date.[85] Mao Dun claimed that even books like *Treasure Island* were 'boring, difficult to understand and unsuited to a Chinese diet.' Whether translations or native works, 'the vocabulary must be Chinese and not Western.'[86]

Li Jinhui, Shanghai's best-known playwright for children, wrote musicals that were certainly not 'boring, difficult or un-

Chinese'. He mixed in a magic ingredient often missing in more serious, social works; that was humor. His plays were fun and often performed by Shanghai schoolchildren. One of his best-known plays is a song-drama, *The Little Painter* (*Xiaoxiao Huajia*), playful but still didactic. The basic plot is similar to Ye Shengtao's 1921 story, *Yier*,[87] in which the title character, a young boy who loves to paint, is nagged by his teachers and mother to study, study, study. All the stern lectures fail until his third uncle punishes him by making him live away from home in the school. However, away from the nagging and with his classmates, Yier has time to paint and play, and is happy. Thus *Yier* is a criticism of blinkered attitudes towards children's education.

Li Jinhui's *The Little Painter* is, however, distanced from a contemporary criticism by being a light-hearted critique of the traditional private education system and Confucian attitudes to education (which still survived). His mother despairs of the boy ever learning the traditional texts off-by-heart and his teachers exhort him to study with words from *The Three Character Classic*: 'If foolishly you do not study, how can you become a man?' They then discover his talent in painting and nurture it, recognizing:

> If we plant beans, we get beans.
> Repeat
> If we plant melons, we get melons.
> Repeat
> Talent must not be buried.
> To ripen, ripen the fruits of culture,
> Then first open, open the flowers of art,
> The true, beautiful and fine,
> The true, beautiful and fine,
> Flowers of art.[88]

The popularity of Li Jinhui's plays shows the extent to which the new literature was both accepted and enjoyed. It could simultaneously teach and entertain. The content was shaped by a still-controversial attitude from the early May Fourth period, but it lacked the stern stringency of reformist works in the inter-war period.

A collection of stories, *Two Little Brothers* (*Xiao Ge'r Lia*), was recognized as among the best children's books published between 1930 and 1936.[89] Its author, Ling Shuhua, was a well-known author. Hsia claims that like Bing Xin, Ling Shuhua 'early manifested a more adult sensibility and psychological acumen, which promised greater achievement'.[90] Indeed, the collection is very like Bing Xin's *Letters to Young Readers*, because the stories are colored by her own memories of childhood. According to a contemporary reviewer, they are different from writings by authors like Ye Shengtao and Zhang Tianyi, in which the descriptions of children come from 'observation' rather than from consciously recalled mood sketches. Ling Shuhua explores, if you like, the romantic 'world of children'. The author wrote in the preface of *Two Little Brothers*: '. . . all the little people in the book are angels often embedded in my heart and, it could be said that two or three of them are paintings which in retrospect capture the spirit (*xieyihua*) of my own childhood.'[91]

In the story that gives the collection its title, two little brothers are delighted when their uncle buys them Eighth Brother, a mouse, but owing to their carelessness, it is eaten by a black cat. The brothers plan revenge and early next morning set out to capture the black cat in the courtyard. When, however, they discover a litter of new kittens being suckled by the cat, they abandon their plans for revenge and look after the kittens. A 1936 review in the left-wing magazine, *Literature* (*Wenxue*), approved this story: it described children's innocence and love without overt moralizing. Another story from the collection, 'Little Ying' ('Xiao Ying'), describes how an unloved girl in a rich household strikes up a friendship with a maidservant, despite her mother's and brother's contempt for the poor as a class. It is undoubtedly stories like this which prompted Jiang Feng, twenty years later, to list the volume as one of the ten good publications for children.

However, as in the West with *Peter Pan* as an example, there was a tendency among some writers to idealize children's inner world into sentimental escapism. The aim of the reformist writers of children's literature in the twenties was to liberate children from the expectation of being 'little adults'; children had their own characteristics, their own world, but there was still a relationship between childhood and adult consciousness—a continuity, a unity. Chinese reformist writers believed like Wordsworth that 'the child is father of the man' and because they wanted a New Man to build a New Society, they began with the child. Works by Bing Xin, Ling Shuhua and Zhou Zuoren hint at the walls around this world as protection against the nasty realities outside, but in the thirties there are signs of this protected world becoming a prison: pleasant, saccharin and isolated.

Another clear example is Sun Qingyang's 1932 collection of poetry, *The Spring Breeze* (*Chunfeng Lailiao*). In one typical poem:

> The mother of clouds is the river,
> As they play, one by one, in the sky,
> They are reflected deep in her heart . . .
> When it rains, of course they
> Return to rest in their mother's bosom.[92]

The poems are more an excuse for the exquisite drawings— all are idyllic and serene, where nothing nasty impinges on the blissful pastoral world open to children. While 'revolutionary literature' did not really come into its own until 1935 and 1936, modern commercial literature continued certain May Fourth concerns but outside the original framework of ongoing social reforms. Because of this, it was labeled as reactionary by reformist critics.

The boom in children's literature came to an end with the Japanese takeover of the coastal cities in 1937 and 1938 and it is now difficult for a foreign reviewer to obtain a wide selection of this literature. It has simply not endured. One forthright thirties reviewer thought that most of what was available for children should be thrown in the rubbish bin and quoted the private opinion of the editor of *New Youth*. In 1922, that editor claimed he did not approve of people in 'The Children's Literature Movement' translating fairytales by Andersen and the Brothers Grimm, forgetting that children's literature was only part of children's problems in society at large.[93]

This was the standpoint of revolutionary literature, the fourth school, which reasserted and reinterpreted this early May Fourth view. The literature of this school is discussed in detail in the next chapter.

Conclusion

Before the works by Ye Shengtao and Bing Xin, the proposed new literature for children was based on Western models, such as those translated by Lu Xun and Zhou Zuoren, and on the argument that the neglect of children and their needs was an intrinsic part of China's outmoded feudal structure. With the creation of a new literature, however, that argument shifted from what it was not, to what it should be, to the sorts of genres suitable for children and the content of particular works. We see the commercialization and modification of an idea into the complex pattern of readership, publishing monopolies and social ideology. Not only was the new literature itself controversial, even among its adherents the styles of new literature were discussed, debated and even censored with partisan fervor.

At the center of the controversy stood the fairytale which, in its Chinese adaptation, stood less for the world of fantasy than for a means of virulent social criticism and as a vehicle for nurturing social change. The fairytale sparked a national debate in 1931. Even something so seemingly innocuous as collections of old Chinese fairytales for children signaled a rejection of the classical Confucian genres and a new interest in the 'lower' forms of popular art: the social status of a Confucian elite and the masses of people was being reversed. Lu Xun initially used the fairytale to liberate the reader's imagination from the prison of traditional values. Zhou Zuoren defended it on the evolutionary argument that children's mental maturity was on a par with that of primitive people whose superstitious world incorporated magic feats, fairies and talking animals; fairytales were a necessary part of children's intellectual development. An ideology of progress and evolution confronted the 'universal' truths of Confucianism in the humble fairytale.

While the opponents of the new literature argued about the malignant nature of the fairytale, its proponents were divided on its content. Zhou Zuoren did not want politics to intrude into children's literature; Zhao Jingshen considered that only the first half of Ye Shengtao's *The Scarecrow* was suitable for children. Both did not want the dark shadows of adults' social reality to enter children's special sunlit world. Revolutionary writers, however, insisted that a mature perception of social reality be the basis of the fairytale (and, indeed, of all children's literature) and the world of children be seen as it really was: a nasty, unjust part of the nasty, unjust adult world. They wanted to banish the imaginary fairies, princes and princesses in the traditional tales, break down the literary walls protecting a children's world and remold the fairytale along the committed social lines of *The Scarecrow* or Panteleev's *The Watch*. Children's literature was to develop children's social consciousness. Thus, the different ideologies of progress, democracy under the Nationalists and revolution under the Marxists, also met and were popularized through the fairytale.

Debates on the ideological implications of the fairytale were suspended during the war period (1937–49). However, after Liberation in 1949 these debates resurfaced as the central issue in children's literature of the People's Republic of China.

Notes

1. Lee, Leo Ou-fan, *The Romantic Generation of Modern Chinese Writers* (Cambridge, Mass., 1973), pp. 294–5. Prusek, J., 'Subjectivism and Individualism in Modern Chinese Literature', *Archiv Orientalni*, 25 (1957).

2. Prusek, J., 'Yeh Sheng-t'ao and Anton Chekhov', *Archiv Orientalni*, 38 (1970), p. 43. Prusek's work refers to him as Ye Shao-chun (Ye Shaojun), except in the title. I have adopted his better-known pen-name, Ye Shengtao.

3. Lu Xun, 'Biao: Yizhi de Hua', *Lu Xun Quanji*, Vol. 14, p. 295.

4. Ye Shengtao, 'Guoqu Suitan', *Zhongxuesheng*, IV (January 1931), p. 44.

5. Hsia, C.T., *A History of Modern Chinese Fiction*, op. cit., p. 59.

6. Ibid., p. 61.

7. Ye Shengtao, 'Guoqu Suitan', op. cit., p. 46.

8. Ye Shengtao, 'Xiaobai Chuan', in *Daocaoren* (Shanghai, 1949), pp. 1–2.

9. Ibid., p. 10.

10. Jiang Feng, *Zhongguo Ertong Wenxue Jianghua*, op. cit., p. 4.

11. The three early fairytales chosen for inclusion in *A Collection of Ye Shengtao's Fairytales* (*Ye Shengtao Tonghua Xuan*, 1956) are 'The Seed', 'The Thrush' and 'The Scarecrow'.

12. Ye Shengtao in 'Yike Zhongzi', *Ye Shengtao Tonghua Xuan* (Peking, 1956), p. 5, translated in 'The Seed', *Chinese Literature*, I (1961), p. 115.

13. Ibid., p. 9; translation p. 118.

14. Ibid., p. 10; translation p. 119.

15. Ye Shengtao, 'Huamei Niao', in *Daocaoren*, op. cit., p. 125.

16. Prusek, J., 'Subjectivism and Individualism in Modern Chinese Literature', op. cit., p. 263.

17. Chen Bochui, *Ertong Wenxue Jianlun*, op. cit., p. 39.

18. Ye Shengtao, 'Guoqu Suitan', op. cit., p. 48.

19. Coveney, P., *The Image of Childhood*, op. cit., p. 67.

20. Ibid., p. 53.

21. Ye Shengtao, 'Daocaoren', in *Daocaoren*, op. cit., p. 207; translated in 'The Scarecrow', *Chinese Literature*, I (1961), p. 107.

22. Ibid., p. 217; translation pp. 113–4.

23. Jiang Feng, *Zhongguo Ertong Wenxue Jianghua*, op. cit., pp. 7–8.

24. Prusek, J., 'Yeh Sheng-t'ao and Anton Chekhov', op. cit., p. 442.

25. Coveney, P., *The Image of Childhood*, op. cit., p. 40.

26. Ye Shengtao, 'Guoqu Suitan', op. cit., p. 46.

27. Prusek, J., 'Yeh Sheng-t'ao and Anton Chekhov', op. cit., p. 442.

28. Editorial, *Zhongxuesheng* I (Jan. 1930), p. 296.

29. Ye Shengtao, 'Gudai Shixiang de Yingxiong', in *Gudai Shixiang de Yingxiong* (Shanghai, 1949), p. 4.

30. Ibid., pp. 6–7.

31. Ibid., p. 12.

32. Ye Shengtao, 'Houji', in *Ye Shengtao Tonghua Xuan*, op. cit., p. 95.

33. Lu Xun, Preface, *Old Tales Retold*, translated in Yang Hsien-i and Yang, Gladys, *Selected Stories of Lu Xun*, (Peking, 1972), p. 4.

34. Hans Christian Andersen, *Fairytales and Other Stories by Hans Christian Andersen*, revised and in part newly translated by W. A. and J. K. Craigie, Oxford Edition (London, 1914), p. 86.

35. Ibid., p. 92.

36. Ye Shengtao, 'Huangdi di Xinyi', op. cit., p. 30.

37. Ibid., p. 43.

38. Hazard, P., *Books, Children and Men*, translated by Mitchell, M. (Boston, 1963), p. 105.

39. Ye Shengtao, 'Huochetou de Jingli', in *Ye Shengtao Tonghua Xuan*, op. cit., p. 84.

40. Ibid., p. 86.

41. Ibid., p. 93.

42. Ibid., p. 91.

43. Ye Shengtao, 'Niaoyan de Hua, in *Ye Shengtao Tonghua Xuan*, op. cit., p. 78.

44. Ibid., p. 74.

45. Ibid., p. 78.

46. Chen Xiu, 'Dalu Ertong Wenxue Jinkuang', *Zhanwang*, 265, 16 February 1973, p. 29.

47. Zhang Tianyi, 'Bing Xin', in Li Xitong (ed.), *Bing Xin Lun* (Shanghai, 1932), p. 103.

48. Bouskova, M., 'The Stories of Ping Hsin', in Prusek, J. (ed.), *Studies in Modern Chinese Literature* (Berlin, 1964), p. 118.

49. Shen Congwen, 'Lun Bing Xin de Chuangzuo', in Li Xitong (ed.), *Bing Xin Lun*, op. cit., p. 105.

50. Bing Xin, 'Zishu', in Yao Nailin (ed.), *Xiandai Zhongguo Wenxue Quanji* (Aomen, 1972), pp. 66–7.

51. Ibid., pp. 65–7.

52. Ibid., p. 68.

53. Bing Xin, *Ji Xiao Duzhe* (Shanghai, 1933), pp. 136–7.

54. Ibid., p. 1.

55. Ibid., p. 1.

56. Ibid., p. 20.

57. Bing Xing, 'Zishu', op. cit., pp. 57–8.

58. Li Subo, 'Bing Xin de *Ji Xiao Duzhe*', in Li Xitong (ed.), *Bing Xin Lun*, op. cit., p. 187.

59. Bing Xin, *Ji Xiao Duzhe*, op. cit., p. 138.

60. Ibid., p. 40.

61. Bouskova, M., 'The Stories of Ping Hsin', op. cit., p. 128.

62. Zhou Zuoren, 'Ertong de Wenxue' (26 October 1920), in Huang Zhiqing, *Zhou Zuoren Lunwenji* (Hong Kong, 1972), pp. 50–8.

63. Zhou Zuoren, 'Ertong de Shu', *Chenbao Fukan,* 21 June 1923. Reprinted in Zhou Zuoren, *Zijide Yuandi,* op. cit., p. 143.

64. Townsend, John R., *Written for Children: An Outline of English-language Children's Literature* (Harmondsworth, 1974), p. 90.

65. Zhou Zuoren, 'Ertong de Wenxue', op. cit., p. 44.

66. Zhou Zuoren, 'Letter to Zhao Jingshen', first published in *Chenbao Fukan,* and included in Zhao Jingshen, *Tonghua Lunji,* op. cit., p. 57.

67. Waley, A., *Analects*, XVIII, 6, p. 220.

68. Jiang Feng, *Zhongguo Ertong Wenxue Jianghua*, op. cit., p. 23.

69. Lu Xun, 'Yonggan de Yuehan', in Jiang Feng (ed.), *Lu Xun Lun Ertong Jiaoyu Yu Ertong Wenxue,* op cit., p. 56.

70. Zhao Jingshen, *Tonghua Lunji,* op. cit., p. 5.

71. Jiang Feng, *Zhongguo Ertong Wenxue Jianghua*, op. cit., p. 17.

72. Lu Hsun, 'The Historical Development of Chinese Fiction', translated in Yang Hsien-i and Yang, Gladys, *A Brief History of Chinese Fiction*, (Peking, 1976), p. 379.

73. Lu Xun, 'Biao', *Lu Xun Quanji*, Vol. 14, p. 225.

74. Shen Wu (ed.), *Zhonghua Gushi*, Vols. I–XII (Shanghai, published at various times between 1915 and 1941).

75. Mao Dun, 'Gei Tamen Kan Shenmo Hao', *Mao Dun Wenji*, Vol. 9 (Hong Kong, 1966), p. 80.

76. Yi, 'Zai Tan Ertong Wenxue', *Wenxue*, VI:1 (1 January 1936), p. 6.

77. Johnson, K., *Folksongs and Children's Songs from Peiping,* Vol. II (Taipei, 1971), p. 318.

78. Ibid., p. 358.

79. Ibid., p. 404.

80. Jiang Feng, 'Guanyu "Ertong Wenxue"', *Wenxue,* I:6 (February 1935), p. 275.

81.   Ying Can, 'Ertong Nian de Ertong Wenxue', *Xhongzuesheng,* 62, (February 1936), p. 189.

82.   Pickowicz, P., 'Ch'u Ch'iu-pai and the Chinese Marxist Conception of Revolutionary Popular Literature and Art', *China Quarterly,* 70, (June 1977), p. 303.

83.   Advertisement in *Zhonghua Gushi,* Vol. 6 (Shanghai, 1935, 29th printing), front page.

84.   Zi Yu, 'Jiben Ertong Zazhi', *Wenxue* IV:3 (March, 1935), p. 516.

85.   Jiang Feng, 'Guanyu "Ertong Wenxue"', op. cit., p. 374.

86.   Mao Dun, 'Gei Tamen Kan Shenmo Hao', op. cit., p. 79.

87.   Ye Shengtao, 'Yier', in *Ye Shengtao Duanpian Xiaoshuo Xuanji* (Peking, 1954), pp. 39–47.

88.   Ten of Li Jinhui's plays from the 1930s were published by *Zhonghua Shuju* in Shanghai in 1941. I have an undated script of *Xiaoxiao Huajia,* with the musical score.

89.   See Table 4.1 of this book for a list of outstanding children's stories from this period.

90.   Hsia, C.T., *A History of Modern Chinese Fiction,* op. cit., pp. 77–8.

91.   Yi, 'Zai Tan Ertong Wenxue', op. cit., p. 5.

92.   Sun Qingyang, *Chunfeng Lailiao* (Shanghai, 1933), p. 6.

93.   Jiang Feng, 'Guanyu "Ertong Wenxue"', op. cit., p. 274–5.

4
Revolutionary Children's Literature

This chapter concentrates on the development of revolutionary children's literature between 1921, the year of the formation of the Chinese Communist Party, and 1949, the year of 'Liberation'. The emergence of this school has a significance beyond its influence in the pre-1949 period because its literature was institutionalized as the basis for the further development of children's literature after the founding of the People's Republic of China in 1949. In other words, it became a seminal part of the new Chinese children's literature in the People's Republic.

As we have seen in earlier chapters, revolutionary children's literature was Marxist or, at least, contained a social analysis which was influenced by Marxism. It projected values concerned with the pursuit of an egalitarian society. Hence this literature is aligned with left-wing politics in the revolutionary period and was instrumental in the Liberation effort. Until his death in 1936, Lu Xun was the major theorist for this emerging school. In the forties, Mao Zedong merged revolutionary literature, including that for children, with the war effort. Mao's famous 'Talks at the Yan'an Forum on Literature and Art' in 1942 set the theoretical guidelines for all revolutionary art over the next three to four decades. All literature was to be an ideological weapon and the passive romanticism of the early May Fourth period gave way to an active romanticism and, finally, to heroic adventure stories in children's literature.

This chapter, therefore, examines revolutionary children's literature within the wider framework of the history of the Chinese revolution. Historical developments are essential for understanding the rise of revolutionary children's literature and the demise of May Fourth romanticism.

The crucial turning point in modern Chinese history, and consequently in the development of revolutionary children's literature, is 1937. This was the beginning of World War II in China, a war known in Chinese as the Anti-Japanese War. It lasted until 1945 and was followed by Civil War between the Nationalists and the Communists. Thus revolutionary children's literature in China can be usefully divided into two main periods: pre-war literature (1921–36) and war literature (1937–49). We will map the historical background of each period before turning to the literature itself.

Revolutionary Children's Literature in the Pre-war Period

Pre-war revolutionary children's literature spans the years from 1921 to 1936. The year 1921 marks the founding of the Communist Party, whilst 1936 is the last year before the Japanese invasion. These tumultuous times impacted on revolutionary children's literature, shaping its development from a minor stream in 1921 to a major school by 1936.

Historical Background

Children's literature was concentrated in Shanghai. Shanghai in the thirties was a city of bizarre contrasts. Harry Carr of *The Los Angeles Times* noted in 1933 that it boasted the most luxurious hotels in East Asia, 'and the prettiest girls I have seen in all my life were the Chinese girls of Shanghai'.[1] Undoubtedly, his focus was on colonial comforts. Harold Isaacs, who lived there in this time, has drawn a different picture:

> Society in Shanghai in the 1930s was made up of the familiar colonial pieces: foreigners of the treaty powers a privileged cast; an upper class of treaty-port Chinese grown immensely wealthy as participants, adjuncts, agents—'compradore' was the Chinese coast word—of foreign enterprise; a large class of Chinese white-collar employees and workers making their living; and a great mass of helot-like poor that kept flocking in from the ravished and impoverished countryside, providing an endless supply of laborers, human beasts of burden, beggars, prostitutes, criminals

and ultimately helpless people who left some 50,000 dead babies on the streets of the city each year—there was a philanthropic organization whose sole activity consisted of picking up and disposing of these tiny corpses. Shanghai in 1930 was a city of more than three million with about 50,000 foreigners, half of them Japanese.

The French concession existed largely as a base for the operations of criminal gangs rooted in the old network of the Yangtze (River) Valley secret societies. They controlled the opium smuggling, gambling, prostitution and other assorted rackets which were such a large part of the life of the city. The gangs had begun by 1927 to play a cardinal political role and became agents of the Guomindang government in dealing with unions, radicals and other opponents of the regime. . .[2]

Revolutionary children's literature in China is marked by a strong social commitment. Most Chinese writers lived and published in Shanghai, so revolutionary children's literature had its social roots in the hostility towards privileged foreigners (capitalists and imperialists was the jargon); the contempt for wealthy treaty-port Chinese (compradores and traitors); the desire to awaken workers to union power; and, in particular, the compelling necessity to do something about 'the great mass of helot-like poor'—like the rickshaw boy almost forgotten in the lower left-hand corner (appropriately) of 'A Page From a Shanghai Artist's Sketchbook' in 1933 (Illustration 4.1).[3] Between 1927 and 1936 this class hostility was a growing but forbidden stream in Chinese children's literature. It was not until the second United Front between the Nationalists and the Communists against the Japanese in 1936 that writers were to openly espouse a Marxist viewpoint in their works.

Between 1921 and 1936 there are three discernible stages in the development of revolutionary children's literature in Shanghai.

The first stage is between 1921 and 1926. At this time, the Communists were junior partners in an alliance with the Nationalist Party. As previous chapters have demonstrated, the May Fourth school dominated the new children's literature; revolutionary literature was a minor stream.

Ilustration 4.1

'A Page from a Shanghai Artist's Sketch Book',
from *The Cathay*

The second stage is between 1927 and 1935. In 1927, the Nationalists split with the Communists, massacred many members of the Party and instituted an anti-Communist campaign called 'The White Terror'. In response, many writers turned to the left and began producing an underground children's literature. This revolutionary shift in children's literature is clearest in the development of popular, mass literature (see Chapter 5), using from the 'guise of the fairytale to cloak stains of blood and sweat' (see Chapter 2), and in the adoption of an active, militant romanticism.

This romanticism owes much to Maxim Gorky's influence. He wrote:

> There are two currents, or schools, in literature: romanticism and realism. By the latter is meant a truthful, unvarnished representation of people and their condition of life. Several definitions of romanticism have been brought forward. . . but two sharply contrasting tendencies should be distinguished. . . the passive and the active. Passive romanticism endeavors to reconcile man to his life by embellishing that life, or to distract him from things around him by means of a barren introspection into his 'inner world'. . . active romanticism strives to strengthen man's will to live and raise him up against the life around him, against any yoke it would impose. . . In great artists realism and romanticism seem to have blended.[4]

In 1928, Guo Moruo, who epitomized the romantic left, wrote a children's story which married the 'blood-stained' fairytale to an 'active' romanticism. The main ingredient of this new romanticism was the heroic worker who represented an invincible proletariat.

In this context, the pastoral view of childhood is 'passive', the exploration of an 'inner' world of children is 'barren'. The Marxist rejection of this notion for an active, class-based romanticism had major ramifications for the 'educational significance' (*jiaoyu yiyi*) of children's literature. The focus on education as a means of saving China moved from the emancipation of the individual child to the awakening of the Chinese people. Sun Yatsen, the founder of the Nationalist Party, made this clear as early as 1925. He wrote in his will that to achieve 'freedom and equality for China. . . the mass of people must be awakened'.[5] Yet this was also the standpoint of the Communist Party. There is thus a clear correspondence, in political terms, between the early May Fourth conception of children's education and the later May Fourth conception of mass education. The thread is Lu Xun's 'call to arms', a call to awaken the sleepers of China in their suffocating iron house.

The third stage is the year 1936. This was a pivotal year in which the Nationalists and Communists formed a second United Front to fight the Japanese. The literature is imbued with a sense of national urgency. Children's literature was consequently more patently realistic, in Gorky's sense, more openly revolutionary and more contemporary. Because of the United Front, literature was also easier to publish as censorship controls were eased. Indeed, most of the stories discussed here in the section on prewar revolutionary children's literature were published in 1936.

One example from this literature shows clearly the changed direction from children's literature in the twenties. Zhang Tianyi's *Big Lin and Little Lin* is probably the classic story for children in the thirties. Little Lin, a worker (proletariat), struggles militantly against the 'Ogre' (who works for the imperialists-capitalists-compradores and kings) and wins his struggle (active romanticism). It is no longer Confucianism that symbolically 'eats' people, but an elite-class Ogre who actually eats poor people in the story. Goodies and baddies are clearly delineated on a Marxist class basis.

In this section on revolutionary children's literature in prewar Shanghai we will draw on themes discussed in the previous two chapters. We place these themes within the overall development of this school of literature. It must be reemphasized, however, that from 1918 to 1936, Lu Xun was the major theorist for the development of Chinese children's literature.

Pre-War Revolutionary Literature

Pre-war revolutionary literature had its identifiable roots in the early May Fourth period. In 1921, the year of the formation of the Chinese Communist Party, Peng Pai (1896–1929) returned from studying in the Soviet Union and wrote children's songs on subjects like Labor Day and the power of the peasantry. A poem like 'The Peasants Curse the Landlord' ('Sianhu Ma Diangong') has the simple logic and repetitive rhythm of traditional songs:

> Bang! Bang! Bang!
> The peasants curse the landlord:
> They work to death,
> He eats white rice.
> He doesn't know death,
> The peasants unite.
> They unite for revolution,
> They revolt and share the land.[6]

Another poem, 'Children of the October Revolution' ('Shiyue Geming de Yiner', in 1925) held up the Russian Young Pioneers as an example to Chinese children in words which will become increasingly familiar. The Russian children sing:

> . . . We are well prepared,
> We are always well prepared,
> We are poor peasant children,
> We are the children's army of the Communist Party;
> We are the flowers of the Future,
> We are the owners of a New World. . .[7]

Admittedly, these are rather poor songs, even in the original. The editors of the collection in which these poems appear claim, in the preface, that they propagated struggle in that era.[8] But, despite the attempts of this cohort of writers, the dominant literary theme in the twenties was non-Marxist social exposure. However, such themes later struck a chord which is still reverberating in children's literature today; in their very simplicity they lay bare the human cry and dream at the center of the complex political issues of the day and this, coupled with their militancy, marks them as a beginning of revolutionary children's literature.

In the second stage, this stream was forced underground when the Nationalists made a bloody and unexpected break with the Communists in 1927. This political severing had far-reaching consequences for revolutionary literature in the thirties. First, there were problems of publication. Because of censorship, revolutionary magazines, such as the earliest *Little Children's Weekly* (*Xiao Haizi Zhoukan*), which began publication as a supplement to a workers' paper in 1926, were short-lived. As late as 1959, researchers in China were trying to make a collection of these magazines which seemed to appear only to disappear—like snowflakes.

A second effect, which presents a real difficulty for foreign researchers trying to examine this period, is that writers commonly used pseudonyms, not as an artistic device but to hide their identity.

A third effect of the 1927 split is the emotional and intellectual reaction of writers. Guo Moruo reacted with anger. Lu Xun, we have seen, became disillusioned and translated works for children that advocated revolution, while his brother, Zhou Zuoren, reacted to the increasing politicization of children's literature by retiring. In 1930 Yu Dafu reacted bitterly in a journal article on children's future in China: society is so bad, he began, that we can only kill ourselves or kill the warlords.[9] Ye Shengtao slowed and then almost stopped his pen in 1930 because, he claimed, the lens he had used to snap society was outmoded and undiscriminating. When Ye Shengtao and others began writing again in the thirties their focus was on the plight and power of the poor, light and dark were clearly defined as poor and rich, and the theoretical framework was one of growing class consciousness and solidarity.

A survey of children's literature produced between 1927 and 1936 demonstrates this change in emphasis. Our survey begins with Guo Moruo's 'Only One Hand' ('Yizhi Shou'), published in 1928.

'Only One Hand' was serialized by Guo Moruo in 1928 under an assumed name. Despite the author's fame as a writer, the story is a thinly disguised treatise on Shanghai factory conditions and the necessity for patience and unity in the workers' movement. The setting—a fairytale capital of a small island—is explicitly Shanghai where booming industry has nevertheless caused a large influx of poor because 'most of the money is concentrated in a few hands'.[10] The story centers around a fifteen-year-old factory worker who is the sole supporter of his blind father and crippled mother, both conditions resulting from factory poisons. One day, the boy caught his sleeve in a machine and lost his right hand. Fellow workers rushed to help him and the boss, hearing the unaccustomed quietness while smoking in his office, confronted them with his iron-plaited whip. It would be repetitive to catalogue the boss's brutality except to record that when he took out his gun to shoot at the angry workers, the boy picked up his own bloody hand lying beside him on the factory floor and, 'like a wounded lion', used it to knock away the gun. The workers attempted but failed to take over the factory, and the boy was killed. The real hero, a Communist Party organizer, broke this news to the old parents: the mother died of shock and the old father set fire to both the house and himself as a cover for an organized take-over of the island that night.

> There was only a rosy glow, only a sheet of red flame.
> —'Ha, ha, ha. The blind will see, the crippled will walk'.
> His voice still seemed to come from the heart of the fire.[11]

This 'fairytale' introduces a dramatic new mood into Chinese children's literature. Children are neither 'garden flowers' nor helpless victims of oppression. Instead they are militant members of a proletariat that struggles for social justice. In this sense, Guo Moruo's 'Only One Hand' is a precursor to the thirties' fairytales of Ye Shengtao and the later translations of Lu Xun. Guo Moruo completely rejected the passive romanticism which Gorky identified as one of the tendencies in European literature. As a corollary, he also rejected pastoral notions of childhood. He adopted active romanticism which, for Guo, was exemplified by such Western writers as Byron and Heine. In his childhood and early manhood, Guo celebrated individual heroes, such as Napoleon and Bismarck (see Chapter 1). With his conversion to Marxism in 1924, he transferred his earlier romanticism into 'a broader type of collective romanticism'[12] in which the hero represents the proletariat. He envisions a future in which 'the blind will see, the crippled will walk' and embeds this vision in his writings.

'Only One Hand' is a horror story, perhaps, of blood and guts. But there is an assurance that, despite setbacks, the workers must win through sheer numerical strength and sacrifice. But Guo Moruo's ultimate justification for violent revolution is a moral one based on the dignity and equality of man. The workers cry, 'Aren't we men? All we lack is a bit of stinking cash'.[13] And later:

> Philosophers and religious teachers say. . . the world is equal, men are equal. . . but this world of theirs excludes the poor. . . You know, poor people aren't men, they are cattle.[14]

The concept of equality—of people, gender, class and even nations—is an essential argument throughout pre-1949 children's literature in China, and, in this sense, 'Only One Hand' is a development, not a departure, from earlier May Fourth arguments based on evolution. When both May Fourth and Communist writers wrote about the inequalities between rich and poor—be they people or nations—they described a gap between vision and reality precisely in order to close it. But whereas May Fourth literature was descriptive, Communist literature was prescriptive; it analyzed in sophisticated class terms and advocated armed class struggle.

Jiang Feng, who has made the only systematic summary of children's literature in this period,[15] listed the most outstanding works between 1930 and 1936 (Figure 4.1). Most of these stories—the major genre since the twenties—were for children aged over eleven who, according to Mao Dun in 1932, lacked

Table 4.1 Jiang Feng's List of Outstanding Revolutionary Children's Stories (1930–36)

Author	Title	Year
Ye Shengtao	#Gudai Shixiang de Xingxiong (The Ancient Stone Hero)	1931
Zhang Tianyi	'Mifeng' ('The Honey-bee')	1932
	'Qiyu' ('A Strange Encounter')	1934
	Da Lin he Xiao Lin (Big Lin and Little Lin)	1936
	'Tutu Dawang' ('The Great King Tutu')	1936
	'Qiang de Difang' ('A Strange Place')	1936
Lao She	'Xiao Po de Shengri' ('Little Po's Birthday')	1931
	'Xin Aimier' ('The New Emile')	1936
Chen Bochui	'Alisi Guniang' ('The Girl Alice')	1936
Ba Jin	'Changsheng Ta' ('The Tower of Long Life')	1935
	* 'Ta de Mimi' ('The Secret of the Tower')	1935
	* 'Yinshen Zhu' ('The Pearl Inside the Body')	1936
	'Nengyan Shu' ('The Talking Tree')	1937
Ling Shuhua	#Xiao Ge'r Lia (Two Little Brothers)	1935
Mao Dun	'Da Bizi de Gushi' ('The Story of Big Nose')	1936
	*'Shaonian Yinshua Gong' ('The Young Printer')	1936
Wang Tongzhao	'Xiao Hong Denglong de Meng' ('The Dream of the Little Red Lantern')	1936
Shu Qun	Mei you Zuguo de Haizi (Child Without a Country)	1936

* Author's addition of two stories to complete Ba Jin's four-story set.
# Critique in earlier chapter.

good modern literature. Younger children were inundated with folk, fairy and animal tales pouring from the Shanghai printing presses. The works listed divide loosely into two categories: those written before 1936 and those written or published during 1936. In fact, ten of the eighteen titles on this list were published in 1936, when restrictions on revolutionary publications were lifted with the second United Front.

In the first category the authors have distanced themselves from contemporary society through fairytales of feudal settings; nevertheless, young Chinese readers would easily transfer the social critique to their own times. One example is 'The Honey-bee' ('Mifeng'), by Zhang Tianyi, claimed by some critics as 'the most brilliant short-story writer of the decade',[16] and the author who was to become China's best-known writer for children. This was his first fairytale and probably the work which brought him to prominence. It unfolds through a series of letters—authentically child-like, with repetition and grammatical errors—from a young, country boy to his older sister in the city. He begins with everyday news, including a schoolboy shouting match between 'Fathead Demon', the son of a rich Shanghai man who keeps twelve thousand hives of Italian bees, and the local country boys who claim the bees are eating the village crops. The conflict escalates from schoolyard insults (taunting, often in rhyme), to the peasants deciding they must all go to the town magistrate to demand the hives be shifted. The boys secretly arm themselves with sticks and stones. They enter the town, full of soldiers, and are kept waiting endlessly to see the magistrate—for years, it seems to the boys. Finally, they angrily force an entry, the soldiers fire into the crowd and arrest many of the people, including the boy's father and elder brother. He is left alone and lives with his teacher.

> I haven't seen Father or Elder Brother. I haven't seen 'Black Ox' or Wang Yansheng. I haven't seen lots of people. It'd be good if I had one of those foreign (Aladdin's) lamps. Then I wouldn't cry. Now I'll stop and go and play. Goodbye.[17]

The reader knows that the conflict is really caused through abysmal ignorance on both sides: bees fertilize crops, they do not eat them, despite the claim by the magistrate that bees eat dew and only go to the fields to play. In this story we see Zhang Tianyi's strength as a writer for children: his children are always children and he has observed them closely, due in part to his background as a teacher. The social comment is an intrinsic part of the story line itself; through the fresh young eyes of a country boy—in the end filled with tears of incomprehension—we see a county bureaucracy that is lazy, evasive, ill-informed, hand-in-glove with the rich, and supported by armed force. The peasants have no say at all in their own lives.

While Zhang Tianyi's story is mistakenly called a 'fairytale', Ba Jin's four fairytales published between 1935 and 1937 could more accurately be called, 'dreamtales':

> From my childhood I loved to dream. After my father died, I could still see his face in my dreams. So I really liked to dream. And my dreamland was often very beautiful.
>
> We cannot turn back the years and I have no way of returning to childhood. Moreover, my father has been gone for twenty years, but even now I can still be with him in my dreams. Then I can see again the world of twenty years ago and my father and I can live a new life.
>
> Real life is often so oppressive that I cannot breathe; my hands and feet wear invisible chains. But in my dreams I have complete freedom.
>
> I offer these stories to those people who, suffocated by real life, can still breathe a little fresh air from these childhood dreams.[18]

The magic framework and mood of the tales is the warmth and love between the boy, Ba Jin, and his father. As he sat and told stories to his son, the father would light up his pipe, and the tale is punctuated with the boy's description of the coming evening until all he can see is his father's glowing pipe—the colors fade. But for Ba Jin it is not a world completely without color while he can see his father in it.

The first tale, 'The Tower of Long Life' ('Changsheng Ta'), begins, 'Once upon a time there was an Emperor. . .'.[19] When the son asks what sort of thing is an Emperor, his father answers, 'An Emperor, well, he is a monster who sits in a palace all day wearing a crown'.[20] This particular Emperor lives a life of luxury until his old age when, fearful of death, he seeks the secret of immortality. After a long search the Emperor discovers that the secret is found in a Tower of Long Life. So thousands of poor people are mobilized to work night and day, in snow and ice, in chains and leg-irons, to build a multi-level tower. Most die and when it is finally completed, the tower collapses because—and the moral is something of an anti-climax—it was built on sand, the sand of the misery of the poor.

In the second tale, 'The Secret of the Tower' ('Ta de Mimi'), the secret that can lead to the destruction of both the tower and imperial power is the bitter memory of the Emperor's cruelty that is harbored and inherited in the hearts of the surviving poor. In this story, the boy is flown mysteriously to the tower on a cold, snowy night to find his father. He meets the Emperor, 'sitting on a throne, laughing with satisfaction. His mouth is so big, his golden teeth are so prominent, that they seem like sharp knives'.[21] This is all the better to eat his old concubines, unwilling concubines, slaves, soldiers and dissidents, for this Emperor is a cannibal and in this way keeps down his harem of 759 young girls. Something of a gourmet, however, he prefers the flesh of little children and young girls. When the boy meets his father, imprisoned on the top floor, the Emperor once again asks him to reveal the secret; the father refuses because that would sacrifice the blood of many workers to save himself. The boy swallows the secret and offers to sacrifice himself. Then he wakes up with his father beside him, saying, 'Child, go to sleep, you are dreaming'.[22]

'The Pearl Inside the Body' ('Yinshen Zhu') is also about the poor people's inherited hatred for the rich and powerful, but this tale is based on an old folk-tale. A child and his mother from a poor family are the only survivors in a village set upon by central tax-gatherers and soldiers in a drought year. The soldiers return to the house to find a secret pearl after they have tortured the boy's father to death. The boy swallows it. Raging with thirst, he goes to drink at the river and, to his mother's horror, he turns into a dragon. There is light, a roaring earthquake when the very mountains seemed to totter, and a flood drowns the land as the dragon swims towards the city to destroy it. When the boy asks his father what happened to the city people, officials, government servants and his father's false friends, his own father answers: 'I'm not sure. Probably they all turned into shrimps'.[23]

In 'The Talking Tree' ('Nengyan Shu') a tree, like the author, looks at his world and is finally forced to make a social comment that could apply equally to the other three tales. This story is told outside when the boy is frightened by the darkly whispering trees and the ghostly wind. A tree stands beside a highway leading to the capital where it sees the Emperor and his concubines riding by, and the poor, the beggars, the homeless walking by—ragged, hungry, slow and sad. One night a fifteen-year-old boy, blinded by cruel officials, drops beside the trunk, crying, 'Why can't I see the stars? They must be in the sky. Why can't I see the starlight? All is darkness, all is darkness. . .'.[24] His sister finds him and together they huddle against the tree when they hear footsteps, whips and curses; soldiers are marching a group of children to a place of iron windows and doors. The sister cries to the gods for an answer and the tree soaks up their tears, shudders and says:

> This order is completely unjust. There are no differences between men in this world and no-one should receive favorable treatment. Whosoever builds his own happiness on the misery of others, whosoever uses chains, whips, hell and the like to secure his own fortune cannot live for very long and, in the end, will lose his good fortune. . . Only the hearts of young children can live forever, nothing can destroy them. Go, go with your brother. Do not think he has lost his eyes because your eyes are his eyes. He can see everything through them. Go, then, go and help others, pity others, love others. Help, pity and love are not crimes.[25]

Believing that the gods have answered her, the girl's fears and sorrows fly away. The siblings linger beneath the tree awhile and leave together. Ba Jin and his father linger, too, in the night, and then move on.

These tales stand between May Fourth and revolutionary children's literature. Ba Jin retains his belief in qualities like imagination, love, pity and the power of childish innocence. But he also uses his art to paint a powerful picture of social injustice, just as the thirties' reviewers were demanding of the contemporary fairytale. In all four tales, the tortured world of pitiful poor and brutal rich is a nightmare fantasy, while the warm love between father and son is a contrasting reality. But Ba Jin clearly states in his introduction on dreams that this is the negative of the picture: the suffocating horror belongs to the real world of China, and his fresh, new life with his father belongs to the world of dreams.

The 1936 stories on Jiang Feng's list, the second category, are a turning point in children's literature. Here, the social analysis is openly Marxist; the settings are realistic and contemporary. The magazine, *Literature* (*Wenxue*), a forum for left-wing writers in the thirties, published a profoundly influential children's edition in 1936 which included three of the stories listed by Jiang Feng. Together with its theoretical articles, it pointed the way to come. With the exception of a story by Lao She, the themes are still of a divided society that demands individual sacrifice, but the revolutionary tone demands much more. This issue of *Literature* carries a scholarly criticism of traditional children's books, a translation of Gorky's 'On Themes' (which was to become a bible for children's literature in the fifties), an introduction to Soviet children's literature by Mao Dun, and a translation of a work by a contemporary Russian children's author, Kassill. These models and theoretical directions were to have a lasting influence on Chinese children's literature.

Two of the stories in this 1936 special edition of *Literature* are set in contemporary Shanghai. 'The Story of Big Nose' ('Da Bizi de Gushi') by Mao Dun describes the life of a derelict, homeless, orphan boy who lives by scavenging in the streets of Shanghai. Yet the ending is somehow unconvincing when Big Nose joins a group of marching revolutionaries, despite Mao Dun's attempt to retain an authentic class feeling by having Big Nose stare fascinated at his own nose droppings, glistening on the black hair of a dedicated revolutionary girl in front of him.

Wang Tongzhao, in 'The Dream of the Little Red Lantern' ('Xiao Hongdenglong de Meng'), holds his story together more tightly through flashbacks and careful use of imagery. In several places, he describes Shanghai in terms of shoes: A Bao, pushing his little cart along a bustling street, sees a flood of shoes:

> There are countless leather shoes, white and yellow high-heeled shoes; shoes in soft, soft embroidered silk and in coarse cotton, there are straw sandals and bare feet—all moving, moving along the battered, black and dirty road.[26]

When A Bao first meets the woman whose cruelty causes him to lose his job, and then, dreaming of the little red lantern in his home village far away, to drown himself, she is described in this way:

> . . . clickety clack, clickety clack, like a tune accompanying the art of walking. . . and a powdered face comes out of the gateway at the side of the road. She is dressed in a long, light blue dress, and beneath it a pair of shining, shining silver shoes advanced rhythmically, step by step, on the solid, sleek earth, an arrogant, prosperous sort of tread. Behind this female creature, dressed in foreign style, comes a big yellow dog and two children. . . [27]

Poor A Bao! He happens to be delivering goods from this woman's husband to her husband's mistress. He is attacked by the dog, his cart and goods are broken, he loses his job and eventually his life. Socially, A Bao is one of Isaac's 'helpless people', he represents a class of 'helot-like poor'; politically, he is one of the oppressed who should be 'a flower of the Future', a New Man; statistically, he becomes one of Shanghai's annual harvest of 50,000 tiny corpses—unless his body is too big to be counted.

The enduring classic in the emerging school of revolutionary literature is Zhang Tianyi's rollicking satire, *Big Lin and Little Lin* (*Da Lin he Xiao Lin*). Jiang Feng called it 'a pioneering work in the history of Chinese children's literature'.[28] While Lu Xun saw the older order as one that ate men, Zhang Tianyi, like Guo Moruo and Ba Jin, claimed explicitly that in contemporary China the eaten are the poor and the eaters are the rich.

The problem is stated almost immediately in the story when two tired and hungry orphans lie down to rest:

> Big Lin looked at their sacks, and sighed. 'When I grow up, I'm going to be a rich man', he said. 'Rich men have all the food and clothes they want and they needn't work'.
> 'But father told us to work hard'. (Little Lin)[29]

Illustration 4.2

"买什么？买吃掉你們！"

'The People-eating Ogre', from *Big Lin and Little Lin*

The argument is broken by a thundering voice: 'I am going to eat you'. It is the roar of the fearful people-eating Ogre. To escape, the children run in two different directions and begin two different lives. But the Ogre always turns up. He is called in to frighten and eat Little Lin and his friends when they kill the slave-owner factory boss—who also, as it happens, changes children into eggs and eats them. Little Lin escapes again (the Ogre catches only the slow ones) and, after many adventures like laughing until he cries when his feet are tickled by a policeman in the Foot-torture Department (Illustration 4.3), he learns to be an engine driver, that is, a worker. Meanwhile, Big Lin's dream comes true and through fraud he becomes the adopted son of Mr Ba Ha, 'the biggest millionaire in the world. The American oil king has even asked him for a loan'.[30] The Ogre is really the tame servant of imperialists, compradores,

Illustration 4.3

足　刑

'The Foot-torture Department', from *Big Lin and Little Lin*

capitalists and kings, and he comes once a day to Big Lin's new house to see if anything needs to be done or anyone needs to be eaten. Big Lin grows so fat and lazy that a servant has to help him even to laugh or cry. After many very funny episodes he eventually marries the ugly, but vain, Princess Rose and plans a honeymoon by the seaside. The couple are to travel in a train driven by Little Lin, but the railway workers strike when the King refuses to carry four truckloads of grain to a famine area; that would mean leaving behind Princess Rose's four truckloads of rouge, scent and powder and she sobs and faints at this suggestion. So the loyal Ogre has to push the train, but he pushes too hard and they all end up in the sea. Big Lin is missing and a reward notice, written by a poet, is posted:

> MISSING MAN
> FAT AS A PORKER
> A WOBBLY WALKER
> WHO SHAKES AND SPINS
> WITH FIVE DOUBLE CHINS. . .[31]

Big Lin ends up on Rich Man's Island where he finds lots of money, a few 'gentlemen' and no servants, peasants or food. He dies. Back from the land of fantasy to the real world: the people are militant and the government is frightened.

'Ah, before long they'll overthrow us and not let us be bosses anymore'.
But presently Sisi Ke Number Three (factory boss) went on.
'Oh well, we'll wait till that time comes. For each day that I'm boss I can make a day's profits'.[32]

Here we have not just a call for the poor to rise against the rich, but a strong sense of urgency—every day counts.

We have emphasized that revolutionary writers in the thirties insisted that social reality be the starting point for literature. The seriousness of Zhang Tianyi's satire is obvious, even down to the militant railway workers who actually did start a wave of strikes in China beginning in the twenties. We have already documented the misery of the poor.

Zhang Tianyi's description of the rich and poor is no more fantastic than Shanghai itself at that time. But his story is for children. He introduces absurdity and humor in simple language. The story line never falters—it bubbles along through a fantasy world peopled by the brave and ridiculous, ideological goodies and baddies, who are described with zest and freshness. It delivers an inspiring message to readers. Jiang Feng gives Zhang Tianyi's works the highest praise:

> In the field of Chinese children's literature Zhang Tianyi was a new star following the appearance of Ye Shengtao. If we say that *The Scarecrow* by Ye Shengtao 'pioneered a new path for the fairytale in China' [Lu Xun], then it was the new writer, Zhang Tianyi, who, appearing on the stage ten years later, took over and developed this path of realism.[33]

The same imagery and social divisions between rich and poor are transformed to a national level in the only story about the war in Jiang Feng's list: *Child Without a Country* (*Mei you Zuguo de Haizi*, 1936) by Shu Qun. War literature will be discussed in detail in the next section. It is sufficient to say at this point that the homeless, vagrant children in these 1936 stories became stateless children; imperialism and oppression take on the human face of the Japanese; the downtrodden victims become the Chinese as a race;

and traitors become not those who betray their class like Big Lin, but those who betray their country. Patriotism, that powerful, unifying force so evident in the early May Fourth period, overrides the sectarian in-fighting of the early thirties to become the main theme in children's stories of the war period.

All the pre-war revolutionary writers we have considered look at the 'outer' world of children. These writers demand sacrifice, bravery and social awareness. By 1936, the pastoral romanticism of the May Fourth period—tenderness, self-discovery and a gentle nurture of children's potential—have been all but swept away. The one exception on Jiang Feng's list is Lao She's 'The New Emile' ('Xin Aimier') (included in the 1936 special children's edition of *Literature*), which returns to the 'inner' world of children. This story explores the effects of the new revolutionary education on a boy's life, sociability and inner being. Lao She sees these effects as a perversion of the very nature of childhood.

In this story, Emile died when he was eight years, four months and twelve days old. The story is a review of his upbringing that was based on stern, and supposedly, scientific methods then in vogue. When Emile was born he cried, but he was taught that life is a struggle and crying is a weakness, so after this he did not cry. At three days old he was taken away from his mother: 'the fearful nature of motherhood; humanity's backsliding can all be blamed on mothers of the world'.[34] Her milk would turn him soft as dough yet he must not be a plaything, but a steel soldier of the future; he must eat bread and be male. Thus begins his upbringing as a revolutionary. When he is hungry Emile steals, so he learns to be cunning, since all revolutionaries who fight for right must be cunning. Sometimes he is starved (but not beyond a certain stage of dizziness) for starvation is the fuel of revolution and he must understand it. He is fed on heroic stories but nothing that will lead to fantasy and romance: he knows the facts about the size, age and creation of the moon but certainly not the story about the rabbit on the moon. In biology, when he learns about frogs, for example, there are no stories about the marriage of frogs or that they may use lotus leaves as boats or that they may become handsome princes. Emile and his friends simply catch a frog and dissect it. His whole education is a triumph of reason and fact, both of which are allegedly responsible for human progress. Emile is to be a man, not a slave! Unfortunately, he is too factual and honest to get along with other children or adults. He would never say to a girl, 'Your face is lovely like a peach', because he knows that peaches are not good looking but good to eat. At six years old he is introduced to abstract words like 'right' and 'revolution' and 'struggle' but he sometimes confuses fact and fiction and says of the next-door neighbor's child, 'Down with (him). . . and save the world'.[35] He is familiar with all sorts of revolutionary slogans:

> Emile says, we will make revolution, down with, down with, completely sacrifice, running dogs, blood flows like a river, drowning you all. . .[36]

At eight years, Emile begins his study of politics. He becomes sick and, still working without medicine, he eventually dies. His teacher reflects:

> When I think of his death I don't know what to say. I certainly don't suspect my theory and methods of education, it is just that in the end I cannot control my own feelings, my weaknesses. But that child, Emile, was just too lovable. I am sad but not discouraged, however, for I gained much experience with Emile and I must happily continue my research and experiments; I fully believe that, in the person of a second Emile, I can complete my great plan.[37]

Lao She's 'Emile' is, in fact, a Chinese version of Rousseau's Emile in his famous tract on education. Emile is the central character in his novel *Emile: or On Education (Emile: ou de L'education,* 1762), which influenced all modern pedagogical movements in the West and directed interest towards the nature of childhood. Coveney wrote that 'the central emphasis of the book lay on the assertion that the primary concern of all education should be the identity and peculiar nature of the child itself'.[38] Rousseau advocated a natural upbringing which included, for example, breast feeding. Education relied on a freely accepted contract between teachers and pupils where the child learned through concrete experience. The child should be neither indoctrinated nor introduced to dead, abstract words. In contrast, Lao She's story documents a 'revolutionary' upbringing which is the precise opposite of that of Rousseau's Emile, and, in consequence, of the entire progressive Western school of educational thought in the nineteenth and twentieth centuries. The Chinese Emile is not an individual with feelings, but a scientific experiment. He is sacrificed for a future Utopia. He embodies Lao She's rejection of the militant values which reverberated through the pages of pre-war revolutionary children's literature and which were subsequently adopted as the only virtues by Maoist literature after 1949.

If we summarize the development of twentieth-century children's literature up to 1936, we can trace the gradual assimilation of a Marxist social analysis that combined four major issues in Chinese thought in the first half of this century: science, society, human equality and national independence. These explorations displaced the exploration of self and the 'inner' world of children as a basis for the mature individual's integration with society. Lao She's story documents the cost of these trends.

Children's literature in this period clearly contradicts a claim by Prusek, one of the most highly-respected commentators on modern Chinese literature, that a work of art in the inter-war period does not, as a rule, 'document social reality but rather reflects the author's inner life and comprises descriptions or analyses of his own feelings, moods, visions and even dreams'.[39] For a start, almost all the authors we have discussed were also the major literary figures in modern China. In children's literature, there was a gradual change, beginning in 1927, when writers attempted to widen their focus and to write from within the minds of the poor. Collective social reality, not individual experience, was the primary inspiration. Militant, social action, not fantasy and self-discovery, were the dominant virtues.

Despite the variety of definition and statement in literature of this period, the result is a fundamental polarity in the literary image of the child. On one side, the child is still 'the flower of the future' who, to quote early Lu Xun through Wordsworth,

> ... more than all other gifts
> That earth can offer to declining man,
> Brings hope with it and forward-looking thoughts.[40]

But on the other side, the child is also, as Lao She observed, a steel soldier of the future, molded sternly for a great social purpose, and always ready to be told what needs to be done. This may include heroic action or sacrificial martyrdom in the mould of Gorky's 'active' romanticism.

Revolutionary Children's Literature in the War Period

The war with Japan and then civil war caused further fundamental changes in children's literature. We will analyze this literature through two periods, Anti-Japanese War literature (1937–45) and Civil War literature (1946–49). First we turn to historical background.

Historical Background

The 1937 Japanese military occupation of Beijing as a crucial stepping stone in their conquest over China was the final trigger for war. During the Anti-Japanese War, children's literature was mobilized as part of China's war effort, and targeted two widely different audiences, dispersed into geographically distinct areas.

One area was Shanghai. Until the Pacific War late in 1941, international settlements in the city were run by foreign governments and so gave Chinese radicals some protection from, first, the Nationalists and then, the Japanese invaders. These settlements were closed with the onset of the Pacific War. Before this, underground and patriotic children's literature continued to be published in Shanghai. Its readers were coastal, urban-educated youth and children.

The second area to assimilate patriotic children's literature was the hinterlands of China. The spread into decentralized locations was gradual. Maoist efforts had already shifted to the countryside in 1927, when Mao Zedong became Chairman of the Central Executive Council of the Chinese Soviet Republic in the southern hinterland. However, it was not until the establishment of the northern rural base area in Yan'an in 1935 that the Maoist line predominated within the Communist Party. The Nationalists in turn fled inland as the Japanese took over Chinese coastal cities in 1937 and 1938. Strategic war centers became Yan'an in the northwest for the Communists and Chongqing in the southwest for the Nationalists.

The war had a dramatic impact on children's literature. The major shift was in writers' attitudes toward the masses. In the late twenties and early thirties, left-wing literary intellectuals in Shanghai had argued, with little result, for a popular, revolutionary literature for mass education. With the imperative of war, mass mobilization was no longer a political platform but a national necessity. When the center of the war effort moved inland, writers for the first time actively sought the peasantry as part of their readership. In children's literature, as in adults' literature, the problem of accessibility had been confronted in theory but never in practice, except in isolated areas under Communist rule. Hence, Chinese intellectuals were forced by the war to create a colloquial revolutionary literature which, for the first time, would be accessible to illiterate and semi-literate peasants and their children.

The emphasis on mass literature blurred the lines between children's literature and popular literature for older audiences. What was the point of a 'Westernized' (some said 'more highbrow')[41] literature for children when more than 90 per cent of them could not read? Hence colloquial and popular literature, such as songs and comics, were more important for mass mobilization than stories in books. The specific audience for this type of popular literature is unclear as it is directed toward both children and illiterate adults, the majority of the population.

The war also affected writers. Before 1937, the pioneers in children's literature were the older, established May Fourth writers such as Lu Xun, Ye Shengtao and Zhang Tianyi, who first made their reputations in adult literature. Ye Shengtao was particularly important as an editor and contributor in children's magazines. With the onset of war, a younger generation of writers, specializing only in children's literature—Chen Bochui, He Yi and Yan Wenjing—gradually took over. While the older writers continued to write for children and always retained the high status earned in the earlier period, it was these new writers who assumed important day-to-day roles in the organization of children's literature, first, in its rudimentary, *ad hoc* stages before 1949, and, second, in its national, then increasingly bureaucratic, stages after 1949.

A third effect of the war was the paucity of children's literature. This was only partly due to the emphasis on mass literature with its merged audience. The supply of all literature thinned dramatically. During the war, publishing centers were occupied by Japanese militarists, distribution networks were disrupted, and basic supplies, such as paper, were scant. Survival of children was more important than exploration of childhood.

A fourth effect of the war on children's literature, whether written or colloquial, was the development of the militant hero. Chinese writers claim that in the twenties children's literature was closely allied to the fight against feudalism; it could equally be said that in the late thirties and the forties it was part of the fight against the Japanese, for the war superseded internal disputes. The militant proletarian hero of earlier revolutionary children's literature was taken beyond its Marxist boundaries to become the brave patriotic hero, just as Communists moved beyond the boundaries of class struggle to claim leadership of an oppressed nation.

Revolutionary children's literature in the Civil War that followed the Pacific War continued the direction set in the thirties and early forties. By 1942, this was that literature should be under the political control of the Communist Party and directed towards workers, peasants, soldiers and cadres. In 1946, a group of Marxist writers in Shanghai set up a federation of writers for children; their first specific task was to discuss the control of 'mass' literature because of its effect on children. Adventure stories set in the countryside with young boys as heroic fighters against the Japanese and traitorous Chinese continued Gorky's 'active romanticism'. Unlike Shanghai literature in the pre-war period, these young heroes represented the peasantry and not the proletariat.

By 1949, revolutionary literature had absorbed the social commitment of early May Fourth literature and assimilated forms from both traditional, popular literature and urban, commercialized literature. It was a mass literature of national revolution with a rural, not just urban, emphasis and audience. Following the political victory of the Chinese Communist Party, it became the dominant school of Chinese children's literature.

When we consider the course of revolutionary children's literature up to 1949, the strong influence of external political events is clear. Between 1921 and 1927 this literature was a minor stream. Between 1927 and 1936 it was a growing but underground literature. From 1936 to 1949 it merged with patriotic children's literature to become the dominant school in the field. Major literary developments over these three decades were triggered by domestic responses to outside circumstances.

War-time Revolutionary Literature: The Anti-Japanese War

A clear picture of wartime conditions in Shanghai and their effect on children's literature is presented here in two accounts: one is first-hand observation, the other is fiction. The first is about the founding of the first specialized children's publishing house, The Juvenile Publishing House (*Shaonian Chubanshe*), in 1939. The second is a story written in 1940, *The Little Traitor* (*Xiao Jianxi*), by one of the same House's six or seven editors and its major contributor, Su Su.

Reminiscing twenty years later, with not a scrap of paper to commemorate the event, in 1959 Ding Su recalled how The Juvenile Publishing House began through publishing a small, rough, pamphlet-like magazine called *Good Children* (*Hao Haizi*).[42] It was run by committed people, such as primary school teachers, who were interested in writing patriotic children's literature which was so difficult to publish at that time in Shanghai. The magazine was so popular that it increased circulation, became more professionally finished and changed its name to *Reading for Children* (*Ertong Duwu*). When He Yi sent in a manuscript, *Wild Little Devils* (*Ye Xiaogui*), which was too lengthy to include in such a small magazine, the founders decided to print it as a separate book under a new organization, The Juvenile Publishing House, to show that there was a specialist publisher of children's books. Between this beginning and the House's closure in December 1941, it had no specialized organization, no definite location (sometimes publishing outside Shanghai), and eventually a proscription on its publications; writers often used different titles and different pseudonyms for the same story. Yet, in this two-year period, it published twenty-five books (including poems, plays, stories and translations of works from the Soviet Union) and a small collection of children's literature, edited by Su Su.

Su Su's main work, *The Little Traitor* (*Xiao Jianxi*) is a fast-moving description of the effects of the war on Shuidong, the young son of a Shanghai builder. 'How strange', the story begins, 'the devils come once to this city and the city completely changes'.[43] To Shuidong, walking home with his mother, the city is full of soldiers; people do not walk on the streets but hurry, as if pursued, with fear on their faces; he sees a burning house and a murdered man. They arrive home and that, too, has changed: robbers have plundered, plates are stolen, his dog lies dead with a split belly, there is no food. His mother begins to cry but then the city is full of crying. She goes to find the boy's father, but returns with his corpse.

Now we arrive at the central conflict: at this moment, in walks his father's hated enemy, 'Stinky Shoemaker' (Chou Pijiang)—swaggering, smiling, sprightly dressed. Stinky pulls at Shuidong's mother saying, 'What are you crying about?'[44] and when she tries to follow the coffin he grabs her, laughing: 'Hey, I'm much better than a corpse! We will. . .'.[45] To Shuidong's horror, Stinky Shoemaker stays for lunch, stays for dinner and then just stays. Shuidong hates him, he cannot understand his mother, and his friends jeer at him because his mother sleeps with a traitor, his own father's murderer, just because he has lots of money and feeds them. Shuidong's new father is a traitor to the Chinese people, he collaborates with the Japanese, and that makes Shuidong 'a little traitor', the title of the book. He is unable to face his friends, to reason with his mother or to explain himself to his teachers. Eventually he is thrown out of home by Stinky and begins his life (by now familiar to us) as a hungry, homeless, thieving vagabond on the streets of Shanghai. But he is not a passive victim; he is constantly haunted by memories of his mother, his previous happy life, as well as his friends' insults. When he is offered an opportunity to revenge his father, he goes happily to spy for the anti-Japanese Army until he is caught and finds he has been tricked into really spying for the traitors. He really is 'a little traitor'. He is judged in Army Headquarters by a fierce, dark man, Commander 'Afraid of Nothing' (*Renbupa*), who finds proof of his spying. But when Shuidong bursts into tears and tells his story, the Commander gently explains the situation, offers to help revenge his father and gives him a job as a proper Chinese Army spy. But Shuidong wants to be a soldier and, to abbreviate a long story, he too changes and becomes a brave and happy little soldier.

Eventually, in a chapter called 'Saving Our Country, Saving My Mother' (Jiu Zuguo, Jiu Mama), Shuidong marches into town with the army and finds his mother who tells him, in the last chapter called 'Shuidong Returns Home', that Stinky Shoemaker left her long ago for another woman. Stinky is a traitor, a murderer, a womanizer and now a downright cad! Shuidong's best friend, Uncle Big Beard, then comes in and tells them of the capture and coming execution of Stinky. His mother then decides to join the Army and fight with Shuidong to save the country by ridding it of all devils and traitors. One has the feeling that there is possibly a very happy ending to 'Saving Mother', too, when she walks out hand-in-hand with her son and Uncle Big Beard to join the brigade.

There is not much more to add to this story (172 pages in all). As we observed before, the twentieth century mission to save the nation has now become a matter of military organization and national unity, not social organizations and class solidarity. Light and dark are portrayed in patriots and traitors. But the central characters, Shuidong and his mother, are, however, neither good nor bad. They are basically good, what the Chinese later call 'middle characters' (*zhongjian renwu*): Shuidong cries and is torn between home and his pride while his mother sleeps with her own husband's murderer because she is afraid and needs protection and food for her son. Both mother and son are redeemed through revolutionary action.

Finally, war stories like this did introduce a positive symbol into children's literature in a strong re-emphasis on the Home, which had been under criticism, or non-existent, in many children's stories since the twenties. Stripped of the stern duties demanded by the traditional Confucian concept of the family, which were rejected by

May Fourth revolutionaries, the Home returns to war-time children's literature as the Chinese Army (later the Communist Party) with a different set of duties and demands. It offered an antidote—security, happiness, protection, hope and kindness—to the lonely, starving, vagabond existence on the streets of Shanghai, which was so much a part of pre-war children's stories. It was like an extended family, full of 'uncles' and strong, paternal leaders; it was united; joining the revolutionary army was like 'coming home'. Children needed it and had a central role in it.

The war affected Shanghai's status as the major publishing center in China. Writers moved inland. Literature was transformed into an overt weapon of war by 1938. Patriotic writers joined The All-China Resist-the-Enemy Federation of Writers and Artists, the cultural arm of the second United Front. The Federation spoke for a United Front of artists with Lao She as one of its two editors and its head. In May, the body's official magazine, *Literature of the War of Resistance* (*Kangzhan Wenyi*) began publication and, in October, moved to the wartime capital of Chongqing. Its editorial tone was akin to that in earlier revolutionary literature but with a new sense of urgency. As the first edition stated: '[T]he sacred anti-Japanese War has lit the beacon of national revolution in every corner of China'. It went on to prescribe the duties of 'true art-workers':

> A true art-worker is a fighter for national revolution, he must forcefully use the weapon of Art in a resolute struggle. A true art-worker must thoroughly understand his own social mission and he must fulfil it, worthily and well. Art is an expression of Society; it is also a driving force in Society. A true art-worker must express Society realistically and he must reinforce this (expression) with his own work of motivating that Society: these must be emphasized as the most minimum requirements in the Art Movement during the Anti-Japanese War.[46]

Despite any earlier controversy, children's writers were now firmly included with 'art-workers' and 'fighters for national revolution' and shared a similar social mission. Pioneering works for children and theoretical discussions had been usually published in major literary journals. *Literature of the War of Resistance*

(1938–46) was the most important national magazine for literature and policy in the war years but it published hardly anything on children's literature. As Jiang Feng observed, 'writers for children wrote very little' in this time.[47] Yet this is a crucial period in the whole history of children's literature in modern China: it created a mass literature of national revolution with a rural, not urban, emphasis and audience. Wartime literature from the hinterland targeted an undifferentiated, mass audience. This continued as one strand of children's literature in the fifties and became its sole model in the Cultural Revolution period. It forged a new tradition.

This strand, henceforth called 'revolutionary, popular literature', was caused by the relocation of the urban intelligentsia to the countryside. The writers were shocked by the new environment: their new, vernacular literature was unread, unwanted, unChinese (not popular) and not understood. A 1938 report by one writer, Lao Xiang, on children's books in the countryside commented that people still preferred such 'outdated, old books' as *The Three Character Classic*. No one bought modern books. Mass mobilization required a genuinely popular, vernacular literature.

> Students of humanity have proved that the Chinese people are intelligent and have, in fact, proved that they most respect reading and writing and are very eager to be educated; it is just that they do not have the opportunity or the strength, that's all. While educationalists have already introduced the latest methods from Europe and America, the masses (of our people), as of old, stand outside the circle of education; while authors have already written cartloads of books, the masses, as of old, will not part with *The Hundred Family Names* and *The Three Character Classic*. The louder we shout our song, the less the people dare to join in—it is not that they do not dare, but that they cannot. Our whole culture has lost contact with ordinary people: in the sky there are planes flying about and on the ground, as of old, one-wheeled carts still struggle in the mud. This problem is more obvious with the beginning of the sacred War of Resistance, and it is more serious. To totally resist, we must mobilize all the people.[48]

Lao Xiang therefore wrote *The Three Character Classic of the Anti-Japanese War*, publishing it first in *Literature of the War of Resistance* and then as a separate book which sold nearly 50,000 copies in one month. He also asked singers in the market place to adapt it to a *xiang sheng*—a witty, colloquial dialogue which was part of China's oral tradition in the performing arts. Another writer wrote a supplementary version. Lao Xiang claimed: 'I took the well-known old bottle and filled it with the new wine of resisting Japan; this is the only way to write popular literature.'[49]

Revolutionary popular literature—the 'new wine' of revolution in the 'old bottles' of traditional and oral literary forms—was quickly established within artistic policy at the beginning of the war. This coordinated and seemingly sudden shift in literary policy did, however, have its background of theoretical discussion. Central to this were Qu Qiubai's series of essays written between 1931 and 1932 which underlined the very point that Lao Xiang re-discovered in practice: May Fourth literature was elitist, isolated and ineffective as mass literature. Qu had proposed a two-stage cultural movement:

> . . . Led by the intellectuals, the first stage, which was to be launched immediately, was designed to complete the abortive democratic literary revolution by bringing writers and artists, and their art, into direct contact with the masses for the first time. The second stage was to be the beginning of a distinctly socialist cultural revolution, one in which the direct participation of the masses was to be steadily increased and the monopoly of the cultural arena by intellectuals thereby broken.[50]

'New wine in old bottles' was (in different words) Qu Qiubai's very suggestion for making revolutionary literature accessible to the masses and was part of the first stage of his cultural movement. The war made more of it necessary.

When formulated, Qu Qiubai's mass literature was theoretically urban-based. The Communists in particular adapted it to conditions in the countryside. Details of the practical day-to-day organization in Mao's base area, Yan'an, were published in an enthusiastic 1938 report on art in the border areas. Despite bad roads and low levels of literacy, the art movement was reported to be alive 'like Spring'. Under the auspices of the new Lu Xun Academy, the anti-Japanese Work Committee:

1. promoted local propaganda teams in different areas;
2. collected local anti-Japanese material;
3. collected folk literature, including forty or more folk tunes to which they wrote new words;
4. wrote new works based on oral art, like song dramas; and
5. edited journals.[51]

Among the new journals was one for children called *Children of the Border Areas (Bianqu Ertong),* which ceased publication after two issues in 1938. The practical difficulties were insurmountable: Yan'an had no machine for making paper for printing and textbooks had first priority when any paper was bought outside, which was difficult anyway. Nevertheless, the first issue was edited in a cave with the headline by Mao Zedong, in his own calligraphy:

> 'RISE UP, CHILDREN, and learn to be free, independent citizens of China, learn how to wrest this freedom from the yoke of Japanese imperialism and transform yourselves into the masters of a new era'.[52]

Half the first issue dealt with politics and world affairs but it also included stories, songs, pictures, games and jokes.

In the same year as revolutionary literature became the dominant model for all art, Mao Zedong entered the cultural arena. He, too, emphasized that revolutionary literature must be Chinese, but from a Marxist and Party perspective.

> To make Marxism concretely Chinese, to ensure that its every expression manifests Chinese characteristics. . . this is the urgent problem which the whole Party should try to understand and solve. Foreign-slanted pedantry and obscurantism must be abolished, hollow and abstract cliches must be discouraged and dogmatism must be arrested so that a fresh and vivid Chinese style and manner, of which the Chinese masses are fond, may take their place. To separate international content from national forms is to betray one's ignorance of internationalism; we must meld the two closely together.[53]

C.T. Hsia claims this view 'was to change drastically the literary scene, and the national scene as a whole'.[54] So it did, but at that time, it was a general overview of a literary policy discussed in the thirties, generally accepted by 1938 with one hundred publications to its credit in the first four months of the war. Hsia also claims that 'national forms are to be identified not so much with classical, vernacular literature as with those marginal, semi-literate and regionally diversified forms of entertainment which still enjoyed a diminishing popularity among the less-educated strata of society'.[55] However, this is not the case in the actual books for children at the time: the rhyming form of *The Three Character Classic,* for example, stood as the foundation of Confucian children's books and, as Lao Xiang reported, was clearly popular.

Four years later, when Mao Zedong delivered his opening and concluding speeches (henceforth referred to as the 'Talks') at the Yan'an Forum on Literature and Art, they were, once again, in line with generally accepted art guidelines in the War. As both Hsia and Pickowicz have pointed out, they were influenced by Qu Qiubai's 'cultural movement'. But they were not, as Hsia claims, 'a restatement of extremist Communist literary opinion of the previous two decades'[56] because, as Pickowicz stated,[57] they adopted only the first stage of Qu Qiubai's cultural program. According   to Mao's 'Talks', writers should go down to the people, literature should serve the people, it should both popularize and elevate, and it should 'awaken and arouse the masses and impel them to unite and struggle to change their environment'.[58] The genius in Mao's 'Talks' lies in delivering a succinct summary of war-time art policy. The difference from previous policy lies in the insistence that political, not artistic, considerations were to be the basic criterion when judging a work of art. Mao's high authority and the enforcement of this policy among urban intellectuals in Yan'an, raised the 'Talks' to the high status of the oracular among the Left. They were no longer an argument for a style of war-time art, but a general directive for all art and literature with no time restrictions. They became increasingly important in the Communist areas as the major theoretical statement on literature and art, which includes children's literature. With the Communist victory in 1949, the 'Talks' applied to all China and became national policy.

Children's songs were one of the most popular 'national forms' during the war, particularly in the Communist areas. But once again, they were not 'a marginal... form of entertainment'; intellectuals in the twenties had already collected and edited many regional children's rhymes with the upsurge of interest in China's own popular tradition and they were, in fact, amongst the earliest vernacular children's literature to be published. New words to old tunes had been practiced by Peng Pai in the twenties and by Qu Qiubai himself in Soviet-area textbooks in the early thirties. During the war, they became one of the most common forms of popular children's literature. The songs are simple, taunting, pungent and usually angry. Here are some (undated) from the Communist areas:

On learning:
> Little Red children,
> Quickly, quickly, go to school.
> Read more books,
> Waste no time,
> Raise your skills,
> Learn to fight,
> When you grow up
> You will be like the Red Army.

On unity:
> Don't fear little fists,
> Just fear few fists;
> Countless fists together,
> Will pummel the landlord to mud.

On fighting for land reform:
> A Mauser pistol, a red silk tassel,
> Stuck in my belt to kill white bandits,
> Kill white bandits and divide the land;
> Everyone calls me The Little Red Devil.

On revenge:
> White dogs with wicked hearts
> Ate our grain, killed our mother,
> My eldest brother will grow up, join the Red Army,
> And kill all white dogs to revenge our mother.

And,

On the hardship of Winter and the happiness of Spring:
>Fly away, fly away,
>Fly away, birds.
>Winter comes with frost and snow,
>The cold chill comes, there is no food,
>Fly away, fly away.
>Fly back, fly back,
>Fly back, birds.
>Spring comes, the air is warm,
>The trees are full of flowers and scent,
>Fly back, fly back.[59]

The following children's song was published in 1938 in *Literature of the War of Resistance,* and has transferred the focus on class struggle in the previous songs to struggle against the Japanese invasion. Its tune is the tune of 'The Little White Cabbage':

>. . . Eastern devils
>Are too cruel, Oh!
>A plane bursts, Ah!
>A cannon sounds, Oh!
>Chinese people
>Are in real hardship, Oh!
>Eastern devils,
>Have cruel hearts, Oh!
>Murder men, light fires,
>So, so bad, Oh!
>Killed my Dad, Ah!
>Raped my Mum, Oh!
>Their Cruel deeds
>Have no words, Oh!
>. . .
>When the grass is green, Ah!
>Or when the grass is yellow, Oh!
>When, oh, when,
>Can I go home, Oh!
>. . .

Four hundred million men
With one heart, Ya!
To drive out the bandits
And live in safety, Oh!
If we don't fight the Easterners,
Who can live, Oh!
Fight to go home
To joy and peace, Oh!⁶⁰

Children's songs are difficult to distinguish from folk songs in general. They beat to a harsh tune: pummeling landlords, murdered fathers, raped mothers, and killing 'bandits', the term for the Japanese invaders. Children who fought these 'Eastern devils' were known as 'little red devils'. The cute, the innocent, the precious and the imaginary have all been swept away. Indeed, revolutionary, popular literature, with its return to traditional forms, makes little distinction between adult's and children's literature; even *The Three Character Classic* (and its modern versions) was more a textbook than literature as we now understand it. The insistence, too, that social reality be the starting point, and end, for literary creation meant that little attention was paid to child psychology and the problems of growing up. Military strategy replaced fairytale fantasy. Indeed, children's literature as a field was less distinct than it had ever been since its beginnings in the early twenties. Children themselves did not inhabit 'a special world', but were treated as 'little adults'. All of these were precisely Lu Xun's criticisms of traditional Chinese literature and its attitudes to children.

But just as traditional children's books held their own with the birth of a new, vernacular literature in China, so May Fourth styles continued alongside revolutionary, popular literature. One such story is a fairytale by Yan Wenjing, who moved from Beijing to Yan'an in 1938, where he began to write. In *Dingding's One Strange Journey* (*Ding Ding de Yici Qiguai Luxing*) a clever, hardworking and helpful little girl learns to overcome one basic fault—her timidity. Hiding from a dog, Dingding meets an ant called Red Eyebrows, who gives her a magic hat to shrink her to his size and together they go to find Teacher 'Knows-everything'. On the way she meets many difficulties, but with determination and help from others, she overcomes them and becomes a brave little girl. When she finally meets Teacher 'Knows-everything' she asks him what is 'an air of bravery' (*yongqi*, literally means 'brave air'):

> The little old man knitted his eyebrows, and said:
> 'An air of bravery is a sort of air, you see.' Dingding seemed to understand and asked:
> 'Is it like when Daddy smokes his pipe and puffs of smoke come out his nostrils?'
> 'Not at all, not at all.'
> 'Is it like steam in a pot, air from boiling water in a kettle?'
> 'Nonsense, not at all.'
> Red Eyebrows helpfully asked:
> 'Is it like air?'
> The old man impatiently said:
> 'No, it's not like that, not at all like that. You children love to ask silly questions. Let me tell you, it's like the 'air' in 'losing your temper' (*fapiqi*) and a bit like the 'air 'in 'angry' (*shengqi*). You understand?'[61]

Dingding said, 'I have never seen this sort of air.' Here, comments Jiang Feng, 'the author has not stooped to capture childish talk but has emphasized the special psychology of children and through their own words has made child-like innocence a tangible thing'.[62] This is central to May Fourth children's literature. But the actual works still belong to the forties: the emphasis, even for a girl, is on bravery, self-reliance and helping others. The political allusions are discreet: 'Red Eyebrows' were Han dynasty rebels who were partly responsible for the dynasty's fall and Dingding is frightened of a 'dog', the euphemism for traitors and collaborators during the war. Nevertheless, in this period of urgent, angry literature, Dingding's story is conspicuous for its gentleness.

This brings us to a major feature of wartime literature: it is essentially 'male' in terms of both its content and its creators. First, in terms of content, girls play a small part. Main characters, invariably heroic, are almost exclusively male. Certainly, the hero is triumphant, the heroine is rare. Even the exception, Dingding, is primarily engaged in overcoming her timidity. Mothers, in particular, have a hard time: they are sacrificed or saved, raped or revenged. They are victims, which may well have been true. But the message goes beyond this. As Lao She noted in 'The New Emile', the softer, imaginative (dare one say, female?) side of life was out, along with mother's milk. 'Little red devils' were the models. Second, the creators of this wartime literature are also predominantly male. This is not surprising even in countries not at war, and certainly not in a country involved in a life-and-death struggle against invasion. We have already discussed how the two famous women writers for children in the pre-war period, Bing Xin and Ling Shuhua, celebrated softness and sentiment and failed to make the transition to wartime literature, with its aggression and militancy. The problem is that this militance became a major current in Maoist children's literature after the war, reaching full flood in the Cultural Revolution twenty to thirty years later. While Jiang Qing then tried to address the imbalance, her revolutionary heroines are, quite literally, dressed in male garb. Women as women and gendered children as girls or boys—however understood—only returned to Chinese literature as distinctive characters and distinctive audiences in the post-Mao period.

War-time Revolutionary Literature: The Civil War

By the end of the Pacific War in August 1945, China had freedom from Japan and revolutionary Communist literature had a definite policy and organizational experience. War had elevated this literature from class struggle to a struggle for national sovereignty. Many children's writers returned to Shanghai and quickly formed an organizational base. This was a significant move, as soon the ideological battle between the Communists and the Nationalists embroiled the nation in civil war, and revolutionary children's literature was again deployed to win the hearts and minds of Chinese children.

In May 1946, more than ten of the new generation of writers, such as Chen Bochui and He Yi, met to discuss children's books. In June, 24 writers held a preparatory meeting for a congress of the Federation of Chinese Children's Writers with an opening address entitled 'Children and Children's Literature'. A second meeting was held in November to discuss comics (lianhuantuhua) and, in 1947, the Federation held an exhibition of children's books in

Shanghai. The first Congress in April, 1947, with more than forty people attending, dealt specifically with the editing and collection of a national bibliography of children's books and the members decided to publish an anthology of children's literature covering the period 1946 to 1948. In October and December 1948, the Federation held two more discussions on, first, language, and second, main characters and children's plays. While the activities appeared benign, the Civil War demanded ideological loyalties and the Communists clearly held sway. The old bitter argument over the political content in children's literature re-surfaced and a special Federation meeting in Shanghai, of only ten or so members, decided that:

> [C]hildren's literature must expose the poverty and darkness created by the previous government and no children's writer should hide from this responsibility. At the same time it must show the masses of children the way to struggle (unity and correct leadership) as well as the brightness of victory before them. If children only see the darkness of their past and not their future they will be depressed and disappointed.[63]

In March 1949, Federation members began to perform progressive children's plays in primary schools and a special section on children's literature in a newspaper on International Children's Day informed readers: 'the darkness will soon be past, the light is on the horizon'.[64] With the Communist Liberation of Shanghai in May 1949, the now 28 members of the Federation issued a congratulatory statement:

> . . . from now on we shall work harder and double our efforts under the principle of serving the working people and poor children in the anti-feudal, anti-imperial, anti-bureaucratic, anti-capitalist cultural movement.[65]

Rhetorically, at least, revolutionary Communist children's literature triumphed with Mao Zedong's victory. Yet despite the rhetoric, the 1948 Anthology returned to traditional May Fourth styles; the sections, in diminishing order, were fairytales, plays, stories, poetry and prose. Many of the fairytales were more like fables, a vehicle to satirize the Nationalist government. Popular children's songs were also filled with the 'new wine' of satire:

> The sun came up, red and bright.
> A Q shoulders a gun, the Easterners to fight.
> One kowtow,
> Two kowtow,
> He fearfully surrenders to Eastern might.[66]

A Q, the symbol of Chinese timidity and stupidity in one of Lu Xun's earliest stories, here represents the Nationalist government which is portrayed as a wartime traitor. The cowardly surrender is back lit by the rising sun, the symbol of Chinese communism.

But by far the most important new development in children's literature during the Civil War took place outside Shanghai. It was the beginning of adventure stories set in the countryside during the anti-Japanese War, none of which were included in the 1948 anthology which returned to pre-war genres. These adventure stories, depicting heroic 'little red devils', came from writers in the Communist liberated areas. Xiao San wrote in *Liberation Daily* (*Jiefang Ribao*): 'the "little devils" who behaved with such heroism during the Anti-Japanese War are not depicted nearly enough in Chinese children's literature'.[67] After 1949, such stories moved beyond their rural origins and into mainstream children's literature.

The most famous of these adventure stories is Hua Shan's *Feather Letter* (*Jimao Xin*), which was published in July 1945, just before the Japanese surrender. After 1949, it was reprinted many times and made into a film. A fourteen-year-old shepherd boy, Haiwa, is entrusted by his father with the delivery of a very urgent letter to the guerilla forces in his area, the Taihang Mountains in Shanxi. When surrounded and captured by Japanese forces, he hides the letter under the tail of a bellwether, which he manages to save when most of the flock are slaughtered by Japanese soldiers for dinner that night. Haiwa escapes, is recaptured, and through guile and determination, leads the enemy into an ambush. He completes his mission by handing over the letter just before he loses consciousness from a bullet wound. The letter, in fact, contains intelligence leading to a local Communist victory and, when Haiwa wakes up, Commander Zhang is looking at him.

Illustration 4.4

'Haiwa, the Shepherd', from *Feather Letter*

Gently patting Haiwa on the head, Zhang said,
'You're a real little Eighth Route Army man, a very young hero. . .
Haiwa flushed. 'Did we capture any rifles?'
'Over there,' Zhang replied, pointing to a corner of the room.
There was a pile of brand new Japanese rifles there.
'I want one. Give me a rifle,' demanded Haiwa, tossing aside the red blanket.
But as he stretched out his hand he gave a little cry, for his wound gave him another stab of pain.[68]

Illustration 4.5

'Japanese Soldiers Slaughter the Sheep for Dinner', from *Feather Letter*

And there the story ends. The story is action-packed and fast moving, alive with patriotism, bravery and Marxist zeal. An eleven-year-old Australian girl who read it liked it because children were not treated like children and actually joined in the action, which is a winning feature of much Communist children's literature. Jiang Feng claims that these stories 'historically and realistically reflect a contemporary struggle and deserve a place, not only in the history of our children's literature, but in the (general) history of modern literature in China'.[69]

Conclusion

The Communist victory in 1949 completed the transition from Lu Xun to Mao Zedong as the major theorist of children's literature in China. Lu Xun's framework was not rejected but adopted, in its latest version, into a Chinese Marxist pantheon. Mao's 'Talks' in 1942 had claimed Lu Xun as China's foremost Marxist writer but severely curtailed his use of satire and irony as unnecessary within a revolutionary society. It was saved for 'official' enemies of the Communists. Writers who broke this taboo in Yan'an were criticized and 'sent down' to the peasants for re-education. This anticipated waves of thought-reform campaigns after 1949.

Revolutionary children's literature before 1949 adopted Marxist materialism, believing that while people may be theoretically equal, they had first to determine their environment to contrive that equality and happiness. This was the point of much of Lu Xun's work. Revolutionary children's literature was 'Confucian' in that it dealt almost entirely with social relationships: the 'outer' world of children. It did not explore humankind in relation to nature and the world (Science and Verne) or men's own inner world (the romantic discovery of the May Fourth literature). Like Confucian children's books, it used art as an instrument of moral and social persuasion and emphasized the social responsibilities of adults and children. Unlike Confucian children's books, however, it aimed at radical social change, not social harmony, and at social equality, not a well-ordered hierarchy, ideally topped by a gentleman-ruler. Its readership was to be the poor and dispossessed, not an elite. Its golden age belonged to the future Communist state, not to the past as in Confucian China. The symbols of the new egalitarian society—Spring, dawn and the rising, red sun—pointed to a new beginning, a new day, for China.

From its meager beginnings in children's songs in 1921, revolutionary children's literature both swept away, and amalgamated with, other literary streams. By 1949, it dominated all the major literary fronts: writers, writings, policy and organization. While its social inspiration was the same as that of the new May Fourth literature—the ideal of a strong, independent and justly-ordered Chinese state—revolutionary literature changed direction over basic issues such as political content, the concept of childhood, and the primacy of society over self. But it was not simply good writers and strong ideologues who created a concerned, committed, social literature. It was primarily the miserable conditions of life in China which demanded a literature aligned with political action.

This literature played its part in the achievement of China's larger social goals: freedom and equality and awakening the people to fight for a new society. It was both a vehicle and an expression of social change. From the demand for and the creation of a children's literature, based on the Western model, it moved through the Soviet example to become assimilated with revolutionary politics and Chinese art forms. It began, physically and thematically, as an urban phenomenon and adapted to the countryside. It changed the idea of children from immature 'little adults' to 'owners of the Future' and then to heroic actors in the Present: they were to 'transform themselves into the masters of a New Era'.

By 1949, there were three major schools of children's literature in China: May Fourth, revolutionary and traditional. May Fourth literature, with its emphasis on imagination and folk and fairytales, the exploration of the world of children, and the necessity to educate and liberate children for an unknown future, was submerged during the war but resurfaced in the fifties. It was integral to the experience of all the major children's authors. But traditional books were still preferred in the countryside where most Chinese lived.

Revolutionary children's literature had a clearly articulated political purpose. It assimilated elements from other schools, such as the social commitment of May Fourth children's literature and forms of popular literature. It celebrated heroic action. But despite the dominance of this school in 1949, numerous reports suggest that the best-seller of all was still that Song Dynasty 'dreg', *The Three Character Classic*. Revolutionary literature had made great inroads into the minds of Chinese children but these minds were still hostage to two millenia of Confucian tradition. Under Mao, the Chinese Communist Party set out to destroy both the May Fourth and traditional heritage.

Notes

1. 'Mr Harry Carr Again. . .', *The Cathay* ('a fortnightly bulletin issued for the guidance and entertainment of guests of Cathay and Metropole Hotels and Cathay Mansions. . . gratis to guests', Christmas Number IV:48 (16 December, 1933), p. 445.
2. Isaacs, H., *Straw Sandals: Chinese Short Stories 1918–1933* (Cambridge, Mass., 1974), p. xxxi.
3. *The Cathay*, op. cit., p. 439.
4. Gorky, M., *On Literature*, op. cit., p. 40.
5. Sun Yat-sen, quoted in Franke, W., *A Century of Revolution 1851–1949*, translated by Blackwell, B. (Oxford, 1970), pp. 144–5.

6. Ying Xiuren, *Qizi de Gushi* (Shanghai, 1961), p. 3.

7. Ibid., pp. 6–7.

8. Ibid., p. ii.

9. Yu Dafu, 'Zhongxuesheng Nali Zou', *Zhongxuesheng*, VI (July 1930), p. 94.

10. Ying Xiuren, *Qizi de Gushi*, op. cit., p. 11. This story was also published separately in 1933 and included in a 1959 collection of Guo Moruo's works.

11. Ibid., p. 38.

12. Lee, Leo Oufan, *The Romantic Generation of Modern Chinese Writers* (Cambridge, 1973), p. 197.

13. Ying Xiuren, *Qizi de Gushi*, op. cit., p. 17.

14. Ibid., p. 26.

15. Jiang Feng, *Zhongguo Ertong Wenxue Jianghua*, op. cit., p. 44. For a more comprehensive list of the major fairytales, short stories, poetry, drama, songs, translations and theoretical writings between 1921 and 1937 see Hu Congjing, 'Wo Guo Geming Ertong Wenxue Fazhan Shilue (1921–37)', in *Wenxue Pinglun*, 1963, pp. 89-95.

16. Hsia, C.T., *A History of Modern Chinese Fiction*, op. cit., p. 212.

17. Zhang Tianyi, 'Mifeng', in *Zhang Tianyi Xuanji: Xiandai Zuowen Ku* (Shanghai, 1936), p. 305.

18. Ba Jin, 'Introduction', in *Changsheng Ta* (Shanghai, 1955), pp. 1–2.

19. Ibid., p. 3.

20. Ibid.

21. Ibid., p. 25.

22. Ibid., p. 44.

23. Ibid., p. 57.

24. Ibid., p. 65.

25. Ibid., pp. 74–75.

26. Wang Tongzhao, 'Xiao Hong Denglong de Meng', *Wenxue: Ertong Wenxue Teji*, VII:1 (1 July 1936), p. 29.

27. Ibid., p. 30.

28. Jiang Feng, *Zhongguo Ertong Wenxue Jianghua*, op. cit., p. 43.

29. Zhang Tianyi, *Da Lin he Xiao Lin* (Peking, 1956), p. 9, translated in *Big Lin and Little Lin* (Peking, 1958), pp. 3–4.

30. Ibid., p. 59, translation p. 52.

31. Ibid., p. 125, translation p. 129.

32. Ibid., p. 151, translation p. 158.

33. Jiang Feng, *Zhongguo Ertong Wenxue Jianghua*, op. cit., p. 32.

34. Lao She, 'Xin Aimier', *Wenxue*, op. cit., p. 407.

35. Ibid., p. 18.

36. Ibid.

37. Ibid.

38. Coveney, P., *The Image of Childhood*, op. cit., p. 43.

39. Prusek, J., 'Subjectivism and Individualism in Modern Chinese Literature', op. cit., p. 261.

40. Coveney, P., *The Image of Childhood*, op. cit., p. 83.

41. Jiang Feng, *Zhongguo Ertong Wenxue Jianghua*, op. cit., p. 2.

42. Ding Su, 'Shaonian Chubanshe Huiyi', *Ertong Wenxue Yanjiu* II (1959), pp. 88-94.

43. Su Su, *Xiao Jianxi* (Canton, 1947), p. 1.

44. Ibid., p. 21.

45. Ibid., p. 23.

46. Mu Mutian, 'Kangzhan Wenyi Yundong de Judian', *Kangzhan Wenyi*, I:6 (1938), p. 5.

47. Ibid., p. 47.

48. Lao Xiang, 'Guanyu Kangri Sanzi Jing', *Kangzhan Wenyi* I:7 (5 June 1938), p. 79.

49. Ibid., p. 19.

50. Pickowicz, P., 'Ch'u Ch'iu-pai and the Chinese Marxist Conception of Revolutionary Popular Literature and Art', op. cit., p. 299.

51. 'Kangzhan Wenyi zai Bianqu', *Kangzhan Wenyi*, I:7 (5 June 1938), p. 78.

52. Liu Yu, 'Jiefangqu Diyizhang Ertongbao', *Ertong Wenxue Yanjiu*, 2, (1959), pp. 85–7.

53. Hsia, C. T., *A History of Modern Chinese Fiction*, op. cit., pp. 301–2. From *Mao Zedong Zuanji*, Vol. II.

54. Ibid., p. 301.

55. Ibid., p. 303.

56. Ibid., p. 312.

57. Pickowicz, P., 'Ch'u Ch'iu-pai and the Chinese Marxist Conception of Revolutionary Popular Literature and Art', op. cit., p. 319.

58. Mao Tse-tung, 'Talks at the Yenan Forum on Literature and Art', in McDougall, B.S., *Mao Tse-tung's Talks at the Yenan Conference on Literature and Art*, (Ann Arbor, 1980), pp. 55–86.

59. Tian Haiyan, 'Suqu Ertong Geyao', *Ertong Wenxue Yanjiu* I, p. 85.

60. Ping Lin, 'Nan Tongyao', *Kangzhan Wenyi*, I:2 (7 May 1938), p. 7.

61. Jiang Feng, *Zhongguo Ertong Wenxue Jianghua*, op. cit. pp. 51–2.

62. Ibid., p. 52.

63. Zhongguo Ertong Duwu Zuozhe Xiehui (ed.), 'Zhongguo Ertong Duwu Zuozhe Xiehui Jianshi', in *Ertong Wenxue Chuangzuo Xuanji 1948* (Shanghai, 1949), pp. 4–5.

64. Ibid., p. 5.

65. Ibid.

66. Jiang Feng, *Zhongguo Ertong Wenxue Jianghua*, op. cit., p. 59.

67. Ibid.

68. Hua Shan, *Jimao Xin* (Shanghai, 1972), p. 75, translated in *Haiwa the Shepherd Boy* (Peking, 1974), p. 69.

69. Jiang Feng, *Zhongguo Ertong Wenxue Jianghua*, op. cit., p. 59.

5

Comic Books and Popularization

This study of Chinese children's literature has concentrated on new urban literature written in the vernacular. The dominant genre in this May Fourth literature was fiction. By the thirties, many Marxist theoreticians rejected May Fourth literature as exclusive. Left-wing literary debates shifted to popular forms in the colloquial language which would be accessible to China's rural and urban masses as well as to an educated urban elite. This was the forerunner of the popularization strategy that Mao, as national leader, would apply wholeheartedly to the nation's literature from 1949 to his death in 1976.

This chapter, therefore, widens the parameters of this study to include a discussion of the major concern of Marxist literary policy: the 'question of creating a revolutionary popular literature and art'.[1] Here we examine the ideological role of revolutionary literature within the field of children's literature. Because of their significance, our focus is on the development of 'serial picture books' or comics.[2] Originally, these were children's books but, by the 1930s, the readership extended to the urban masses, and comics were then recognized as a major new form of popular literature. Nevertheless, children still dominated the readership.

As popular literature, comics in China were first targeted by revolutionaries for the purpose of mass education. A history of comics therefore gives us not only examples of what children liked to read, but also models of works that revolutionaries and bureaucrats thought children and the masses should read. The concept of comics as revolutionary popular literature was developed before the Communist victory in 1949, and subsequently applied with constant shifts and re-interpretations after 1949. In practice, popular but 'counter-revolutionary' works were criticized or purged while exemplary 'revolutionary' works were held up for emulation. Thus, the focus of this chapter is on left-wing theories of revolutionary, popular literature and Party policy towards comic book publication. Discussion of particular 'exemplary' works illustrates this analysis.

Mao Zedong's 'Talks' at Yan'an in 1942 provide the framework for understanding the theory of comics as revolutionary, popular art after 1949. As explained in the previous chapter, such works were to be an ideological weapon in the Communist struggle during the war period. Because these works aimed to mobilize ordinary Chinese against internal and external enemies, this literature had to be accessible to a vast illiterate audience. It also had to be liked, that is, be popular. Marxists adapted the comic book form for revolutionary purposes precisely because comics were the most popular reading material of all. Mao's 'Talks' also called for the use of traditional art forms, which ordinary people understood. Comics were familiar to the public and had the requisite Chinese ancestry. This chapter describes the process of popularizing revolutionary values through comics. The chapter is organized within a chronological framework, from the early twentieth century to 1976, the year of Mao's death. It is divided into two parts: before and after 1949.

Exploration of Chinese comics, essentially a pictorial genre, adds a new dimension to the history of Chinese children's literature by departing from the established practice of analyzing mainly written genres, such as fiction, plays and poetry. In literary sinology, as McDougall has observed, this practice 'resulted in a very narrow and biased view of the contemporary cultural scene'.[3] Propagandizing through comics, children's most popular reading material, highlights the importance that Chinese Marxists attributed to mass education through literature and art, and to the political utility of this medium. Indeed, popularization of revolutionary cultural products, such as picture books, was perhaps the most significant Maoist contribution to modern Chinese children's literature. It is a proposition developed throughout this chapter.

Chinese Comics between 1908 and Liberation in 1949

Between 1908 and 1949, comics flourished within a commercial publishing network based in Shanghai. Their intended audience was children though the readership extended well beyond. Their popularity in the urban market place led to recognition of comics as popular literature. Subsequently, this popularity warranted organizational control over comic-book production when the Chinese Communist Party took control of the nation in 1949. In this section, first we examine the development of comics as popular literature. Theory for this genre was developed from the late twenties to Mao's 'Talks' in 1942. Second, we discuss policy changes at the point of Liberation. Third, these changes are evaluated through an analysis of China's most famous example of pre-Liberation comics, *Sanmao* in its various versions.

'Precedents' for Popularization of Comic Books

Chinese claim that comics are an indigenous art form with an ancestry stretching back to serial pictures in the Wei Dynasty (200–65 AD).[4] As Chiang stated, China has a long history of using pictorial narratives:

> The stories of the Song (960–1279) and Yuan (1279–1368) dynasties often had illustrations at the top of each page. The popular novels and romances of the Ming (1368–1644) and Qing (1644–1911) dynasties frequently had portraits of the characters at the beginning of the book, and sometimes there were additional pictures at the start of each chapter. These may be considered as the forerunners of picture-story books. The New Year paintings so popular throughout the country are also sometimes in serial form, for they used to be mounted on screens with sixteen, twenty-four or thirty-two pictures to one set. Thus they have something in common with picture-story books. Then there are serial wall paintings. . . [5]

The earliest modern comic in China was published in 1908, 26 years before the first comic book, *Famous Funnies*, was published in the West. The 1908 Chinese comic was a small five-page booklet, based on the episode, 'Zhuge Liang Arranges a Wedding' ('Zhuge Liang Zhaoqin'), from the classical historical novel, *Romance of the Three Kingdoms* (*Sanguo Yanyi*). The illustrations were taken from a contemporary opera version then playing in Shanghai.[6] For the first time, the illustrations were serialized rather than depicting specific scenes randomly selected from the original chapter; thus the pictures had effectively become the text. From this unpretentious beginning, explanatory text was included in later publications. Dialogue, first used in 1921, was common by 1929.[7] By the early thirties the comic had crystallized into its present form: small booklets, about ten by twelve centimeters, printed on newspaper with one illustration and a short accompanying text to each page. Thus the emphasis in Chinese comics is on illustrations (at least two-thirds of the page), serially linked to depict a story, and with a short explanatory text in simple characters (at most one-third of the page). Hence, we should note the accuracy of the literal translation of the Chinese term, *lianhuantuhua*: 'serial pictures'. Lu Xun described the form in 1932:

> Book illustrations were originally intended as adornment to stimulate the reader's interest but. . . they do not supplement the text so there is a second kind of illustration which is explanatory. When many of these latter kind can together be solely relied upon to understand the text, while still being separate from it, they form a single comic book.[8]

The name *lianhuantuhua* or 'serial pictures' was not used generically until 1925 with the publication of a Shanghai comic based on yet another classical novel, *Journey to the West* (*Xiyouji*). Before this, serial picture books had local names which, with the exception of the Shanghai term, *tuhuashu* meaning 'picture-book', all mean 'children's book': *xiaorenshu* in the North, *gongzishu* in Guangdong and Guangxi in the South, *pusashu* in Zhejiang and *yayashu* in Hankou.[9] Lu Xun claimed that the 'children's book' label was because contemporary critiques always emphasized the works' educational potential.[10]

Nevertheless it also seems that, in their early history, comics were seen as properly belonging to children's books.

In 1932, Mao Dun still thought that the majority of comic readers were primary-school children. He was surprised to observe, at one Shanghai bookstall, that the readers were mostly apprentices, aged fifteen and sixteen and some were adult workers.[11] Thus the change of name in 1925 signified both recognition of the form on a national scale and a broadening of its audience; comics were becoming 'popular' literature and not just children's literature. This was recognized by leading leftist writers and theoreticians in the very early thirties and comics were included in the debates on the many forms of 'mass' literature in need of ideological reform and artistic control.

A major factor leading to the wide circulation of comics, at least in the cities, was the advent of rental rather than purchase. This development is described by A Ying in his short but definitive work on comics, *The History of Chinese Comics* (*Zhongguo Lianhuantuhua Shihua*).

> The first bookshop to sell comics for profit had ample funds and a lithographic press and so it only sold, not rented, comics. Later, however, there were the two bookshops of Yao Wenhai and Jiang Chunji which had (only simple) copying facilities; after completing ten illustrations they would send them immediately to the press but they only printed one book a day and sometimes it took more than twenty days to complete a publication. Due to a lack of capital they could not afford to wait for a publication to be complete and then sell but, as it is difficult to promote sales before this, they thought up a rental plan. (Thus) both bookstalls and bookshops could turn over capital all the time. Because renting was cheap the readers increased and soon bookstalls only rented comics.
>
> On this basis the publishers of comics established their own distribution network, at first domestically and then overseas in Southeast Asia, and built up a broad popular base. By 1931 or thereabouts the bookshops had increased to more than forty with an organization for total distribution. Later they set up a research organization for improvement.[12]

The comic-rental business built up particularly rapidly in Shanghai and was well established by 1932. Mao Dun wrote that Shanghai streets were crowded with bookstalls hiring out comics, with this new trade ousting the earlier market in songbooks within the short space of five or so years. This, he observed, 'points to a rapid rise in the reading ability of Shanghai's general populace. . . ; songbooks cannot satisfy them, they demand "fiction"! The fact, too, that so many primary-school children enjoy reading comics shows that the reading material we have to give them is quite inadequate.'[13]

Mao Dun describes the bookstalls as two planks of wood, leaning against a wall and piled high with comics. Alongside was a wooden stool, and for two coppers anyone could hire between twenty and thirty comics and sit down to read them on the spot. These bookstalls 'have imperceptibly become the most welcome and lively library for Shanghai's masses and also the most powerful and popular tool for "mass education"'.[14] They were to remain a feature of Chinese cities until the Cultural Revolution and re-emerge in the post-Mao period.

Not surprisingly, the maturity of the comic book—in form, organization and visible popularity—in the early thirties coincided with its intellectual recognition as 'art' and this in turn attracted talented and progressive artists to its ranks. One of the earliest and most famous was Zhao Hongben.[15] In 1931 at the age of sixteen, he became an apprentice illustrator, although he did not leave his 'teacher' to work on his own until 1939.[16] In 1941 when Zhao began working with the Communist underground in Shanghai, he switched from old themes, such as swordsmen and the like, to 'comics with a new content':[17] *Sunrise (Richu)*, *Thunderstorm (Leiyu)*, *The True Story of A Q (A Q Zhengzhuan* by Lu Xun), *The Watch* (translated by Lu Xun) and *A Youth Learns to Write (Shaonian Bigeng)*. These were major May Fourth works. As a comic-book illustrator, Zhao 'followed the road which Lu Xun had pointed out'.[18] A Ying wrote that gourmets of the comic book at that time could recognize a particular artist's style immediately on opening its pages.[19]

The most influential and quoted defender of the comic was Lu Xun. In 1932 Su Wen, spokesperson for a literature *non-engagee,* wrote in the Shanghai magazine, *Modern Times* (*Xiandai*), that comics 'could never produce a Tolstoy or a Flaubert' and had no future.[20] This prompted Lu Xun to take up his pen in caustic reply. Perhaps '"comics will not produce a Tolstoy or a Flaubert" but I do believe that they can produce a great artist like da Vinci or Michelangelo', he wrote in the first essay.[21] He went on to ask what were Michelangelo's paintings if not 'religious propaganda paintings, Christian serial-pictures' of the day?[22] In the same month he wrote another essay, 'A Defense of Comics' ('Lianhuanthuhua Bianhu'), which briefly reviewed comics in China and the West, particularly Germany, and concluded: 'My intention is to raise the facts and prove not only that comics can be considered as art but that they already sit in the "temple of art"'.[23] He entreated young illustrators not to despise this form because 'I dare believe this about them: the masses want them, the masses appreciate them'.[24]

Mao Dun's article on comics, written in December 1932, finishes in a similar vein with an obvious reference in the last line to Lu Xun's essay:

> If this form is utilized cleverly it will certainly become the most powerful work in mass literature and art. Whether in the realm of illustration or explanatory text (note well! the text alone is an independent story), both can evolve into 'works of art'. Indeed, there is nothing to stop us saying that they may even slightly surpass German comics.[25]

The comic was defended on the basis of its popularity at a time when the League of Left-wing Writers was involved in the polemics surrounding the use of mass literature for revolutionary propaganda. These writers saw comics as a form already recognized in the West, with a mass market in China and the potential to be both a potent educational medium and great art.

The critical focus, in the early thirties, was on the quality and lucidity of the illustrations. This took precedence even over changing the content from the favorite themes of 'the supernatural, the chivalrous sword fighter, the adventurous romance' and the classical novel, to revolutionary themes, without causing a loss of popularity among their audience.[26] In a 1934 essay titled 'A Trifling Chat About Comics' ('Lianhuantuhua Suotan'), Lu Xun made the point that the most important aspect of comic-book illustration was its 'intelligibility' to the masses, which in no way lessened its value as art.[27] For example, Chinese people were unused to both perspective and shading so it did not matter if the illustrator omitted them.[28] In another essay on pictures in children's books, he criticized their poor quality, such as muddy color, outdated subject-matter and lack of clarity which stemmed from artists' unfamiliarity with their subjects.[29]

Mao Dun, in his 1936 children's story, 'Big Nose', concentrated on the 'unintelligibility' of the storyline because the depicted scenes were discontinuous, that is, not 'serial'. Big Nose, an illiterate young vagabond, spent his life scavenging for food and shelter in Shanghai's streets but when he found five coppers he spent them all at 'the street library' reading comics on his favorite topic: women sword fighters. He lost himself in the first story only to find, at the climax, that the pictures stopped telling the story and the written text took over. Just when a monk looked as if he would aid the woman and child, fleeing from three evil monks and a Daoist, he turned the page, wondering 'Will the monk help?'[30] but the next picture showed only the monk talking. By the last picture, the woman was shown safely at home. What happened? He was annoyed with the artist: 'The climax, and he can't even draw it, just words to fill in the gap'.[31] In 'Big Nose', Mao Dun was reminding the artist of the nature of his audience, with nine out of ten people illiterate. Therefore, the illustrations had to be lucid enough to carry the storyline without support from the text.

Theoretical discussions on comics as mass literature stopped during the period of the anti-Japanese war. Not much was published. However, Mao's 'Talks' in 1942 crystallized certain trends in revolutionary literary theory of the pre-war period, setting the guidelines for later organization of the publishing world, including comics. A Ying records that the Communists definitely utilized serial pictures in the Liberated Areas and the 1938 children's magazine in Yan'an certainly included comics.[32] Few, however, have survived. Publication rapidly increased after the Japanese surrender in 1945 but, once again, few comics survive from the civil war period.[33]

Despite theories of comics as mass literature, children's writers in the pre-Liberation period clearly saw comics as part of their domain. In 1946, in Shanghai, the first study session of the newly formed Chinese Association of Writers for Children chose comic-books as their first discussion topic, presumably because of the popularity of these works among children. The Association's interest was primarily educational and organizational, as evidenced by the areas it explored:

> Comics' influence on children and the masses;
> Comics' faults;
> Methods for reforming old comics;
> Methods for creating new comics; and
> How to take the masses of young readers out of the hands of the publishers of old comics.[34]

The push for organizational and ideological reform had begun. This push became serious immediately after Liberation.

The Significance of 'Liberation'

'Liberation' had both temporal and symbolic significance. Temporally, it marked 'the end of one phase and the beginning of another'.[35] Mao Zedong proclaimed China a People's Republic on 1 October 1949. 'The Chinese people', said Mao Zedong, 'have stood up'![36] For the first time since the beginnings of a modern children's literature, one group alone, the Chinese Communist Party, had the undisputed power to implement its policies on a national scale. Symbolically, Liberation divided 'old' China from a 'new', reborn nation. Comics such as *Sanmao* pictorialized the division as stark: black and white, dark and light, winter and spring.

In terms of organization, 'Liberation' signified the strict implementation of guidelines for literature that were formulated in the earlier revolutionary period. The educational function of children's literature within a larger program of social reform for all China, was now far more important than its 'fragrance', its imaginative and entertaining side. Official pronouncements always emphasized this; an early editorial (June 1948) in the Party newspaper, *People's Daily* (*Renmin Ribao*), echoed with little variation through the next three decades:

> The problem of nurturing successors to the proletarian revolution is a great question of strategic importance raised by Comrade Mao Zedong. To guarantee the ultimate victory of the Proletarian revolution and communism, we must not only formulate a correct line and policy but also nurture and educate the one hundred and twenty million successors[37] to the proletarian revolution.[38]

As it had always been for Lu Xun, literature was still seen as part of the total upbringing of China's younger generation, but with a more definite goal than 'the future'; children were 'successors to the proletarian revolution' and their literature was to 'nurture' these successes. The point at issue was never the 'strategic importance' of their education but education's 'line and policy'. The aims of national education policy therefore shaped policy towards children's books, as an influential editorial in a September 1995 edition of *People's Daily,* 'Create, Publish and Distribute a Great Quantity of Children's Books', clearly points out:

> We must bring up children to be new socialist men. They must have healthy bodies. They must be nurtured in Communist virtues, a materialistic world view and a knowledge of science, the basis of production, and culture, so that on the day they grow up, they may inherit the work of an older generation and shoulder the difficult responsibility of socialist and communist construction. Therefore, education (in which children's books play a part) is a basic task related to the future of our nation and society.[39]

The major problem facing the Communists in 1949 was the organizational aspect of policy implementation. Looking back on the achievements of the People's Republic, Franz Schurmann wrote:

> In earlier decades, Chinese intellectuals wrote about socialism, anarchism, and the nature of the world and society. This made for an intellectual liveliness which has since disappeared. But few of the intellectual great men of that time had the slightest notion about the true problems of organization. By the time of Yenan [Yan'an], 'theory' had been canonized, and the Chinese Communists turned their attention to 'practice', namely organization and action.
>
> There is indeed a new China—a China of organization.[40]

The art world, including children's literature, was no exception. In the first few years, ideological articles emphasized the 'correct' theoretical framework, critical essays held up model works for emulation, and organizational changes aiming at bureaucratic centralization under Party leadership were the instruments of planning and control. At the apex stood the Chinese Communist Party, 'the one great organizational product of the Chinese Revolution'.[41]

One of the first targets for organization and ideological control in the arts, and the first in children's literature, was the comic book: its writers, illustrators, publishers, editors and vendors. Two reasons, in particular, made the comic book the obvious first target for reorganization.

The first was educational. In the early years after 1949 there was a continued emphasis on 'popularization' in art as the cornerstone of Communist literary policy, a strategy already enshrined in Mao's 'Talks', and comics were the most popular art form of all. Emphasis was now on comics as mass literature, not just children's literature. From a voice articulating the official line, '[T]he massive circulation of comics among our people proves that comics are the most popular art form, and highlights the importance of editing borne by anyone involved in education of the masses'.[42] Comics were read by 'children, women, shopkeepers, workers, operators of small businesses and the entire class of semi-literate people in the cities'.[43] A 1949 article, however, pointed out the 'fact' that readers only liked comics on traditional themes: the supernatural, wandering swordsmen (and swordswomen), illustrated versions of the classics and decadent 'stories based on American thrillers, sex-ridden Hollywood films. . . These reactionary, vulgar and pornographic picture books poisoned the minds of many of our people and had a particularly pernicious influence on children'.[44] Given their potential 'danger', and the Party's urge to embed a Marxist ideology nationally, reform of the comic book was considered a political imperative.

The second compelling reason for reform was organizational. A dispersed and powerful publishing and distribution network, which was capitalist and as yet outside Communist control, churned out comics for a hungry market. Between 1920 and 1950, the nation's publishing center, Shanghai, published more than 28,000 titles and distributed more than twenty-eight million copies.[45] In 1952 in Shanghai, 350,000 small bookstalls rented comics to between 200 and 400 thousand people each day (for a small sum each person rented five to twenty comics) while the city's daily cinema attendance was only 100,000.[46] Hence, comics had a much larger market than the publishing statistics based on actual sales suggest, a market largely in the hands of the wealthy publishers. In reforming and controlling the comic book, the Communist Party gained control of some of the major publishing houses in the coastal cities which, for much of the twentieth century, were the influential molders of public consciousness.

Hence, in terms of Party organization of comic book publication, 'Liberation' was not so much a point in time as a period lasting from 1946 to 1953, when the Party announced it was in control of the publishing world. It was a process, not a single event.

One measure that the Party adopted to facilitate overall policy implementation was to publicize 'model' works from the pre-Liberation period. In this way, the Party began to institutionalize a canon of revolutionary children's literature and art. The model for comic book publishers and artists was the 1947 version of *Sanmao* by Zhang Leping, *An Orphan on the Streets* (*Sanmao Liulangji*).

Sanmao *Versions by Zhang Leping*

Children's writers were the first to plan the reform of the comic book in 1946, so it is not surprising that the most famous example of pre-Liberation comics is now seen as belonging indisputably to children's literature. This is *An Orphan on the Streets* (or *Sanmao*), the work upheld by the Party for nationwide emulation. In 1950, the editor introduced the hero, Sanmao, after whom the comic is named, to a new generation of Chinese children. The editor cast Sanmao as a representative of an oppressed class in the pre-Liberation period, in contrast with the 'new' life in communist China. He wrote:

> Was there really such a child as Sanmao?
> Okay, let's talk about Sanmao's life. In 1948 and 1949, before Liberation... none of you were born then. At that time, you could see homeless children in every street and alley you walked along in old Shanghai, then ruled by the reactionary nationalist government. Some were so exploited by landlords and capitalists that they had no clothes or food and died of illness or starvation. Others became cannon fodder, forced into the army by the reactionary Nationalist clique. Still others were killed indiscriminately by reactionary American devils... Every family has countless such tragedies to tell![47]

Sanmao began as a cartoon strip, published serially in Shanghai newspapers, but was subsequently reprinted many times as a comic book. It was so powerful that fiction and reality blurred in the public's perception, with the author, Zhang Leping, known as 'the father of Sanmao'.[48] Children wrote letters asking for news or offering Sanmao a home, typically:

> Dear Mr. Leping,
> I have not seen Sanmao for three days and I am really worried about him. Where has he gone? Has he starved or frozen to death after all or has he gone to school? Please tell me the truth.
> Yao Shuping (8 years)[49]

Sanmao, named because of the three hairs on his head, is taken by most people as the orphan depicted in *An Orphan on the Streets* (1947). But there are, in fact, four Sanmaos in four discrete texts: published in 1935, 1945, 1947, and post Liberation.

Sanmao was 'born' in 1935 when the cartoon strip was first published in *Xiaochenbao* in Shanghai. This version is mostly of historical interest, but it does support the claim that the war politicized cartoonists such as Zhang Leping. Bi Keguan and Huang Yuanlin observed that the first pre-war *Sanmao* is different to later versions; here, the emphasis is on humor and entertainment, not social exposure or ideological persuasion.[50]

The second version was published in the Shanghai newspaper, *Shenbao*, after Zhang Leping participated in an anti-Japanese propaganda team during the war. Like many wartime artists, he travelled widely to Zhejiang, Jiangxi, Fujian, Hubei, Hunan, Guangxi and Guangdong. He has claimed that in these eight itinerant years he did not even think of Sanmao. But when he returned to Shanghai in 1945, he resurrected Sanmao as he watched greedy high officials 'compete for the spoils of victory'.[51] The strip, called *Sanmao Follows the Army* (*Sanmao Congjunji),* satirizes both this wartime experience and official greed. The humor still exists in this version, but has a bitter edge; the situations are often funny but it is clear that Sanmao is at rock bottom, and indeed, cannon fodder for the army.

Zhang Leping himself wrote that the situations in *Sanmao Follows the Army* 'border on the absurd'.[52] An example of this is a series of forty-seven strips which narrate how Sanmao became a hero, single-handedly defeating a Japanese platoon armed with cannon while he had only four hand grenades. Picked as a 'dare to die' victim because he is the smallest, he retreats to a river under cannon fire, arms an ox with the grenades, is re-ordered to the front where he discovers the Japanese drunk after feasting on the ox (Illustration 5.1), whereupon he calls his Chinese comrades who capture the enemy. Even so, Sanmao falls on his head but turns his 'dare to die' death warrant into a star, outshining the fat boastful soldier. Indeed, the whole victory is a farce. Despite being shot at by the enemy and bullied by the Chinese army, Sanmao's resourcefulness wins through. Delirious

Illustration 5.1

from *Sanmao Follows the Army*

Illustration 5.2

from *Sanmao Follows the Army*

joy at Japan's unconditional surrender, however, is followed by the last set in which Sanmao is among those first demobilized. He stands, like China, at the crossroads leading to either devastated countryside or cityscape. Both roads lie through a field of graves (Illustration 5.2).

This 1945 version exhibits several traits that were adapted in the classic 1947 version. First, as with cartoons in general, the issues are contemporary and controversial; 'the fictional narrative reflects grim reality'.[53] Second, the material now has the educational element espoused by Marxist literary policy but it is still free from the dull seriousness of later works. Zhang wrote that he tried to induce people's awareness of issues through hilarious situations but, as he also noted, the humor is farcical rather than funny. Entertainment is still overt while education is covert. Third, and most important, the cartoon is not only *about* China's masses, but is *sympathetic to them*. It is drawn, albeit humorously, from their point of view. It was also easily accessible to them. The pictures required no previous knowledge of Chinese poetry or history in order to be understood. There was no abstruse symbolism. As Zhang wrote: '[T]here are pictures without words, which may be considered popularization (*dazhonghua*) in China with its high proportion of illiterates'.[54] This was precisely the point of the thirties' theorists and Maoist literary policy.

All three traits are transferred to the Sanmao classic in 1947: *An Orphan on the Streets*. But a fourth element is added. This is a clear differentiation of class. In Zhang's classic, a shivering, skinny Sanmao watches the fat feed in grotesque comfort, as in Illustration 5.3. Without Japanese invaders, the enemy shifts to the privilege and corruption of the elite. It is this class element, along with the other three traits, which made the 1947 *Sanmao* a classic in the canon of popular literature and art after 1949. Although originally for a general newspaper readership, it was reprinted again and again after 1949 so that children could compare pre- and post-Liberation society and 'love our great socialist fatherland'.[55] It became a children's classic, as well as a cartoon/comic book classic, and Zhang Leping became an illustrator of children's works.

Illustration 5.3

'Two Worlds',
from *An Orphan on the Streets*

As a street orphan, Sanmao is still a victim, basically good-hearted and resourceful, but with a strong sense of justice. In one sense, we have here an illustrated adaptation of a common theme in revolutionary literature in Shanghai: the depiction, not description, of the life of an orphan boy, eking out a lonely, miserable existence in Shanghai's streets. He has no family, no food, no shelter, no clothes.[56] The illustrator made him a fictional symbol of the hundreds of thousands of poor orphaned children around the city before 1949. Zhang Leping was friendly with some of these homeless orphans and, after finding that two out of three had frozen to death overnight, he went home and decided to use his art as powerful social accusation. Throughout the text, Sanmao's orphaned life is emphasized by comparing him to the powerful, the well-connected, the well-fed and the well-clothed. The imagery is stark and powerful.

Illustration 5.4

'Liberation through Dreams',
from *An Orphan on the Streets*

Illustration 5.5

'Entering Children's Paradise',
from *An Orphan on the Streets*

Unlike the earlier versions of Sanmao, the 1947 version includes Sanmao's dreams. His dreams are of maternal warmth, nurture and friendship. Lying in prison for stealing grain, Sanmao 'dreams of liberation' in a children's paradise where he is mothered, washed, fed, plays and goes to school with friends—until he is rudely awakened by the prison guard (Illustrations 5.4 and 5.5). Dream and reality are starkly defined. The various introductions to post-Liberation selections of *An Orphan on the Streets* clearly present the reality as 'old' China and the dream as realized in 'new' China under the Communist Party.

The result was a 'classic' that combined all the qualities the critics demanded. The theme was one from the heart of pre-Liberation Marxist revolutionary literature. The artist was familiar with the subject and environment, which Lu Xun and Mao Zedong claimed was the beginning for a progressive writer or artist. The illustrations were lucid and immediately intelligible to a Shanghai audience, and they were supported, not by a text, but a four-character title which readers did not have to understand in order to follow the story. For example, the caption, 'Dogs are Better off than People' (Illustration 5.6), merely reiterates the visual message. The message is 'read' by following the moving lines in the composition, swinging in an arc from the woman's eye to rest on Sanmao. Against a barely sketched and static background emphasizing a winter bareness, an apparently wealthy and aloof woman wearing boots, furs, muff and scarf dominates the composition. Her back is to Sanmao, who is therefore invisible to her. Her suspicious, sideways stare and the lines of the dogs' leads move the reader's eye to the two well-fed, warm dogs at the center of the picture. The white dog's backward glance to a shivering, barefoot Sanmao focuses the reader on the child marooned in the left-hand corner. The eye stops, hemmed in by tree and house. Thus, the child is alienated and ignored within the illustration, just as he is alienated and ignored in society. Yet visually insignificant, he dominates both the linear rhythm and the meaning. The reader feels for Sanmao, for his plight and simple dreams.

Illustration 5.6

'Dogs are Better off than People',

from *An Orphan on the Streets*

It is because of such deceptively simple, yet compassionate art that Sanmao was not just popular, he was loved. The famous playwright, Xia Yan, wrote in 1950:

> Sanmao is a most familiar character in Shanghai; not only do children know him, like him and pity him but even their household heads and teachers point out that its almost as if Sanmao is not an abstract creation of the artist's brush but a real flesh-and-blood child of misery who incites pity and love. That the artist has created a character which gains such appreciation, sympathy and love from the masses of people, that the artist cared and recorded his life as if he were a real, live person to the extent that people wrote to the newspaper offering money and effort to help Sanmao out of his difficulties, then that is undoubtedly the artist's success and reward.[57]

Such empathy mixed with class consciousness makes this version a classic in revolutionary popular literature, claimed nationally by historians of cartoons, comic books and children's literature. Fundamental to its longevity is its accessibility to a mass audience. Mao's 1942 'Talks' suggest an ambiguity between the masses as a passive and as an active audience. The response to *An Orphan on the Streets* was overwhelmingly active and positive, partly because the work is so highly crafted and contemporary. But it also blends entertainment with education; whereas farce replaced humor in the 1945 *Sanmao*, satire now replaces farce. As cartoon art, *Sanmao* retains its central core of biting humor.

Sanmao 'most clearly shows the progressive features of comics, including "children's books", at that time', according to the eminent critic, A Ying. He claimed it 'most reflects the social life of that time and the sort of unhappy fate children met under that dark social system'[58] Its frequent reprintings after 1949 are part of children's continuing education for it serves as a comparison between life in the old society and life in Communist 'New China'.

The pictorial contrast between reality and dreams was echoed in Zhang Leping's comments on *Sanmao* in new China. Zhang wrote that this was 'a tragic history from the oppressive old society' and that, after Liberation, Sanmao 'led a life of warmth and good fortune'. He became 'an outstanding and lucky Young Pioneer'.[59] Xia Yan's preface to the 1950 edition reiterates this:

> It is a matter for rejoicing that the era of Sanmao is already past. The old society turned men into ghosts, the new society turns ghosts into men. Sanmao is good, brave and has undergone trials and hardship so let us wait and see how he develops and progresses in the new society.[60]

A sequel to *Sanmao* produced later in the fifties, *Sanmao Yesterday and Today* (*Sanmao Jinxi*), pictorialized Sanmao's life before and after Liberation. Its impact relies on a stark contrast between China's old and new societies, by juxtaposing pre-Liberation cartoons with new post-Liberation depictions of Sanmao's idyllic life under Communism. The idyll is described in a 1959 review:

> Sanmao is a good child, a good student and takes a dynamic part in social activities. He has a warm home, he goes to school and he has done his best to participate in society's work such as raising

pigs, eradicating the four pests, working in the fields and collecting waste. In a new environment he has developed a more flawless character and is a model of our children in new China.

What a clear contrast is Sanmao's past and present life!

. . . Let children recognize the bitterness of old society and treasure the happiness of our new society through *Sanmao Yesterday and Today*.[61]

Unfortunately, this sequel lacks any humor or narrative and the 'flawless' Sanmao is extremely dull. Education through models has now completely replaced entertainment and humor.

In their clear commitment to China's revolutionary ideology, both the 1947 and the post-Liberation *Sanmao* are model comics. In their literary world, Liberation marks a glorious new beginning that offered more than the simple necessities of life hitherto denied to China's poor: a home, food, work and an education. Whereas Liberation had previously been a dream of freedom for China and, as such, the muse of much modern Chinese literature, it now became a threshold that promised children like Sanmao a place and purpose in building a new China. It was as if they had walked through the 'gates of darkness' and stepped blithely into the 'bright wide-open spaces' of Lu Xun's dream. Liberation as a symbolic line between the 'bitterness of the old and the happiness of the new' was established throughout children's literature in the next three decades under Mao.

Chinese Comics from 1949 to 1965

Centralized bureaucratic planning was the dominant feature of comic book publication in the years between Liberation and the Great Proletarian Cultural Revolution (1949–65). We have said that a major problem that the Communists faced in 1949 was the organizational one of policy implementation. Mao's line on literature and art was 'canonized' and procedures were instituted to control the production and distribution of comics. We now turn to those procedures in more detail, and to some of the prize-winning comics produced in this period.

Control took effect at two levels: organizational and critical. This double effort to control the industry was considered so important that it was likened to a 'battle'. Revolutionary, popular comics were poised to invade the territory of the old popular comics.

The battleground was the publishing world, with 'old' and 'new' comics singled out as the combatants. The dividing line was ideological, not temporal; 'old' comics were those with traditional themes while 'new' comics were those with themes from revolutionary Chinese society. The best of these, according to critic, Li Qun, 'not only contained the new thinking but also absorbed the good points from the old comics so it is no accident that they are welcomed by the masses'.[62] The signal for control came almost immediately after Liberation with statements such as new comics 'have not only failed to take over the territory of the "old comics". . . but have not even made full preparation for an "attack"'.[63]

While the organizational apparatus may not have been fully prepared, the ideological arsenal that the Communists launched against the old comics drew on pre-Liberation theories. Thus, the lines were drawn between the 'popular' old comics and the 'popularization' of new comics. The divide was imposed with the explicit understanding that adherence to either side had ideological implications: support, or lack of it, for the embryonic People's Republic of China.

Organizational Control of Comic Book Publishing

A report from Shanghai gives rarely revealed details of the early organizational methods of control. It shows that the grass-roots bureaucracy set up to control the publication of comics was inseparable from the stated aim of an 'attack' by new comics on the territory of the old. The report focussed on the practicalities and difficulties of implementation. Following a resolution passed at a major conference on the reform of pre-Liberation literature, held on 24 July 1949, a group of 'enlightened' comic-book publishers established their own committee: The Censorship Committee of the Shanghai Association of Comic-book

Publishers (*Shanghaishi Lianhuantuhua Chuban Xiehui Bianshen Weiyuanhui*). Their task was mammoth: to catalogue all existing stocks and approve or reject all titles ready for print according to rules already laid down by the July 24 conference.

The new rules were:

1. Stocks of all pre-Liberation publications were to be investigated by each publisher or bookshop and a list of these titles, together with a sample of each for filing, were to be sent to the Publishers' Association. The entire stock of any works found to have serious errors was to be sent to the Public Security Bureau for burning.
2. A sample of all comics published after Liberation and before 1 August 1949 were to be sent to the Censorship Committee before distribution, and those with errors could either be revised or sent to the Public Security Bureau for burning.
3. A sample of all manuscripts ready for printing after 1 August was to be sent to the Censorship Committee for publication approval or rejection.

The Committee classified works into three categories according to ideological correctness:

1. Works with minor mistakes could be corrected and then printed.
2. Works with major, but not serious, mistakes could be corrected and resubmitted.
3. Works with serious and irreparable errors would not be published.

In the first few months of operation, however, few works were censored outright although the report noted that in August 1949 less than ten per cent were 'comparatively good' but, in September, this had improved to just under 20 per cent.[64] In 1951 another critic lamented that only 30 per cent of Shanghai's 1,600 new comics, published in 1950 and the first half of 1951, were passable.[65] The remaining 70 per cent had, presumably, either passed through, or bypassed, the Censorship Committee.

The Committee encountered problems such as a lack of market interest due to the ingrained reading habits and the 'feudal mentality' of comics' audiences (that is, the audiences liked 'old' comics) and, at the other end of the scale, lack of government leadership. But most of the Committee's problems involved the commercial publishing world which seems to have partly resented, or ignored, the intrusion of this fledgling bureaucracy. Some publishers, for example, did not comply with the new regulations, either registering their works late, or both registering and distributing at the same time. The report admitted that the publishing world was complex and adhered to varying standards of production, with little co-operation between the publishers of old and new comics. Indeed, 'publishers and editors in the old commercial [world] are relatively backward in ideological education and they must undergo training.[66] The decisive difference lay in political orientation. Reform therefore demanded actual Communist control of the publishing houses and distribution network. This control was largely effected by 1953 when the Communists announced that 'chaotic tendencies' in the book world, such as duplication, waste, the reproduction of 'bad' books and erratic distribution, had been overcome.[67] The New China Bookstore became the national distribution outlet, distributing 80 per cent of all books by 1952.[68]

This conscious attempt to realize the 1930s claim that comics 'will certainly become the most powerful work in mass literature and art' led to spectacular publication growth in the fifties.[69] A Ying claimed in 1957:

> The period of real growth in Chinese comics came after National Liberation. The necessary conditions, whether in the realm of politics, economics or the arts themselves, only began to flourish at this time.[70]

Official publishing statistics show that while the total number of titles published between 1949 and 1965 was less than the pre-Liberation output, the number of copies published in the later period surpassed the number for the earlier period in the first three years.[71] From the perspective of popularization, the quantity of books actually distributed among China's vast population, with 90 per cent illiterate, is considerably more important than the number of titles published. The existence of rental stalls, libraries and reading rooms meant that each book served many readers and greatly magnified the influence of 'new' comics. It is difficult to know, however, whether this trend was confined to China's larger cities or included a similar, multiple readership pattern at the village level as well. The impressive achievement with comics in the fifties was followed by the fall-off in production in the sixties. This is consistent with all other areas in the arts. Decline was due largely to economic difficulties, including widespread famine in the early sixties. But is was also a product of the cumulative effects of campaigns against writers and artists from 1950 onwards.

Critical Control of Comic-book Publishing

Organizational control was supplemented by a second level of control: critical control. This involved the mobilization of public opinion through public denunciation of 'bad' works and approbation of 'good' works in periodicals and magazines of the day.

These early criticisms in the press gave readers actual examples of what was considered unacceptable at this second level of control. One detailed article, 'Strengthen Ideological Leadership in Editing and Publishing New Comics',[72] lists the types of mistakes common in Shanghai's comics published between 1950 and mid-1951, complete with the title and name of the publisher in each instance. In international themes, especially those relating to America in Korea, there was 'a very bad trend': the heinous nature of the enemy was emphasized by insults to China or raping women, for example, to make the plot more moving. Many titles indicate the themes that attracted disapproval because of cheap sensationalism: *The Animal Behavior of American Soldiers* (*Meiguobing Shuxing*), *Remember the Blood Debt of American Imperialism* (*Jizhu Meidi Xuezhai*), *Look! American Soldiers in Korea* (*Kan! Meiguobing zai Chaoxian*), *One Hundred and Eleven Days in Gaol* (*Yuzhong Yibaishiyitian*) and so forth.

Another major mistake, according to the article, was political naivete or insufficient awareness of the political nature of class struggle. One example given was a comic in which peasants were shown respectfully addressing landlords during land reform. Another described a despotic landlord 'as a virtuous and sincerely repentant "liberal gentleman"', and his wealth as 'full of worthiness', while the cadres involved in land reform are described as 'not correctly leading the peasants in their fight against the wicked landlord but, conversely, supporting him'. The article claimed artists were often confused in their presentation of class stance, drawing peasants and workers with 'narrow heads and rat-like eyes', for example; the comment was that such writers and artists all belonged to 'the old school and so can never correctly express the new life'. Yet another trend was plainly deceitful: while the cover suggested 'correct' political content, such as a comic called *The Marriage Revolution* (*Hunyin Geming*), the actual story praised feudal values and old attitudes to marriage. Last, there were textual oxymorons based on either ignorance or guile. Examples included such statements as 'The Communist Party is really good, they never divide into classes' and 'Not only did he have the old values but he also had progressive thought'.[73] Adherence to China's new values was fundamental in all works after 1949; as Mao wrote in 1957, 'Not to have a correct political orientation is like not having a soul'.[74]

At the same time as 'backward' publishers and works were held up for rebuke, progressive publishers were cited as models in the production of comics. According to Li Qun, 'a genuinely good comic' was one which:

> . . . not only the masses can understand, with an illustrated storyline which makes them want to go on reading but, more importantly, one which moves the reader through its plot and characterization, arousing a strong love for the positive characters and a deep hate for the negative characters so that the reader does not tire of it after even three or five readings, but harvests a deep impression and lasting ideological education.[75]

'A genuinely good comic' had 'a correct political orientation', an artistry capable of 'moving the reader', and capacity to deliver 'lasting ideological education'.

Foremost among the models cited for progressive publishers was Beijing's People's Art Publishing House (*Dazhong Tuhua Chubanshe*), which printed thirty titles in 600,000 copies in its first year (March 1950 to March 1951).[76] Three of these titles were said to be particularly outstanding: *Feather Letter* (*Jimaoxin*), a retelling of Hua Shan's famous children's story; *Master Dongguo* (*Dongguo Xiansheng*), a modern version of an ancient Chinese fable; and *Wang Xiuying* (*Wang Xiuying*), adapted from a modern play set in rural China.

Chiang Wei-pu also cites the first two in a short summary, worth quoting at length, of the main themes found in new comics of the fifties:

> A large proportion. . . deal with the revolutionary struggle and socialist construction. Examples of these are stories about the anti-Japanese war, like *The Shepherd's Message* [*Feather Letter*] and tales of the Liberation war, like *Reconnaissance Across the River* and *Defend Yenan!*, the story of the 25,000 *li* 'Long March' *Across Mountains and Rivers*, and *Volunteer Heroes*, depicting the struggle to resist US aggression and aid Korea. Picture story books have also been published about heroic men and women of modern China who are worthy models for the younger generation.
> . .
> Another large percentage of these books is devoted to stories of historical figures, revolutionary struggles, patriots of the past, and pioneers in the search for freedom and truth. Such picture story books as *Water Margin* and *Romance of the Three Kingdoms* in many volumes are extremely popular. Other favorites are those based on old legends, dramas, fables, or folktales, like *Schoolmaster Tungkuo* [*Master Dongguo*], *The White Snake*, *Mistress Clever*, *The Lovelorn Peacock Flies East*, *The Western Chamber* and *The Angel Maid and the Mortal*.[77]

Let us consider two of these exemplary comics identified by critic Chiang Wei-pu.

Feather Letter

Feather Letter exemplifies comics on revolutionary struggle. Li Qun claimed it as 'the most successful work in today's new and old comics', excelling in every aspect of comic book art.[78] He wrote that the plot was brilliantly adapted from Hua Shan's children's story into a comic of 140 pictures in two parts, moving at just the right pace through the pictures, developing the plot and emphasizing each crucial point in the story. When the young hero, Haiwa, hid the secret Party letter under the bell-wether's tail 'our hearts skip a beat', and when the Japanese 'devils' are just about to eat the sheep and so discover the letter 'our hearts thud'. Li Qun praised the illustrations as a work of art in themselves. He wrote that Liu Jiyou's pen makes Haiwa, his sheep, the donkey, the Japanese soldiers and even the grass and the trees live with a clarity that delineates both love and loathing. This 'true art' and the 'literature' of the text combine their separate functions like 'dance' and 'music' to make an outstanding educational and patriotic comic for Chinese children.[79]

Master Dongguo

The originals of both *Feather Letter* and *Wang Xiuying* were modern revolutionary works already imbued with the 'correct political interpretation'. The comic book version sought to transfer the flavor of the original to a different genre. *Master Dongguo,* however, was originally a very old fable, which was considered to be 'harmful to human morality. . . and in today's language. . . lacked principles'.[80] This work exemplifies those comics, on Chiang's list, that rewrote old stories and fables. Liu Jiyou's version therefore sought to inject fifties' principles into yesteryear's story.

The story is based on a fable, set in the Warring States period, more than two thousand years ago. At this time, China was divided into several small kingdoms at war with each other. In the original a learned and idealistic scholar and teacher, Master Dongguo, acts out his belief that 'virtue will be rewarded' by hiding a man-eating wolf in his sack when the wolf is hunted down by the patriotic general, Zhao Jianzi, and his soldiers. But the ungrateful wolf then turns on Master Dongguo to eat him, and he is saved only by the quick thinking of a shrewd old peasant (Illustration 5.7).

In the model comic, the story is told in eighty-two frames by prize-winning artist, Liu Jiyou. It begins with frames of Master Dongguo absorbed in writing an essay called 'A Discussion on Rewards of Virtue'. A student interrupts, telling the teacher that a former student, Zhao Jianzi, is going to fight a neighboring kingdom. The teacher goes to remonstrate with Zhao for actions that would kill common people. This was contrary to Buddhist principles and Buddhist beliefs that respected all living things. On the way to the kingdom to thwart Zhao, he meets a woman whose son has been eaten by a wolf and then he meets the wolf, fleeing Zhao and his troops. Master Dongguo believes the wolf, not the woman, when the wolf says it does not eat people, and he tries to save it. The wolf then turns on Master Dongguo. In short, Master Dongguo is a muddle-headed 'bookworm' who lied to Zhao Jianzi and lacked any concrete experience of social struggle or the true nature of wolves.

This storyline was opposed to a Marxist world view which started from the actual social conditions and not abstract definitions of right and wrong; or as Mao wrote, 'only social practice can be the criterion of truth'.[81] The comic version retells the story to bring out a modern lesson:

> This fable severely criticizes the foolish ideas of not discriminating between enemies and friends and that 'virtue must be rewarded' through Master Dongguo's 'virtue' in saving the wolf and its outcome. Wolves will always be wolves and class enemies will always be class enemies and, in no matter what guise, their natures cannot be changed. Imperialism, revisionism and all reactionaries are just the same.[82] (Foreword to 1973 edition.)

Li Qun wrote that reading this version was like reading Lu Xun's *Old Tales Retold*. 'The moral is one which Lu Xun advocated twenty years ago of beating a drowning dog', that is, completely crushing a defeated enemy.[83]

Illustration 5.7

71. The old man tipped the books from the sack and, saying he did not believe this sack could hold a wolf, he told it to get back inside so he could see for himself.

72. The wolf, licking its lips at the thought of Master Dongguo, immediately agreed and actually pushed its way into the sack.

Serial frames from *Master Dongguo*

73. The old man quickly tied up the opening as soon as the wolf was completely inside.

74. The old man raised his hoe and was just about to beat the wolf when Master Dongguo hurried forward to stop him. (The old man pushes Master Dongguo aside and beats it three times.)

Serial frames from *Master Dongguo*

76. Knowing the wolf was half dead from the beating, the old man tipped it from the sack (and asked the wolf if it still wanted to eat people).

77. The wolf stared at Master Dongguo, who was still feeling very sorry for it; who would believe that on its death-bed the wolf should still speak the truth: ('I will regret all my life that I did not eat such a foolish bookworm.')?

Serial frames from *Master Dongguo*

Comics for Younger Children

While comics began as children's books and developed into popular literature, therefore with a dual readership, there were also picture story books for very young children.

These usually have shorter texts and the main themes are folklore and legend, children's life at home and at school, scientific subjects or tales about great men and women. Such books help to mould the children's moral character and increase their general knowledge. Some of these illustrations are in color, and these are particularly liked by children.[84]

Book illustration was seen as important for children at primary school level and 'particularly for kindergarten children who have just walked into the world of books'.[85] These very young children had specialized requirements: boldness, clarity and immediate comprehension.[86] Illustrations had to be 'explanatory and expressive' so that 'the main theme leaps onto the page'.[87]

Two prize-winning works fulfil these criteria. The first, *The Story of the White Hen* (*Baimuji de Gushi*), was published in 1953, won a prize in 1954 for outstanding illustration, and by 1955 had been reprinted 113 times in 118,000 copies.[88] The story is about a little girl's love for two white hens. The girl lived in a liberated area before 1949 and her first white hen was eaten by the Nationalist soldiers when they took over her village, while the second white hen was cared for by the Red Army (who even stored all the eggs) when they later won back the village. Thus, she learned to hate the Nationalists and love the Red Army. As she said: 'The Uncles in the People's Liberation Army are really nice. I'm going to send them these eggs'.[89] Or, as the foreword explained, she learned about 'the deep bond, like that between fish and water, between the Army and the people and the blood relationship of the Army's love for the people and the people's support for the Army'.[90] But the real magic lies in the illustrations themselves: the recognizable and unpretentious realism of the village background and the lively little girl who cares so much about her white hens (Illustration 5.8).

The second picture book, for even younger children, is *Our Story* (*Womende Gushi*) by Zhang Leping, the author of *Sanmao*. These small comic strips originally appeared in the magazine *Little Friends,* and were later compiled into a booklet that was one of the two Chinese children's books to win a bronze medal at the Leipzig Book Fair in 1959.[91] The illustrations are simple in the extreme: '[I]f the story needs one tree, then he draws only one tree; if it needs one wall then he draws only one wall'.[92] Two Chinese silver medallists from the same fair achieve the boldness, clarity and intelligibility required in pictures for young children, using traditional styles other than the usually predominant line drawings: *In the Forest* (*Zai Senlinzhong*) is a wood-block print and *All the Sunflowers Face the Sun* (*Duoduo Kuihua Chao Taiyang*) uses paper-cut illustrations. Thus the principles involved in comic book illustration filtered through to picture books for younger children, albeit with a softened ideological message.

Illustration 5.8

Plate 4: When she walked over to the empty hen-house and saw how broken down it was, she felt very, very sad.

Serial frame from *The Story of the White Hen*

Plate 53: When Flower and her mother came to their own courtyard, she jumped for joy because her former hen and pig were already there to welcome them.

Serial frame from *The Story of the White Hen*

Monkey Subdues the White-bone Demon

Perhaps China's best-known comic from the 1949 to 1965 period is *Monkey Subdues the White-bone Demon* (*Sun Wukong Sanda Baigujing*), drawn by Zhao Hongben in the sixties. It belongs to that 'extremely popular' category of comics, according to Chiang's overview, that adapted stories from history and classical novels. *Monkey* is taken from the novel, *Journey to the West* (*Xiyouji*). It won a national prize (first class) for Chinese comics in 1963.

This comic is of particular interest because it highlights the difficulties of controlling the political interpretation of stories, especially traditional stories. Chinese have a centuries-old tradition of allocating a political interpretation to literature. Confucius, for example, found political meanings in the most unlikely genres, such as love poems. The opera on which *Monkey Subdues the White-bone Demon* was based sparked a famous debate between Mao Zedong and Guo Moruo on the political interpretation of the various characters.

These characters are all favorites from *Journey to the West*. Although by no means written specifically for children, the original sixteenth-century novel with its unique blend of adventure, fantasy, myth and mischief, on a cosmic scale, has been considered particularly suitable for children since the 1920s.[93] In the fantastic world woven around the actual account of a Tang Dynasty monk's journey to India to find the Buddhist scriptures, one of the monk's disciples, Monkey, is the rebellious and irreverent hero who saves the monk from all sorts of perils. It is a kind of *Pilgrim's Progress,* a search for enlightenment and truth within a Buddhist cosmology. Lu Xun made this comment:

> Actually, although Wu Chengen (the author) was a scholar, he wrote this work for entertainment. . . If we insist on seeking some hidden meaning, the following comment by Hsieh Chao-chih is quite adequate: *The Pilgrimage to the West* is purely imaginary, belonging to the world of fantasy and miraculous transformations. Monkey symbolizes man's intelligence, Pigsy man's physical desires. Thus Monkey first runs wild in heaven and on earth, proving quite irrepressible; but once he is kept in check he steadies down. So this is an allegory of the human mind, not simply a fantasy.[94]

Monkey Subdues the White-bone Demon was adapted from a 1961 Shaoxing opera of the same name which, in its turn, borrows episodes from *Journey to the West*. In their encounter with the demon, the monk was constantly deceived by the demon's various transformations (a sweet young girl, an old woman and a bereaved old man) and insisted, anyway, that even a demon may be converted. Only Monkey saw the real nature of the demon and fought her in her many forms until he was dismissed by the monk for his lack of compassion. 'The foolish monk' learned the truth when he and his remaining two disciples were seized by the demon as food for their feast that night. Just as the White-bone Demon said to Wolf Demon, 'Go quickly to Golden Light Cave and invite my mother, Golden Toad Fairy, to come immediately and partake of the monk's flesh', Monkey was 'somersaulting through the clouds. . . to rescue his master'

Illustration 5.9

Out of the cave and somersaulting through the clouds, Monkey
headed straight for the demons' cave to rescue his master.

from *Monkey Subdues the White-bone Demon*

(Illustration 5.9). Monkey killed the Golden Toad Fairy and
impersonated her to enter the demon's cave, changing to his true
form only when the monk cried out: 'Monkey, I should not have
confused right and wrong, men and demons, and sent you away'.
After a desperate fight, Monkey 'spewed forth divine fire and
burned her until she resumed her true form'. (In the English
translation, on the other hand, he 'finished her off with one
blow' of his cudgel.) The story ends as the pilgrimage is
resumed.

The foreword to the 1972 edition of the comic draws out the
same moral as in *Master Dongguo:* the monk is ultimately

'educated by reality' and Monkey is praised for his wisdom, bravery, resoluteness and his knowledge that 'when you see a demon you must wipe it out'.[95]

Such is the background and story line of *Monkey Subdues the White-bone Demon*. However, the success of a comic ultimately depends on the quality of the illustrations and, in this case, they are as 'marvelous' as the story itself. The artists were Zhao Hongben and Jian Xiaodai, although the former seems to be the senior artist. The work bears Zhao's characteristic emphasis on people and line that is evident in his early works and in his post-1949 comics, such as *The White Snake* (*Baishe Zhuan*), another favorite mentioned by Chiang Weipu.[96] The lines of the scenery, meticulously rendered in traditional style, always lead the eye to the characters in the story. Indeed, the towering precipices, deep grottoes, weird stones and gnarled, even clawlike, trees accentuate the perils of the journey while supplying an appropriate setting for man-eating monsters and demons capable of multiple transformations. It does not seem the least surprising, for example, to turn the page and find a temple shimmering through a dark grove of trees in which Buddha and all the other images turn into ferocious demons (in the middle of a prayer!) and then it disappears. The temple, that is, not the demons. At the same time the artist clearly delineates each character: the monk, ever impassive; Monkey, always alert and lively; Pigsy, fat, foolish but good-hearted; Sandy, always faithfully following the monk; and the White-bone Demon, both sinister and seductive with her ghoulish band of followers. This delineation is achieved, moreover, without resorting to tricks like drawing the Demon as dark, skulking and ugly, or Monkey as glorious and larger than life. Below is a Chinese appreciation of Zhao Hongben's artistry:

> Zhao Hongben is an expert at drawing monkeys and, having often observed their habits and behavior, each movement of the enemy of evil, brave and staunch Monkey, is absolutely life-like in the comic. In composition, especially, the artist gives full play to the fine points of traditional Chinese painting, dots and perspective so that the composition breathes and the small frame, with its

complicated and myriad meanings, is spatially harmonious and structurally well-defined. The line drawings are meticulous throughout, even in the strictest detail of a small leaf or a fine thread of hair.[97]

Monkey Subdues the White-bone Demon survived the Cultural Revolution and was also published in English, in a second edition in 1973, and reprinted in 1975.

The fascinating poetic debate in 1961 between Mao Zedong and Guo Moruo (head of the Academy of Sciences) on the meaning of the play is equally applicable to the comic book version. It centered on the role of the monk rather than on Monkey or the White-bone Demon who, respectively, epitomize good and evil. The monk is a 'middle character', neither good nor evil, who is frequently deluded and deceived and the debate is of interest because it was these very 'middle characters' that were later criticized during the Cultural Revolution. After seeing the opera in 1961, Guo Moruo reserved his strongest criticism for the monk:

> Confounding humans and demons, right and wrong,
> The monk was kind to foes and vicious to friends.
> Endlessly he intoned 'The Incantation of the Golden Hoop',
> And thrice he let the White-bone Demon escape.
> The monk deserved to be torn from limb to limb. . .[98]
>
> (October 1961)

Moreover, Guo Moruo implied that the demon was imperialism and the monk was Khruschev, the head of revisionist Russia.[99] Mao Zedong's reply focussed on Monkey as 'the wonder-worker' and the demon, not the monk, as evil:

> A thunderstorm burst over the earth,
> So a devil rose from a heap of white bones.
> The deluded monk was not beyond the light,
> But the malignant demon must wreak havoc.
> The Golden Monkey wrathfully swung his massive cudgel.
> And the jade-like firmament was cleared of dust.
> Today, a miasmal mist once more rising,
> We hail Sun Wukong, the wonder-worker.[100]
>
> (November 1961)

Guo Moruo's reply to Mao's reply revised his view of the monk to one who 'suffering from torment, knows regret'[101] because 'the reply by the Chairman is based on the essence of the thing itself and deals with the problem analytically on a deeper level. The reply by the Chairman actually corrects my radical point of view towards the monk'.[102] Mao Zedong's answer was cryptic and somewhat ambiguous: 'The reply is good, no more. "The monk deserved to be torn from limb to limb." It's good to take the policy of United Front towards the Centralists.'[103]

The game is then to assign a political interpretation to the various roles. This is difficult indeed in the case of the opera, because the monk could well be Mao himself given that quite a few works criticized Mao's policies at this time, most notably *Hai Rui Dismissed From Office* (*Hai Rui Baguan*). The 'miasmal mist' which Mao refers to could be revisionist policies in China as well as in the Soviet Union. In fact, as one critic wrote in the twenties, *Journey to the West* is so rich that you can interpret it in any way you like. Guo Moruo, however, had the last say in 1977, a year after Mao's death, when he likened Mao's wife, Jiang Qing, to the White-bone Demon:

> . . . The Gang of Four has been ferreted out!
> Political gangster, lettered crook,
> Zhang their dog-head counselor,
> Together with the White-bone Demon
> Who likened herself to Empress Wu
> All gone. . .[104]

Mao, of course, could not reply.

Hence, *Monkey Subdues the White-bone Demon* shows the subtlety and the importance of 'correct' political interpretation. Authorities paid particular attention to interpretations of old familiar stories. Chapters 3, 4 and 5 of *Journey to the West* is another favorite excerpt which, in certain respects, conforms to the demands of new comics. Monkey's defiance of all authority, especially that of the Jade Emperor in heaven, parallels the rebellion against authority in twentieth century China which led to the founding of the People's Republic. In these chapters, Monkey remains undefeated and thus a triumphant hero in the fight against despotism. The comic book versions do not, however, include Monkey's subsequent defeat, imprisonment and guidance by Buddha which would not only detract from this modern reading but also emphasize religious overtones that were inimical to the secular ideology of new China. One version of these same chapters, with far inferior black and white line drawings, was a fifties best seller. The original publication ran to 646,000 copies and a new publication was reprinted nineteen times between 1956 and 1961 in a total of 897,000 copies.[105] Yet another fifties version came from Liu Jiyou, a prize-winning illustrator in 1963.

In short, the Monkey legend was both 'popular' and a vehicle for popularization, according to the Maoist definition. When this same legend was reinterpreted by craftspeople such as Zhao Hongben or Wang Laiming,[106] the product was a recognized work of art in a form which, in Lu Xun's words, the masses 'want' and 'appreciate'—that is, an outstanding comic. Nevertheless, despite the high level of Party control over literary and artistic production in China, the masses sometimes 'appreciated' a work in ways contrary to the Party's dictates. In this sense, control was still problematic.

Comic Books in the Great Proletarian Cultural Revolution 1966 to 1976

This section turns to the Great Proletarian Cultural Revolution (1966–76) and its effect on comic book production. First we discuss Mao's Yan'an model of mass mobilization that dominated all cultural activity at the time. Second, we look at the particular policies and purges that resulted in a dramatic decline in comic book publishing in this period when compared to the fifties. However, one prize-winning comic published in the early seventies, *Norman Bethune in China,* was still considered outstanding by Chinese critics in the post-Mao period. This comic is discussed as exemplifying principles informing all artistic production during the Cultural Revolution.

Maoist literary policy dominated during the Cultural Revolution period. The idea of launching a 'distinctly socialist cultural revolution' in which the masses participated had been raised by Qu Qiubai in the thirties. By the mid-sixties the radical left in the Chinese Communist Party were convinced that their long-standing attempt to develop a genuinely revolutionary and popular culture in China had failed. Mao believed that most literature was still 'feudal' and 'capitalist'. In 1963, he claimed of the arts that 'very little had been achieved so far in socialist transformation. . . Isn't it absurd that many Communists are enthusiastic about promoting feudal and capitalist art, but not socialist art?'[107] In 1964 he accused writers of ignoring Party policy and acting as an elite group.

> They have acted as high and mighty bureaucrats, have not gone to the workers, peasants and soldiers and have not reflected socialist revolution and socialist construction.[108]

In November 1965, the Great Proletarian Cultural Revolution began officially with a published attack on a historical play, *Hai Rui Dismissed from Office*. The play was severely critical of Mao's policies. Mao's response was to launch a revolution that challenged not only all of China's political structures but the whole ideology which informed them.

It was a 'cultural' revolution in only the broadest sense of the word. In 1966 schools were closed, literary journals were suspended, and almost all works published between 1949 and 1965, including comic books, were condemned as part of the 'black' and 'revisionist' line in literature and art. At issue, according to Chesneaux, 'were the original options of Chinese Communism outlined at Yan'an'.[109] These options included the development of a genuinely proletarian and popular Chinese literature and art. Hence, Mao's 'Talks' became the only reference for cultural policy in this period.

All works in China's literary heritage—traditional and modern—were subject to the guidelines required of proletarian literature. The guidelines were strictly ideological and applied equally to literature for adults and children. While comics had been appropriated into art for the masses, children were still considered the readership most directly influenced by 'unhealthy' works. A writer described how such works '"poisoned the minds" of our youth and children' in a letter to the *Workers' Daily* on 18 May 1965. Arriving home from work, he found his children all drawing pictures of 'emperors, generals, prime ministers, scholars, beauties and the like', not of workers, peasants and soldiers. The pictures had been copied from serial picture books that retold stories from old novels, perennial favorites with Chinese readers. He concluded:

> Small friends take a great interest in serial pictures. At present, many good serial pictures reflecting life in the struggle for socialist construction and revolution are available for hire on bookstalls. They are of great educational significance as reading matter for children. However, at the same time some hackneyed serial picture books with pictures of emperors, generals, prime ministers, scholars or beauties are also available. They can do great harm in the education of children, having a bad influence on them. Therefore, I suggest that the leadership departments concerned should check and purge according to plan all the serial picture books to be published, issued or offered for hire. The unwholesome picture serial books should not be allowed to poison the minds of our youth and children.[110]

The rationale for a 'purge' was the 'great educational significance' of children's reading matter. Indeed, during the Cultural Revolution, the emphasis on the educational function of literature was such that no literature was believed to be better than unwholesome literature.

Rather than learn from books, children were urged to learn from experience of class struggle. Bookshops, libraries and schools were closed. Following Chairman Mao's instructions, children were to 'go out and face the world'.[111] As in revolutionary children's literature in the thirties and the war period, the virtues to be inculcated in children's minds were those of the militant proletariat and peasantry.

While very few new works were produced in this period, guidelines were formulated to direct production of socialist art. These guidelines were propagated through model works, all 'revolutionary model operas' (*geming yangbanxi*) produced under the direction of Jiang Qing, Mao's wife. In this period models were not specific to each genre or targeted towards specific audiences; instead, models from one genre in the performing arts were to be emulated by all the literary and art forms. Most of the comics that were published in the early period of the Cultural Revolution were stories of the model operas in comic-book form. These were operas on contemporary themes. The heroes were no longer 'emperors and generals, useless scholars and sickly maids' but workers, peasants and soldiers.

The model operas propagated a formulaic representation of revolutionary heroism, called 'the three prominences' (*san tuchu*):

> Give prominence to positive characters among all the characters, to heroes among the positive characters, to the principal hero among the heroes. Create special environment, character and personality and use all kinds of artistic media to make the proletarian heroes stand out. Reveal the heroes' inherent communist spirit.[112]

The effect of this formula on comic books is evident from a national exhibition of 97 comics held in 1973. A review claimed that all 'decadent, feudal, bourgeois or revisionist content that was a feature of so many works before the Cultural Revolution' had indeed been purged.[113] The Maoist line was paramount. According to this reviewer, 'the basic task of all socialist art is to create successful images of proletarian heroes. In picture story books this is best done by depicting the development of the main characters as the plot unfolds. . . to enhance their images of heroes and heroines in typical circumstances'.[114] All the comics in this exhibition celebrated proletarian heroes.

Examples of comic book production in this period show the extent to which operatic styles dominated the portrayal of heroes in comic books. One comic from the 1973 exhibition, *Song of*

the *Proletariat,* (*Wuchan jieji zhi ge*), was singled out by Ch'i
Cheng, the reviewer, for particular comment. In 1981 it won a
prize for illustration in the Second National Awards for Chinese
Comics.[115] Hence, this is considered a 'good' comic in both the
Cultural Revolution period and its aftermath.

Song of the Proletariat tells the story of the Paris Commune.
Its characters are established heroes within a Marxist pantheon,
and their depiction adhered to the principles of 'the three
prominences'. Ch'i Cheng analyzes the artistic techniques as
follows:

> Contrasts between light and shade, between solid objects and
> space, between different angles, characters and scenes are used to
> portray heroic characters. These are usually portrayed from a
> lower angle to give them an appearance of greater height while
> reactionaries are portrayed from a higher angle to make them
> appear more despicable and sinister. Contrasts between light and
> shade are used not only in individual scenes but between different
> scenes as well. For example, the 65th picture representing the
> enemy's attempt to ban the Internationale is predominantly dark,
> while the following scene of the workers' defiance of the singing
> of this song is lighter. This switch from darkness to light indicates
> that the voice of truth must triumph and the forces of reaction are
> powerless to silence it.[116]

These techniques come straight from revolutionary operas,
models for all literature and art in this period. A memorable
example is the scene in which Ke Xiang, the heroine of *Azalea
Mountain* (*Dujuan Shan, 1973*), first appears. In the opera, the
audience hears her sing one haunting line, and then:

> Ke Xiang in chains, her head high, strides out of the temple and
> turns to toss back her hair. . . she halts and strikes a proud
> pose[117] . . . the enemy cower.[118]

The comic-book version—stills from the film based on the
opera—renders this part in three frames which focus on Ke
Xiang's 'proud pose' in increasing close-ups (Illustration 5.10).

Illustration 5.10

29 "无产者等闲看惊涛骇浪。"面对着敌人的刺刀丛，柯湘从容镇定，器宇轩昂，表现了无产阶级先锋战士洒热血，求解放，生命不息斗志旺的大无畏英雄气概。

'The proletariat stands firm through stormy seas.' Ke Xiang's calm dignity expresses the fearless heroic spirit of a soldier in the vanguard of the proletariat, a spirit which sheds its own blood for liberation and fights to the very last.[119]

from _Azalea Mountain_

Ke Xiang is spotlit high on the temple steps while the enemy cower in semi-darkness. Theatrical devices concentrate on highlighting her heroism and danger. Deprived of the integral accompaniments of opera—stage setting, music, singing, acrobatics, dancing and color—the comic book version reduced a thrilling entry and a chilling song to a series of frozen operatic stances and a repetitive text. From her first appearance in frame 28, Ke Xiang is shown in similar poses on pages 29–39, 51–52, 57, 59, 64–65, 69, 97. . . Perhaps nothing so clearly shows the now-recognized narrowness and woodenness of characterization as these pictures.

It is not necessary to document lots of examples from the Cultural Revolution. Chinese comics and book illustrations from this period bear an unmistakable style, recognizable just by flipping through the pages. In comics, the unique characteristics of the form—features that made it such an effective means for popularization—were all but ignored. Reviews from the period concentrate narrowly on political message and not on the story medium. This medium lost its distinctive character. It was subsumed by revolutionary operas into pale sycophants of their dramatic action; the unabated emphasis on stereotyped proletarian heroes with prescribed rules for portrayal reduced the arts to a continued glorification of a disembodied triumphant Marxist 'truth'; and the 'three prominences' commonly led to a pedestal effect with heroes elevated like well-lit statues while reactionaries skulked in the shadows.

Deng Xiaoping called operas from this period 'a single flower blossoming'.[120] Other art forms withered. It was precisely this 'stereotyped imitation', this sameness 'as a piece of cast metal turned out from within a desert', which was harshly condemned in 1976 when the Cultural Revolution ended with Mao's death and the arrest of Jiang Qing, Mao's wife, and other leaders.[121]

However, one comic from the Cultural Revolution period was still considered to be outstanding by Chinese critics in 1981. This is *Norman Bethune in China (Bai Qiuen zai Zhongguo)*.

Norman Bethune in China

Revolutionary literature, including comics, was to be written for the masses in forms that were popular and accessible. Thus *Norman Bethune in China* takes its place with the more famous products of Maoist literary policy, such as *Sanmao,* before Liberation and the model revolutionary operas after Liberation.

It was one of the two comics from the 1973 Exhibition which later won prizes in the Second National Awards for Chinese comics in 1981 (the other was *Song of the Proletariat)*. These 1981 awards were a major event in the history of Chinese comics; prize-winners were selected only after an exhaustive survey of all publications between 1963 (the year of the first national awards) and 1980, with the inclusion of some fifties entries that had been rejected for political reasons in the first award round. Hence, not only are these two comics representative of the best during the Cultural Revolution period and beyond, but they are also examples of the Maoist line on art which has since been partly discredited.

Of the 1981 list of prize-winners, only *Norman Bethune in China* won awards for both illustration and text. Chinese experts have, therefore, judged it the outstanding comic book in the eighteen years since 1963. Yet it belongs unmistakably to the period of the Cultural Revolution which spawned it, fulfilling the major requirements of the Maoist line on art and literature.

Dr Norman Bethune, a Canadian Communist Party member who worked among the peasants and Red Army for nearly two years until his death in 1939, was a nationally recognized hero. In 1939 Mao praised him for his internationalism: 'his great sense of responsibility in his work and his warm-heartedness towards all comrades and people. . . (and his) absolute selflessness'. He represented the 'true Communist spirit'.[122]

The artists of the comic version of his story decided on a definite strategy to emphasize Dr Bethune's heroism.

> From the outline (of his life) presented by the peasants, from their knowledge of life in the old base areas, and after exhaustive research of the records, the authors understood that their primary task was to portray Norman Bethune among the Chinese people, in the midst of revolutionary struggle and (at work) in the mountainous Chinese landscape. . . The authors understood that a successful creation of Bethune's image was inseparable from the portrayal of the army and peasants in the anti-Japanese war. He had to be presented in the turbulence of war, relying on his character and deeds, and not on empty doctrine, to move the readers.[123]

This strategy is 'the three prominences' (*san tuchu*), that embodied the rules for artistic production during the Cultural Revolution.

Bethune is highlighted among fellow heroes and positive characters, the soldiers and peasants fighting in the mountain villages against the Japanese. He is depicted healing a peasant or riding through raging rivers, for example, to show the difficult terrain in which Bethune worked (Illustration 5.11).

Illustration 5.11

Plate 76: One day, on hearing that there was a seriously wounded
soldier on the verge of death in a village some 25 kilometers away,
Comrade Bethune jumped on his horse and rode off at full gallop.

from *Norman Bethune in China*

The artists achieved historical and pictorial authenticity
through extensive field research between Fall 1971 and Spring
1973. Adhering to Mao's insistence that popularization meant
learning from the workers, peasants and soldiers as part of the
production process, they visited peasants who had known
Bethune, and villages where he had worked. They stayed longest
in Huapen village where the peasants' reminiscences and the
local architecture, customs and mountain scenery inspired many
of these artists' best compositions. One frame (Illustration 5.12)
shows a Party messenger raising a cloud of dust as he gallops to
the mud house where Bethune lay dying. The poplars lining the
road were planted to commemorate Bethune after he died, but
the authors included them in recognition of the respect felt by the
local villagers.[124] This is not simply an *ad hoc* addition to reveal
a 'true communist spirit.' In the composition itself the poplars
dominate, softening the forbidding splendor of Taihang
Mountains and finally focussing on a small lighted window of
Bethune's hut. Hardly visible in the lower right hand corner is
the outline of the village topped by a lone sentry. The frame
continues the story but the detail can be 'read' as a story in itself.

While Mao Zedong claimed the primacy of political over artistic criteria in judging a work of art, he nevertheless claimed that a politically correct work without artistic merit lacked force.

Illustration 5.12

Plate 103: On November 10, Comrade Bethune arrived at Yellow Stone Village in Tanghsien County, where his condition grew ever graver. When the Military Area command heard of this, they immediately gave an urgent order: Comrade Bethune must be saved at all costs!

from *Norman Bethune in China*

He demanded the unity of politics and art, content and form.[125] It was these qualities that won *Norman Bethune in China* an award in 1981.

This comic was collaborative. Hao Ran, perhaps the only writer of any stature in this period, apart from Mao, records:

> The decrease in the importance of the individual was most visible in the writing and publication fields. To some extent, a writer before the Cultural Revolution carried over some of the old idea of writing to establish oneself as a writer, but after 1970 the writer, the publisher and the reader became one, working together to make literature better serve the revolution.[126]

While *Norman Bethune in China* was produced by specialists, not amateurs, it was the result of a literary process that involved consultation with non-professionals, such as peasants in the

Taihang Mountain region, and close collaboration between four artists, including younger artists. All four taught at the Lu Xun Art Academy: Xu Rongzhu, a fifties' graduate, was most familiar with Bethune's life and was both the organizer of the work and the illustrator of the main characters; Xu Yong, a fifties' graduate, specialized in figures and horses; Gu Liandang, another fifties' graduate, excelled in moving figures and composition; and Wang Yisheng, the youngest and a sixties' graduate, drew many of the lyrical landscapes.[127]

The major reviewer of this comic praised it with a grandiloquence reserved for the very, very best.

> Without an artist's talent, individuality and skill, crystal clear and sparkling like a dew drop, then there can be no artistry. But this alone will always be insubstantial. However, if this drop of water melts into the great and eddying sea of men and history and forms a mighty wave which beats against the shore, then it takes on the power which shakes men's souls and can never, ever be destroyed. This is so whether it be a monumental work of art or a 'small, small' comic book.[128]

Conclusion

There is clear continuity between the Confucian emphasis on education, the early May Fourth notion of 'emancipating' children through literature and the Marxist notion of 'awakening' the masses through revolutionary popular literature and art. Just as Zhu Xi sought to mold children through the Confucian *Daily Stories* and Lu Xun sought 'to change the spirit' of China through 'the best medium', literature,[129] so too Marxists aimed to create a mass revolutionary consciousness through literature and art. Mao was specific on this point.[130]

By the Cultural Revolution, however, the ideological imperative had strangled any serious consideration of education or literary and artistic values. The few new works of this period were monotonous, stereotyped and dreadfully dull. While the popular audience in the past had exercised some choice, the masses in Mao's China were offered what they 'should have' rather than 'what they want'.[131] Popular 'old' works were purged, leaving a meager basis on which to develop a genuinely socialist and popular literature and art. Ironically, the 'new' revolutionary works were often manifestly 'unpopular'.

The intended audience for revolutionary popular literature and art was unambiguously 'the masses'. As McDougall pointed out, 'cultural authorities have insisted on postulating a single, mass homogeneous audience for [such] cultural products'.[132] Children were an unspecified part of this mass audience. Maoist literary theory paid no attention to stages of childhood development with correspondingly suitable types of literature. Consequently, children were absorbed into the 'single' audience and children's literature as a field all but disappeared. Just as children were merged with adults into an undifferentiated audience, so too cultural products, which targeted specific audiences, were appropriated by revolutionary, popular literature for consumption by the masses. The comic or 'serial picture book' is a prime example.

Initially, comics were regarded as only for children. The term *xiaoren shu,* meaning 'little people's books', is still used to designate comics. Unlike other forms of modern children's literature, which a progressive intellectual elite created specifically for them, comics were a product of the commercial publishing world and retain no clear distinction as to their proper audience—children, youth, urban adults or the uneducated masses. The answer seems to be that comics were read by all groups. However, reviewers refer repeatedly to comics' particular influence on children and youth. This influence was considered so great that comics were the first item for reform by the newly formed Chinese Association of Writers for Children in 1946. Indeed, comics seem to be the books most widely read by children right through the period between 1920 and 1976.

Popular literature and children's literature, therefore, met in the educational function and influence of the comic book. In a society shackled by a low level of literacy, comics were to be a simple and effective means of popularizing a new, revolutionary ideology, a form especially favored by children as well as the illiterate and semi-literate masses at the lower levels of society. In appropriating comics as an art form, Marxists and leftists elevated an art form initially despised by both Confucian and May Fourth intelligentsia. Comics were not to be judged according to standards prevailing in children's literature, but according to standards of popularization. By these standards, the work of the artist is enhanced by being modestly bound, and held, not in some actual representation of Lu Xun's 'temple of art', but in the hands of China's millions. To ignore this popular literature and concentrate narrowly on the 'exclusive' written forms of May Fourth children's literature is to ignore children's most popular reading material. It also ignores one of the major Marxist contributions to the field of modern Chinese literature.

Notes

1. Qu Qiubai, 'The Question of Popular Literature and Art', translated by Pickowicz, P., in Berninghausen, J. et al., *Revolutionary Literature in China: An Anthology*, op. cit., p. 47.
2. The Chinese term for comic, *lianhuan tuhua* or later *lianhuanhua*, literally means 'serial pictures'. I have translated it as its nearest Western counterpart, 'comic': an artistic form serially linked to tell a story and supported by a short text and/or conversation. It should be noted that comics, in both the west or China, are not necessarily comical or humourous.
3. McDougall, B.S., 'Preface', in McDougall, B.S. (ed.), *Popular Chinese Literature and the Performing Arts in the People's Republic of China 1949–1979*, op. cit., p. xi.
4. A Ying, *Zhongguo Lianhuantuhua Shihua* (Beijing, 1957), p. 2.
5. Chiang Wei-pu, 'Chinese Picture Story Books', op. cit., p. 16.
6. A Ying, *Zhongguo Lianhuantuhua Shihua*, op. cit., p. 24.
7. Ibid., p. 25.
8. Lu Xun, '"Lianhuantuhua" Bianhu', *Lu Xun Quanji*, Vol. 5, p. 40.
9. A Ying, *Zhongguo Lianhuantuhua Shihua*, op. cit., p. 25.
10. Lu Xun, 'Lianhuantuhua Xiaotan', *Lu Xun Quanji*, Vol. 6, p. 32.
11. Mao Dun, 'Lianhuantuhua Xiaoshuo', *Mao Dun Wenji*, Vol. 9 (Hong Kong 1966), p. 76.
12. A Ying, *Zhongguo Lianhuantuhua Shihua*, op. cit., p. 27.
13. Mao Dun, 'Lianhuantuhua Xiaoshuo', op. cit., p. 77.
14. Ibid., p. 75.
15. A. Ying, *Zhongguo Lianhuantuhua Shihua*, op. cit., pp. 24–5. Zhao Hongben was one of nineteen artists cited in 1981 for their outstanding contribution to the genre.
16. Wu Nong and Li Lu, 'Huiqi Huabi zai Changzheng', *Lianhuanhuabao*, No. 10 (1979), p. 34.
17. Ibid.
18. Ibid.
19. A. Ying, *Zhongguo Lianhuantuhua Shihua*, op. cit., p. 24.
20. Lu Xun, 'Disanzhong Ren', *Lu Xun Quanji*, Vol. 5, p. 37.
21. Ibid.

22. Ibid.
23. Lu Xun, '"Lianhuantuhua" Bianhu', op. cit., p. 44.
24. Ibid.
25. Mao Dun, 'Lianhuantuhua Xiaoshuo', op. cit., p. 78.
26. Ibid., p. 77.
27. Lu Xun, 'Lianhuantuhua Suotan', *Lu Xun Quanji*, Vol. 6, p. 34.
28. Ibid.
29. Lu Xun, 'Kantu Shizi', *Lu Xun Quanji*, Vol. 6, p. 42.
30. Mao Dun, 'Da Bizi de Gushi', op. cit., p. 56.
31. Ibid., p. 46.
32. Liu Yu, 'Jiefangqu Diyizhang Ertong Bao', op. cit., p. 87.
33. A Ying, *Zhongguo Lianhuantuhua Shihua*, op. cit., p. 30.
34. Zhongguo Ertong Duwu Zuozhe Xiehui (ed.), *Zhongguo Ertong Duwu Zuozhe Xiehui Jianshi*, op. cit., p. 2.
. 35. Schurmann, F., *Ideology and Organization in Communist China* (Berkeley and Los Angeles, 1968), p. x.
36. Schram, S., *Mao Tse-tung: Political Leaders of the Twentieth Century* (Harmondsworth, Middlesex, 1967), revised edition, p. 251.
37. According to population statistics, China had 120 million children between the ages of six and fifteen who constituted the proper readership of children's books (*Renmin Ribao*, 9 September 1955). The readers of children's literature belong to later childhood (6–10 years) and adolescence (10-15 years) but the readership does not include early childhood (3–6 years). The age group, 6–15 years, corresponds in school age with children from primary to lower middle school (inclusive) in China after 1949. A 1978 report on children's literature shows an increased readership of 80 million, i.e. 200 million children. (*Renmin Ribao*, 28 May 1978, p. 3.) The 1982 census estimates 38.6 per cent of the population was then fifteen years and under, i.e., 389.88 million.
38. Editorial, *Renmin Ribao*, 15 June 1948, p. 1.
39. Editorial, *Renmin Ribao*, 9 September 1955, p. 1.
40. Schurmann, F., *Ideology and Organization in Communist China*, op. cit., p. lii.
41. Ibid., p. xlvii.
42. Chen Xiao, 'Jiaqiang dui Xin Lianhuantuhua Bianhui yu Chuban Gongzuo de Sixiang Lingdao', *Wenyibao*, 55 (1952), p. 20.
43. Yun Geng, 'Lianhuantuhua de Gaizao Wenti', *Wenyibao*, 1:5 (1949), p. 11.
44. Ibid. Also see Chiang Wei-pu, 'Chinese Picture Serial Books', *Chinese Literature* No. 3 (March 1959), p. 144–7, and in Croizier, R. C. (ed.), *China's Cultural Legacy and Communism* (London, 1970), p. 165.
45. Li Qun, 'Ping, "Dazhongtuhua Chubanshe" de Lianhuantuhua', *Wenyibao*, No. 38, 4:2 (1951), p. 8.
46. Chen Xiao, 'Jiaqiang dui Xin Lianhuantuhua Bianhui yu Chuban Gongzuo de Sixiang Lingdao', op. cit., p. 20.
47. Xia Yan, 'Daixu', in Zhang Leping, *Sanmao Liulangi* (Shanghai, 1978), front page.
48. Bi Keguan and Huang Yuanlin, *Zhonggo Manhua Shi* (Beijing, 1986), p. 257.
49. Ibid., p. 262.
50. Ibid., p. 258.
51. Zhang Leping, Frontispiece, *Sanmao Congjunji* (Chengdu, 1983).

52.   Ibid.
53.   Ibid.
54.   Ibid.
55.   Editor, 'He Xiaoduzhe Tantan Sanmao', in Zhang, Leping, *Sanmao Liulangji*, op. cit, no pagination.
56.   For a discussion of revolutionary Chinese children's literature, see Farquhar, M., *Children's Literature in China*, op. cit., pp. 143–90.
57.   Xia Yan, 'Daixu', in Zhang Leping, *Sanmao Liulangi*, op. cit., front page.
58.   A Ying, *Zhongguo Lianhuantuhua Shihua*, op. cit., p. 28.
59.   Ibid.
60.   Li Keruo, 'Xianming de Duizhao—Ping "Sanmao Jinxi"', *Ertong Wenxue Yanjiu*, No. 1 (1959), p. 76.
61.   Ibid.
62.   Li Qun, 'Ping "Dazhongtuhua Chubanshe" de Lianhuantuhua', op. cit., p. 8.
63.   Yun Geng, 'Lianhuantuhua de Gaizao Wenti', op. cit., p. 8.
64.   Li Ming and Ling Xiao, 'Lianhuantuhua Gaizao Gongzuo, Shanghai Tongxun', *Wenyibao*, 1:6 (1949), p. 27.
65.   Chen Xiao, 'Jiaqiang dui Xin Lianhuantuhua Bianhui yu Chuban Gongzuo de Sixiang Lingdao', op. cit., p. 20.
66.   Li Ming and Ling Xiao, 'Lianhuantuhua Gaizao Gongzuo, Shanghai Tongxun', op. cit., p. 28.
67.   *Survey of China Mainland Press*, 626 (1953), p. 17.
68.   Ibid.
69.   Post-Liberation statistics may be found in *Quanguo Xinshumu* (National Bibliography) and *Zongshumu* for 1958. Apart from figures conveniently arranged in tables in the mid-fifties, the statistics are monthly and, later, fortnightly. Moreover they are classified under a bewildering array of headings: as 'popular literature' until 1951; as 'picture books' in the mid-fifties; and as comics (*lianhuantuhua*) from 1959. Children's comics were sometimes classified under children's literature, for example, and sometimes under comics in general. Reliable statistics are therefore difficult to ascertain. Chiang Wei-pu claims that 1,600 titles were printed in the first half of 1958, while I counted 1,291 in *Zongshumu* for the full year. Nevertheless, it is clear that there was a massive publishing effort in the fifties, with 2,000 to 3,000 prints and reprints of titles in the mid-fifties. This fell to merely hundreds of titles in the sixties, with only 269 new prints in 1966.
70.   A Ying, *Zhongguo Lianhuantuhua Shihua*, op. cit., p. 29.
71.   Publication details are available in *Quanguo Xinshumu* and *Zongshumu* up to 1966. It is difficult to give an accurate figure because published statistics concerning comic books were compiled under different headings: popular literature (1950–52), picture books (1953–56) and comics (1959), for example.
72.   Chen Xiao, 'Jianqiang dui Xin Lianhuantuhua Bianhui yu Chuban Gongzuo de Sixiang Lingdao', *Wenyibao*, No. 55 (1952).
73.   Ibid., p. 21.
74.   Mao Tse-tung, 'On the Correct Handling of Contradictions Among the People', *Selected Works*, Vol. V, p. 405.
75.   Li Qun, 'Ping "Dazhong Tuhua Chubanshe" de Lianhuantuhua', op. cit., p. 9.
76.   Ibid., p. 81.
77.   Chiang Wei-pu, 'Chinese Picture Story Books', op. cit., pp. 165–6.

78. Ibid., p. 9.
79. Ibid.
80. Ibid., p. 10.
81. Mao Tse-tung, 'On Practice', *Selected Works*, Vol. I, p. 296.
82. Liu Jiyou, 'Qianyan', in *Dongguo Xiansheng*, (Beijing, 1973), unnumbered page after title.
83. Li Qun, 'Ping "Dazhong Tuhua Chubanshe" de Lianhuantuhua', op. cit., p. 10.
84. Ibid., p. 166.
85. Lu Bing, 'Duhua Zagan', *Ertong Wenxue Yanjiu* (Shanghai, 1959), p. 56.
86. Ibid., p. 57.
87. Ibid., p. 58.
88. Wang Linqui, Foreword, *Baimuji de Gushi* (Beijing, 1955).
89. Ibid., p. 59.
90. Ibid., Foreword.
91. 'Zai Guoji Shuji Yishi Zhanlanhui Shang, Siben Ertong Duwu De Jiang', *Ertong Wenxue Yanjiu*, 2 (1959).
92. Lu Bing, 'Duhua Zagan', op. cit., p. 58.
93. For example, Zhou Zuoren. See Chapter 2.
94. Lu Hsun, *A Short History of Chinese Fiction*, op. cit., pp. 206–7.
95. 'Sun Wukong Sanda Baigu Jing' in Chuangzuo Zu, *Sun Wukong Sanda Baigujing* (Shanghai, 1973), unnumbered page after title page.
96. Wu Nong and Li Lu, 'Huiqi Huabi zai Changzheng', op. cit., p. 35.
97. Ibid.
98. Mao Tse-tung, 'Kuo Mo-juo's Poem "On Seeing the Monkey Subdue the Demon"', in *Poems* (Peking, 1976), p. 42.
99. Engle, Hua Ling-nieh and Engel, P. *The Poetry of Mao Tse-tung* (London, 1973), p. 111.
100. Mao Tse-tung, 'Reply to Comrade Kuo Mo-ruo', *Poems*, op. cit., p. 41.
101. Engle, Hua Ling-nieh and Engle, P. *The Poetry of Mao Tse-tung*, op. cit., p. 113.
102. Ibid., p. 112.
103. Ibid., p. 114.
104. Kuo Mo-ruo, 'Smash the Gang of Four', *Chinese Literature*, No. 1 (1977), p. 64.
105. Chen Guang, *Danao Tiangong* (Shanghai, 1961). From publication details on back cover.
106. For a discussion of animated cartoons for Chinese children see Farquhar, M.A., 'Monks and Monkey: A Study of "National Style" in Chinese Animation', *Animation Journal*, 1:2, Spring, 1993, pp. 5–27.
107. Mao Tse-tung, *Five Documents on Literature and Art*, (Peking, 1967), pp. 10-11.
108. Ibid., p. 11.
109. Chesneaux, J., *China: The People's Republic, 1949–1976*, op cit., p. 138.
110. P'an Yu-ch'un, 'A Reader's Complaint', in Croizier, R.C. (ed.), *China's Cultural Legacy and Communism*, op. cit., pp. 166–7.
111. 'Use Mao Tse-tung's Thought to Educate Children to Become Proletarian Revolutionaries', Editorial, *Chieh-fang Rihpao*, translated in *Survey of the Chinese Mainland Press*, 3961, (1967), p. 24.
112. Laing, D., *The Marxist Theory of Art* (Sussex, New Jersey, 1978), p. 79.

113. Ch'i Cheng, 'New Serial Pictures', *Chinese Literature*, No. 2 (February 1974), p. 112.

114. Ibid., pp. 11–12.

115. For details on the method of selection see 'Lianhuanhuabao de Yijian Xishi', *Lianhuanhuabao*, No. 3 (March 1981), p. 1.

116. Chi Cheng, 'New Serial Pictures', op. cit., p. 113.

117. '*Liangxiang*', often translated as 'strikes a proud pose' is an integral part of dramatic movement on the Chinese stage. An actor, during exit or entry onto a stage or during a dance, momentarily freezes from a moving to a motionless pose. The aim is to accentuate the actor's feelings and heightens the atmosphere of the opera.

118. Wang Shuyaun et al., 'Azalea Mountain', *Chinese Literature*, No. 1 (January 1974), p. 12.

119. *Dujuan Shan*, adapted from the color film, *Dujuan Shan* (Beijing, 1975), p. 29.

120. Mass Criticism Group of Beijing and Qinghua Universities, 'Negating the Revolution in Literature and Art Aims at Restoring Capitalism', *Peking Review*, 22 (28 May 1976), p. 7, in Mackerras, C., *The Peforming Arts in Contemporary China* (London, 1981) p. 34.

121. Zhao Yifu, 'Letter to Editor', *Renmin Xiju*, 4 (1977), p. 57, cited in Mackerras, C., 'The Taming of the Shrew: Chinese Theatre and Social Change Since Mao', *Australian Journal of Chinese Affairs*, No. 1 (January 1979), p. 7.

122. Mao Tse-tung, 'In Memory of Norman Bethune', in *Selected Works*, Vol. II (Peking 1975), pp. 337–8.

123. Bi Qingyu, 'Zhigen yu Renmin—Tantan Bai Qiuen Zai Zhongguo ji qi Zuozhe', *Lianhuanhuabao*, No. 2 (February 1981), p. 52.

124. Ibid.

125. Mao Tse-tung, 'Talks at the Yen'an Forum on Literature and Art', op. cit., p. 90.

126. Laing, D., *The Marxist Theory of Art*, op. cit., pp. 77–8.

127. Bi Qingyu, 'Zhigen yu Renmin—Tantan Bai Qiuen Zai Zhongguo ji qi Zuozhe', op. cit., pp. 44, 50.

128. Ibid., p. 44.

129. Lu Xun, 'Nahan', op. cit., p. 271.

130. Mao Tse-tung, 'Talks at the Yenan Forum on Literature and Art', op. cit., p. 82.

131. McDougall, B. S., 'The First Three Decades', op. cit., pp. 282–3.

132. Ibid., p. 280.

6

Children's Literature in the People's Republic of China

In 1949, Mao Zedong proclaimed the birth of a new People's Republic of China. It was led by the Chinese Communist Party, with Mao as Chairman. Between 1949 and Mao's death in 1976, children's literature, like all the arts, was centralized under layers of bureaucracy and harnessed as an instrument of social control and ideological change. Children's literature in this period was a state institution, apparently controlled by either civil or military bureaucracies. However, at the apex of these bureaucracies stood the Communist Party, a parallel and convergent command structure with functions traditionally associated with the state.[1] Thus Party policy determined the development of children's literature in this period.

The problem with Party policy as a defining framework for developments in children's literature is that policy changed constantly. These changes arose from factional power struggles within the Party and from the Maoist imperative to transform the nation's people ideologically through revolutionary struggle. Party policy towards the arts, including arts for children, oscillated between coercive pressure to conform to the Maoist principles of revolutionary popularization as enshrined in the 1942 Yan'an 'Talks', and relaxing of these controls. Children's literature in these decades must therefore be understood in the context of particular periods, marked by major policy shifts and political events (Table 6.1). These periods are: 1949–56, a time of consolidation and relaxation of controls; 1957–65, a period of increasing control over both children's literature and its writers; and 1966–76, called the Great Proletarian Cultural Revolution, when class struggle was the 'key link' for all cultural activity.

Table 6.1 Periodization of Children's Literature in the People's Republic of China

Period	Political Watersheds	Developments in Children's Literature
1949 – May 1957	Liberation to the Hundred Flowers Campaign	• Organization of the field. • Flourishing children's literature, especially from 1954–56.
June 1957 – 1965	Anti-Rightist Campaign to the Great Proletarian Cultural Revolution	• Attacks on selected themes and writers. • Attacks on fairytales and fantasy. • Decrease in the number of writers and works produced.
1966 – Sept 1976	Great Proletarian Cultural Revolution to Mao's death	• Purge of previous works. • Themes of class struggle. • Dominance of model heroes. • Few new works produced.
After 1976	Post-Mao period	• Reassessment of the entire field of children's literature.

These policy shifts had a dramatic effect on children's literature. In the first period, bureaucratic organization of the field, led by May Fourth writers, resulted in a so-called 'Golden Age' of children's literature for a few short years in the mid-fifties. Between 1957 and 1965, more rigid controls were imposed, leading the veteran writer, Mao Dun, to claim in 1961 that 'politics was in command' and, by 1965, Diény categorized children's books of the time as a 'cement block of propaganda'. Ideological attacks on all aspects of this literature sharpened during the Cultural Revolution, the third period. Most literary works were purged, many writers were exiled to the countryside for 're-education', and children left school to 'make revolution' as Red Guards. After Mao's death in 1976, the field was reassessed, works and writers were rehabilitated, and children's literature was said to have blossomed into a second 'Golden Age'.

The overall effect of Maoist policies was to decimate children's literature as a field. The two vibrant schools that the Communists had inherited in 1949, traditional and May Fourth children's literature, were destroyed by 1976. 'Old' works were purged as feudal superstition; works in the May Fourth mode—especially fairytales—were attacked as bourgeois. Revolutionary literature triumphed. But it was a hollow victory as this school was left devoid of infrastructure, good works and good writers.

This chapter focuses on the 'very tortuous path' of children's literature in Mao's China.[2] This was the path for all the arts, as we saw with comics in the previous chapter. In this chapter, the three historical periods detailed above provide the structure for our discussion. Each period is introduced in terms of the dominant policy context. This is followed by a survey of literary works, most selected from the lists of national prize-winners for children's literature. Two rounds of national awards were made, covering the periods 1949–53 and 1954–79 respectively. Prize-winners from the latter round come from the post-Mao assessment of the field, but these works are generally also considered excellent in contemporary critiques. Finally, there is analysis of the major debates that shaped the field in each particular period.

Children's Literature from 1949 to May 1957

In the early years of this period, from 1949–53, the government consolidated its control over children's literature, just as it had over comic book publishing. In the next few years, it oversaw a concerted effort to support children's literature. Commentators hailed 'The First Golden Age of Children's Literature'.

Organizational support for this literature included the establishment of specialized magazines, publishing houses, theatres, children's organizations (such as the Young Pioneers) and writers' organizations, called 'children's literature groups', under the umbrella of the Chinese Writers' Union. Groups, committees and conferences abounded. The National Chinese People's Protect the Children Committee, for example, instituted

---

Table 6.2 State Measures to Organize Children's Literature (1949–57)

Magazines

1949   Only one children's magazine in circulation: *China's Children* (*Zhongguo Shaonian Ertong*).

1951   *China's Children* name changed to *China's Adolescents* (*Zhongguo Shaonianbao*).

1954   Distribution per issue reached 1,700,000 copies. Joined by five other national magazines aimed at specific age groups: *Middle School Student* (*Zhongxuesheng*) for junior and middle school students; *Juvenile Literature* (*Shaonian Wenyi*) for adolescents; *Children's Epoch* (*Ertong Shidai*) for third- and fourth-year primary school students; *Little Friends* (*Xiao Pengyou*), an illustrated magazine for first- and second-year primary school students.*

1956   By year's end, there were five more magazines: *New Children* (*Xin Ertong*); *Red Scarf* (*Hong Lingshi*);*Young Pioneers* (*Shaoxianduiyuan*); *Adolescents and Children* (*Shaonian Ertong*);*Yan'an Children* (*Yanbian Ertong*).**

Children's Literature Groups

1949   Chinese Writers' Union formed national and branch 'children's literature groups' (*ertong wenxuezu*), just after the first conference of the All-China Federation of Literature and Art Circles.

1956   A considerable increase in the number of new writers of children's literature by 1956.

The Chinese Children's League (*Zhongguo Shaonian Ertongtuan*)

1949   Formed under the Youth League.

1953   Name changed to Young Pioneers.

1954   Eight million members, with Young Pioneers supplementing the education system and introducing members to new children's books.

1956   Membership of 20 million.

---

2 of 8

37052245013241421633

Publishing Houses

1952   Government established The Adolescents' and Children's Publishing House (*Shaonian Ertong Chubanshe*), specializing in children's books, in Shanghai.

1957   A second children's publishing house established in Beijing.

These two houses became the major publishers of children's literature in China.

National Prizes

1953   At year's end the National Chinese People's Protect the Children Committee awarded national prizes for children's literature and art published between 1949 and 1953. The awards encouraged and steered writers, and elevated the status of children's literature and art. (The next national prizes were held in 1980).

Newspaper Editorials

1954   *People's Daily* editorial used to launch a campaign against undesirable books.

1955   September 16. *People's Daily* editorial used to launch a campaign to increase the number of children's books published.

Children's Theatre

1955   June 1 (Children's Day). The first children's theatre opened in Beijing.

Writers' Union Special Meetings

1955   A special meeting was held to implement Party policies in November.

1956   All major national literary magazines were regularly featuring children's literature, and children's writers in the Union began editing periodic anthologies of the best children's literature through to 1963.

---

[*] Ai Lu, 'Ertong Duwu Zhong de Jige Wenti', *Wenyibao*, No. 63 (1952), p. 38

[**] *Current Background*, No. 436 (1957), p.10.

national awards for children's literature. Government-run newspapers launched campaigns against 'undesirable' books in 1954, and for an increase in the number of good children's books in 1955 (Table 6.2).

This support was strengthened by a nationwide political campaign in 1956. Mao called for a period of intellectual freedom and creativity, known as 'The Hundred Flowers'. In this climate, children's literature blossomed into a garden. One writer claimed:

> In December 1953 the National Conference on Prizes for Children's Literature opened a vast tract of land for children's literature in new China; in September 1955 the *People's Daily* editorial. . . was like a deep furrowing of this land; in June 1956 the Party's call 'to let a hundred flowers blossom. . .' was like a steady shower of rain. Looking around we see everywhere a luxuriant new green.[3]

All commentators point to the 16 September 1955 *People's Daily* editorial as the single most significant event in children's literature of this period. Organization of the field opened the way for an assessment of all books, including literature, available to both urban and rural children. The editorial stated that, in 1954, over 400 new titles were published in 13,690,000 copies for a population of 120 million children, aged between six and fifteen. Only seventy million of these children were literate. Nationwide, this meant one book for every five children. There were also regional surveys. In one urban municipality, there were 40,000 books in libraries for 180,000 children; again one book for every four or five children. Rural children fared worst. In the Hebei countryside, only one book was available for every 1,100 children. The editorial claimed that children's books were 'inadequate', that organizations involved in producing, publishing and distributing these books were 'not interested' in children or in their education, and that the Writers' Union neglected the field. Children's literature lacked status. The editorial called for increased production and more equitable distribution.[4] Writers and organizations responded overwhelmingly to the call until mid-1957, when the chill wind of ideological purity swept through the art world in the Anti-Rightist Campaign.

The 1955 editorial promoted children's literature as part of education. One writer in the prestigious literary journal, *Literature and Arts Journal (Wenyibao)*, stated succinctly that the diverse themes in children's literature could be summed up as 'education and nurture of the new generation'.[5] This education was perceived as primarily ideological, even in the early period. In 1950, a speaker at The First National Conference of Cadres Involved in Adolescents' and Children's Work formulated the educational objectives of the new era in terms that echoed through the following decades:

> Our educational aim is to nurture the new generation in correct ideological consciousness and revolutionary qualities, to give them basic cultural and scientific knowledge and healthy bodies, in short (to bring up) virtuous and wise future masters of a new society, outstanding sons and daughters of new China.[6]

Despite this rhetoric, the major figures in children's literature in the early Mao years were those who had made a lasting contribution before 1949. These writers, such as Ye Shengtao, Bing Xin, Zhang Tianyi, Yan Wenjing and Zhang Leping, were imbued with a May Fourth sensibility. Hence, many works in this first period reflected the May Fourth emphasis on a 'children's world'.

Major Works in Children's Literature (1949–57)

The post-Mao reassessment of children's literature in the People's Republic confirmed this early period as the one which produced the most outstanding writers and works. The second national awards for children's literature and art (1954–79) honored both authors and particular works. All the authors cited for commendation for their contribution over three decades of the Republic had published in this first period, although in two cases their representative work is a new edition of pre-Liberation

Table 6.3 Prize-winning Writers and Representative Works in Children's Literature (1954–79)

Author	Representative Work	Form
Ye Shengtao	*The Scarecrow* (*Daocaoren he qita tonghua*)	Fairytales
Bing Xin	*The Small Orange Lantern* (*Xiao Judeng*)	Stories and poems
Gao Shiqi	*Do You Know Who I Am?* (*Ni Zhidao Wo shi Shei?*)	Science stories
Zhang Tianyi	*For Children* (*Gei Haizimen*)	Stories, plays, tales
Yan Wenjing	*The Streamlet's Song* (*Xiao Xiliu de Ge*)	Fairytales
Ye Junjian	*A Selection of Andersen's Fairytales* (*Antusheng tonghuaxuan*)	Translation of fairytales
Chen Bochui	*Flying Tiger Brigade and Wild Pig Brigade* (*Feihudui yu Yezhudui*)	Fairytales
He Yi	*A Selection of He Yi's Works* (*He Yi Zuopin Xuan*)	Fairytales
Bao Lei	*The Firefly and the Goldfish* (*Huoying yu Jinyu*)	Fairytales
Jin Jin	*Fairytales Brought by the Spring Breeze* (*Chunfeng Lailiao de Tonghua*)	Fairytales
Zhang Leping	*A Record of the Vagabond Sanmao* (*Sanmao liulangji*)	Cartoon strips
Wan Laiming	*Havoc in Heaven, Part 1* (*Danao tiangong*)	Animation
	The White-bone Demon (*Sanda baigujing*)	Picture book
Sun Jingxiu	*Several Decades of Stories for Children* (*Shushinian wei shaonian ertong jiang gushi*	Translation of children's tales

Source: Dierci Quanguo Shaonian Ertong Wenyi Chuangzuo Pingjiang Weiyuanhui Bangongshe (ed.), *Ertong Wenxue Zuojia Zuopin Lun* (Beijing, 1981).

publications: Ye Shengtao's fairytale collection and Zhang Leping's *Sanmao* (Table 6.3). Fairytales and fantasy are the main vehicle of these writers. This imbalance in favor of fairytales cannot be attributed to the judges' preferences in the post-Mao period; with the exception of the Cultural Revolution period, these writers have always been recognized as outstanding in the field. Moreover, when it came to awards for particular works between 1954 and 1957, the same judges selected both 'realistic' stories and fairytales.

Particular works that won first prize in this period—and are therefore considered outstanding by Chinese critics—may be listed from both rounds of the national awards (Table 6.4). Five works in a range of genres were given first prizes by their peers in the first national awards. Fifteen works were awarded first prize in the second national awards. Again, the judges of the post-Mao period have awarded a majority of first prizes, fifteen of the twenty-seven titles over three decades, to works in this early period after Liberation. Overall, fiction predominates, with an almost equal proportion of stories and fairytales.

The following survey of these works first discusses stories, then looks at some exceptions to the dominant themes and forms. Finally, it considers fairytales and fables. The focus is on this literature's portrayal of a 'children's world', that May Fourth construct that rationalized the creation of a children's literature. Conceptualizations of this world offer a window into views of childhood in this period and, as is always the case in modern Chinese children's literature, into views of educational priorities for children.

'Realistic' Stories

'Realistic' stories in a contemporary setting were part of the later May Fourth contribution to children's literature. The emphasis, then, was on social realism in the mould of Lu Xun's later translations. The majority of the stories in the years from 1949–56 return to children's everyday world, rather than to children's place in the larger society of China. These works socialize children into the institutions governing their daily lives:

Table 6.4 Prize-winning Works (First Class) in Children's Literature (1949–57)*

Author	Work	Form
First National Awards, 1949–53		
Zhang Tianyi	'How Luo Wenying Became a Young Pioneer' ('Luo Wenying de Gushi')	Story
Gao Shiqi	'Our Mother Earth' ('Turang Mama')	Science poem
Feng Xuefeng	*Lu Xun and His Boyhood Friends* (*Lu Xun he ta Shaonian Shidai de Pengyou*)	Biography
Qin Zhaoyang	'The 10,000 Li Flight of Two Little Swallows' ('Xiaoyanzi de Wanli Feixingji')	Fairytale
Guo Xu	'Commander Yang's Young Pioneers' ('Yang Siling de Shaoxiandui')	Stories
Second National Awards, 1954–57**		
Xiao Ping	'At the Seaside' ('Haibin de Haizi')	Story
Ren Daxing	'Lu Xiaogang and His Sister' ('Lu Xiaogang he Tade Meimei')	Story
Gao Xiangzhen	'Chubby and Little Pine' ('Xiao Pang he Xiao Song')	Story
Ren Dalin	'Crickets' ('Xishuai')	Story
Liu Zhen	'Little Song and I' ('Wo he Xiao Song')	Story

Author	Work	Form
Yang Shuo	'Fluttering Snowflakes' ('Xuehua Piaopiao')	Story
Hu Qi	*The Multicolored Road* (*Wucai Lu*)	Story
Ke Yan	'Story of the Little Soldier' ('Xiaobing de Gushi')	Poem
Ruan Yuanjing	'The Golden Conch' ('Jinse de Hailuo')	Poem, fairytale/ folktale
Hong Xuntao	'Ma Liang and His Magic Brush' ('Shenbi Maliang')	Fairytale/ folktale
Ge Cuilin	'The Wild Grapes' ('Ye Putao')	Fairytale/ folktale
Huang Qingyun	'The Strange Red Star' ('Qiyi de Hongxing')	Fairytale
Fang Huizhen, Sheng Lude	'The Little Tadpoles Look for Their Mother' ('Xiao Kedou Zhao Mama')	Pre-school fairytale
Peng Wenxi	'A Pony Crosses the River' ('Xiaoma Guohe')	Pre-school fairytale
Ren Deyao	'Ma Lanhua' ('Ma Lanhua')	Play, folktale

*Because of the nature of the awards system, this list does not include art (comics) and songs for the period 1949–53, nor picture books, films, art, music and songs for the period 1954–79.

** The Second National Awards spanned the period 1954–79. Given the chronological limitation of this table, here we include only the award-winners for the first three years of the period, i.e. 1954–57.

family, school, friends, and the Communist Party organization for children, the Young Pioneers.

Jiang Feng, in *A Discussion of Children's Literature in China,* looked at the best works produced up to 1956 and began with the established author, Zhang Tianyi. A prize-winning example is Zhang's work, 'How Luo Wenying Became a Young Pioneer'. It was said to have been very popular with children when it was first published. Here, the main character is a boy who wants to be a soldier in the People's Liberation Army but he is lazy and spends his time in the markets or reading comics when he should be studying. A group of friends form a study group to help him, and the story is told through a series of letters they send to their 'uncles' in the Army about Luo Wenying's 'progress' and his eventual admission to the Young Pioneers. Jiang Feng summarized the message: '[t]hrough his own efforts and the help of his friends, [Luo] learns "discipline" and solves the contradiction between playing and studying'.[7] Jiang said of Zhang Tianyi's corpus of works for children in this period:

> [He is] adept at revealing important social themes and the development of new moral qualities by children in their everyday life.[8]

Such stories of ordinary children who overcome character faults—called 'middle' characters in Chinese, as we considered in the previous chapter—were very common in children's literature in the fifties. There are usually figures of authority or models, such as the school friends or the Army, but they are not central characters. The emphasis is on Mao's maxim to Chinese children: Study hard and progress day by day.

'Crickets' ('Xishuai')[9] by the younger author, Ren Dalin, is similar to Zhang Tianyi's story of Luo Wenying. In 'Crickets' the main character, having failed the entrance exam into middle school, harvests crops for the village cooperative throughout the hot summer. He loves cricket fighting and captures a 'genuine snake cricket', General Black Feelers, which subsequently dies in a cricket fight. He wastes lots of time searching for another cricket until he becomes the cooperative's book-keeper and, immersed in work rather than play, loses all interest in crickets.

Similarly, in 'Chubby and Little Pine' ('Xiao Fang he Xiao Song') by Gao Xiangzhen, a sister and brother separate after an argument in a park. On his own, Little Pine becomes lost and almost drowns. This leads to a happy reunion at the police station.[10]

In general, these stories are caring and educational, both politically and morally. Ke Yan's poem, a series of four line verses, titled 'The Story of "The Little Soldier"' ('"Xiaobing" de Gushi'), fits into this category.[11]

All of these stories *domesticate* children. The virtues advocated may be worthy, but they are also unexciting. Army soldiers, village leaders and the police oversee children's welfare. The exception to these stories about everyday life is Xiao Ping's 'At the Seaside' ('Haibin de Haizi'), a story of adventure, danger and the development of a lifelong friendship.

In 'At the Seaside', a young boy, Er Xiao, goes on holiday to his grandmother's place in a seaside village where he finds excitement in fishing and digging for clams. He dreams of collecting about twenty clam shells to display proudly on his desk when he returns to school. He imagines himself giving some away to his friends. However, Er Xiao is reticent about his cousin, Da Hu, who lives with his grandmother; Da Hu is a Young Pioneer squad leader who seems older, and more knowledgeable. He avoids taking Er Xiao to the north bank of the estuary to catch the clams of Er Xiao's daydreams because the area is dangerous and children are forbidden to go there. Eventually Da Hu takes him, leaving Er Xiao to watch for the incoming tide while he collects the clams. Er Xiao is disgruntled and bored until he feels a clam shell while idly digging his fingers in the sand and soon he forgets all about the time and the tide. When he finally looks up, the tide is swirling fast and deep and the boys are trapped. Da Hu acts quickly, pulling his cousin to the other bank by his trousers and retrieving the clams. The boys run to safety.

'At the Seaside' is an extremely well-developed story of only twelve pages about a little boy, his daydreams and sense of status, his thoughts, fears and tears (Illustration 6.1). In the end his dream about the clams is unimportant. What is important is the mutual respect which had developed between the two boys at the story's end:

> 'I say Da Hu,' he blurted out, 'I like you ever so much. I really do. Let's be friends all our lives—what do you say?'
>
> Da Hu sat there without answering, gazing vaguely out to sea, frowning as he clasped his knees. After quite a long time he said:
>
> 'If my old man asks you any questions when we get back, don't tell him everything, understand? Just say that I was the one who took you to the estuary north of the village: it wasn't *your* idea. . .'[12]

Illustration 6.1

from 'At the Seaside'

The messages in this story do not fit neatly into the new moral framework which privileged work over play, and exemplary models over middle characters. This may explain why there is no published critique of 'At the Seaside', despite the story's popularity. The story exhibits a psychological subtlety, rare in children's literature of the People's Republic, seen in Er Xiao's sense of status, which moves from showing off the clams, to a more mature awareness of authority, action and caution. Adults do not impinge on the two boys' intimate world; adults exist to formulate taboos. And, in the end, adults can be lied to but, in the context of Da Hu's acceptance of responsibility, this seems quite justifiable. However, 'At the Seaside' is the exception among the corpus of children's stories about everyday life in this period.

Exceptions to 'Realistic' Stories about Daily Life or Fairytales

'Realistic' stories outside these themes of children's daily lives are not so common. Prize-winners in this category are Bing Xin's *The Small Orange Lantern* and Hu Qi's book for older children, *The Multicolored Road*. Both comply with the policy demand for ideological education through literature in this period. Gao Shiqi's poems popularizing science stand in a category of their own.

Bing Xin's 'The Small Orange Lantern'[13] ('Xiao Judeng') is a very short and beautifully written piece, comparing the past bitterness of a family's life in Chongqing with the happiness of life in new China. Structurally, this is akin to the post-Liberation version of *Sanmao*, with old and new China contrasted as black and white. However, Bing Xin's work is reportage, not fiction. As in the May Fourth period, she uses forms outside the mainstream in children's literature of the period.

Hu Qi's *The Multicolored Road* (*Wucai de Lu*) carries an obvious message about the glories of the Communist Party but it still features 'middle', not heroic, characters. In Hu Qi's story, three children living in remote, snow-covered mountains leave home to find the multi-colored road that they believe the People's Liberation Army is quite literally creating in China.

Through difficulties and adventures the three children discover another road that is metaphoric but equally glorious, a road being made by the Communist Party and the Chinese people. The children learn that 'fortune and struggle are closely linked, like a man and his shadow. . . they all hope that an even more sparkling and happier multicolored road will always open up before them. . .'.[14] Part of the book's original appeal was the story's idealistic optimism that clearly espoused the educational values of 'correct ideological consciousness and revolutionary qualities', the policy priority in this period. But like Yan Wenjing's wartime story about Dingding, the focus is on children's self discovery, on learning through a series of actual adventures. In this sense, the characters are ordinary children, not the heroic little 'red devils' of wartime adventure stories.

Poems on the natural world by Gao Shiqi fit into their own category, in terms of both content and literary form. Gao was the outstanding author in the area of popularizing science.[15] He blended science and fantasy in works that were unique for their imagination, their warmth and their intimacy about the natural world. In Gao Shiqi's poems, nature is respected, not dominated; alive, not dead. This poet, who began his writing for children with 'The Autobiography of a Germ' ('Juner de Zizhuan') in 1936,[16] communicated these messages with breathtaking simplicity on subjects like the sun, time and the earth.

The Sun:

> From streams,
> From seas,
> From forests and grassy plains,
> [the sun] vaporizes water,
> Storing it in cloudy layers
> Turning it into fine raindrops
> To fall upon the parched earth. . .[17]

Uncle Time:

> We do not know your age
> It is as if you had neither begun nor ended. . .[18]

'Our Mother Earth' which won a first prize for children's literature, begins:

> Our Mother Earth
> Is the worker in the factory of the world. . . [19]

These poems are not directly political but they are educational, satisfying the objective of giving children 'basic scientific knowledge'. Like the old *Three Character Classic*, the rhymes are easily memorized and the language, albeit the vernacular in this case, is a delight. Gao's corpus of poetry is a classic in children's literature of twentieth-century China.

Fairytales and Fables

Fairytales persisted as a special form belonging to children's literature. In a sense, Gao Shiqi's poetry spans the division between realism and fantasy in the children's literature of this period. His work personified natural forces to teach children about the natural world. As we saw with May Fourth fairytales, personification of objects, such as scarecrows, birds and trains, was the 'fairytale' device that allowed writers to comment on contemporary society. Gao's poems were the only prize-winning work to continue this tradition in a delightful yet serious way, although he is commenting on nature and science, not on society.

Hans Christian Andersen's works, which also used this fairytale device, were the exemplar in pre-Liberation China for modern, literary fairytales, as Zhou Zuoren had called them. It is therefore not surprising that Ye Junjian, who translated Andersen's fairytales into Chinese, was commended in the post-Mao awards as an outstanding contributor to children's literature. However, the literary fairytale had always been seen as a modern, Western form so it was now ideologically suspect because of its origins. Folktales, however, were a traditional form belonging to Chinese popular literature that was sanctioned by Mao's 'Talks'. When we look at the prize-winning fairytales and fables in this early period of the People's Republic, we find a submerged censorship at work around what was ideologically acceptable. This system approved fairy stories for the very young, but these are really tales about animals. It also approved folktales. The prize-winning 'fairytales' written between 1949 and 1957 really belong to these two categories: animal stories and folktales.

In the first category, various animals and birds are personified as a family to teach the everyday lessons that dominated 'realistic' fiction. For example, 'The 10,000 Li Flight of Two Little Swallows' is about two spoilt and lazy baby swallows. Unaware of the coming winter, they refuse to migrate with their mother. When the cold finally forces them to fly south, they discover the vastness of China. Finding their mother, they say 'we would like to fly over the whole of China so that we can better temper ourselves and will never fear hunger again, or cold or fatigue'.[20] 'A Pony Crosses a River' and 'The Little Tadpoles Look for Their Mother' were similar stories. In the first, a pony learns to test the depth of the river before crossing it, instead of relying on the opinions of others. In the second, tadpoles search for, and find, their mother—a frog. The joy of reading in these two books is not so much through the message as through the illustrations. Indeed, 'The Little Tadpoles Look for Their Mother' was made into an award-winning animation, using brush and ink paintings by the famous artist Qi Baishi.

Prize-winning works in the second category—the stories 'The Wild Grapes' and 'Ma Liang and His Magic Brush'; the poem, 'The Golden Conch'; and the play, 'Ma Lanhua'—are all based on folk stories in which the poor and oppressed eventually receive justice. Thus these works fit within a revolutionary framework. For example, in 'The Wild Grapes', White Goose Maiden is blinded by a cruel and jealous aunt but she is cured and then able to help others who are suffering as she had suffered earlier (Illustration 6.2).[21] In the second story, the emperor steals Ma Liang's magic brush. The brush transforms paintings into real objects, thus enabling Ma Liang to help poor villagers. Eventually, Ma Liang paints a boat then a storm, capsizing the boat and drowning the emperor (Illustration 6.3).[22]

Illustration 6.2

from 'The Wild Grapes'

The poem, 'The Golden Conch', opens like the well-known fairytale by Pushkin in which a fisherman saved a golden fish stranded on the seashore. The fisherman returned home to a nagging wife who insisted on using the fish's magic powers for selfish ends. In the Chinese poem, the orphaned boy saves the conch out of the goodness of his heart. Unlike Pushkin's hero, the boy in this story is unmarried and the conch transforms into a girl to spend three years with him in payment for saving her life. At first, he does not know who is looking after him but, on the third day, he returns home early from fishing and peeps in the window:

Illustration 6.3

from 'Ma Liang and His Magic Brush'

He saw a colored ring of light
On the fair young girl.
She wore a skirt like moonlight,
Her hair was like the morning sun.[23]

Of course, he wants to keep his fairy for ever so three times he visits the savage spirit of the sea who finally is so impressed by the constancy of his love that the sea spirit allows the conch girl to stay with him. After a year the couple have two babies, after three years they have four children but, 'alas', ends the singer, 'I did not learn the last line saying how many children altogether.'[24] Even with its romanticism, the poem's message is clear: selfless effort is rewarded (Illustration 6.4).

In an article by writer He Yi about 'The Golden Conch', he recognized the love, fantasy and traditional forms of this fairytale.[25] Another writer, Yuan Ying, supported the educational function of literature in a speech to young authors, but reserved the highest praise, even hyperbole, for fairytales as a genre not simply unique to children's literature but the most loved by young readers. He suggested:

> Each writer for children should learn how to write fairytales. A comrade said to me, 'If you cannot write fairytales then you cannot consider yourself a children's author'.[26]

Illustration 6.4

from 'The Golden Conch'

Yuan's emphasis on the fairytale is reminiscent of writers in the early May Fourth period. However, this section of Yuan Ying's article has been deleted in subsequent reprintings, even after 1976. The fairytale form was a major subject for debate among writers between 1949 and 1957. Later, it came under official attack.

Debates in Children's Literature Between 1949 and 1957

The fairytale that was publicly debated used satire to criticize society under the Communists in this period. Called 'Discernment' ('Huiyan'), this fairytale by Ouyang Shan was published over four issues in 1956 in the adult magazine, *Literary Works* (*Zuopin*). The story satirized both revolutionary hypocrisy and revolutionaries' arrogance in new China. For example, in the story in the first issue, Zhou Bang's parents realize, in the year of Liberation, that their son's eyes can pierce through people's bodies to see their hearts, their real nature. Good hearts are red, bad hearts are black. Zhou himself is arrogant about his gift, despite his father's admonition. But Zhou is deceived by a corrupt revolutionary who uses red paper to cover his black heart. Zhou learns to be modest about his powers only when he sees the paper falling out of the corrupt revolutionary's clothes.[27]

'Discernment' is not a prepossessing work but it caused particular controversy and deepened the divisions over views on fairytales under socialism. It was a subject for debate in 1956 and then an object of attack in the Anti-Rightist Campaign that began the next period in children's literature.

In this first period, some critics stated that 'Discernment' was unsuccessful as a fairytale and unsuitable for socialist China. Others claimed that it advocated idealism, not materialism, and was contrary to socialist realism. It was said, for example, that '[t]he author does not use "discernment" to expose and criticize backward social elements but uses backward social forces to expose and criticize the weaknesses... of "discernment"'.[28] Chen Bochui, prize-winning author and specialist commentator on fairytales, claimed the opposite: it was a 'flower' on 'the fairytale tree'. This was despite Chen's acknowledgment that 'Discernment' was not a very good fairytale, mainly due to a loose blending of fantasy and reality and the author's improper understanding of the nature of the fairytale form. Chen wrote that Zhou Bang, for example, had magical powers but no fairytale world in which to use them.[29] Chen Bochui's primary aim was to defend the fairytale form as a vehicle for criticism and satire in new China.

But satire of life in the Communist guerilla society of Yan'an was prohibited by Mao Zedong in his 'Talks' in 1942. Political campaigns at that time had implemented Mao's line, exiling writers who had broken this taboo to the countryside for 're-education' by the peasants. Satire was reserved for national and class enemies. Mao reiterated this policy in the fifties, when he stated that society should be divided into 'enemies' and 'friends' and criticism of 'friends'—the Communist Party and revolutionary classes—was proscribed. As in Yan'an, a campaign to enforce ideological compliance followed the social criticism of new China that emerged in much literature of the Hundred Flowers period in 1956, when controls were relaxed. In children's literature, the campaign targeted such works as 'Discernment' in particular, and fairytales in general.

Children's Literature from 1957 to 1965

In this period, political controls on children's literature were tightened. Party policy insisted on revolutionary popularization and on education about class struggle. In 1958, all literature—including that for children—had to obey a literary platform with more precise rules. Called 'revolutionary realism and re-volutionary romanticism', this platform was summed up by Kai Yu-hsu as one that allowed 'realism only so long as it [would] aid the revolution.'[30] The overall policy effect in this period was that political education was paramount and children's literature became propaganda.

The Party enforced its control of literature and art through political campaigns. These campaigns harnessed literature for purposes of dissemination and control. The campaigns surged in waves during these years. In 1957, the Anti-Rightist Campaign attacked and exiled writers and artists whose work had criticized new China under Communist rule. In 1958, the Great Leap Forward, with its backyard smelters and introduction of communes in the villages, whipped the Chinese people into a frenzy of collective industrial activity in order to reach Western levels of industrialization. This campaign was spectacularly unsuccessful and China entered several years of famine, with many people dying of starvation. Mao remained Chairman of the Party but lost his position as Chairman of the state in the late fifties. Controls were then relaxed, although there were intense ideological struggles around children's literature in 1960. In the early sixties, Maoists staged a comeback through a Socialist Education Campaign which led into the Cultural Revolution. During the Socialist Education Campaign, policies and model works in literature and art were increasingly propagated through Army institutions. Military authorities implemented the basic line in Mao's 1942 'Talks' at Yan'an: that literature and art be subservient to politics and that it also emphasize revolutionary popularization. From a post-Mao perspective, literary critic Chen Zijun summed up this period in children's literature as one of intensifying 'leftist interference'.

Leftist or Maoist policies on children's literature were entirely premised on an educational package based on 'proletarian politics'. An editorial in a 1959 issue of *People's Daily,* the Communist Party mouthpiece, claimed children were 'the army for building communism in the future'.[31] A 1960 editorial in the same newspaper stated that reactionary classes and old, feudal habits still exerted a strong influence on Chinese children, even though these children had grown up 'under the care of the Party'. The editorial claimed that children wanted to know about political struggles in society, about distinguishing enemies from friends, and about judging right from wrong. It called for 'stories about the revolutionary struggle and heroic and exemplary exploits in actual life'.[32]

This policy is a direct application of 'revolutionary realism and revolutionary romanticism', the new, restrictive guidelines for producing literature and art. Introducing these guidelines in 1958, Zhou Yang, the Deputy-Director of the Propaganda Department, claimed that 'the creation of new heroic characters has become the glorious duty of socialist literature and art' because 'there is no limit to the revolutionary task of transforming the new world'. With some irony, Mao Dun wrote in 1961 that this resulted in a children's literature 'so rich in ideological and educational values' that children themselves could not understand it. He added that this lack of understanding was despite the fact that all the stories were basically the same and that all the main characters were 'little cadres'.[33]

Maoist cultural policy in this period therefore swung children's literature from its initial phase still resonant with May Fourth creative leanings into ideological propaganda. However, this shift was contested in both the political and literary arenas in the period between 1957 and 1965. Maoists finally won when they launched the Great Proletarian Cultural Revolution that swept the nation into a frenzy of revolutionary action that, ironically, made a revolutionary children's literature irrelevant.

Major Works in Children Literature (June 1957–1965)

A survey of children's literature in this period shows that most of the first-class prize-winning works in children's literature between 1957 and 1965 were stories. A play for young children and poems were also chosen. Most of these prize-winning works celebrated heroes (Table 6.5). Of the works by outstanding authors over the three decades covered by the two National Awards (Table 6.3), Zhang Tianyi's 1958 fairytale about school life, *The Magic Gourd,* stands out as a valiant attempt to revitalize the fairytale form in hostile times. Other writers who had defended the fairytale in the previous period, such as Yuan Ying and He Yi, capitulated to the prevailing trend and wrote works of heroic, revolutionary struggle.

Two of these stories, *Little Soldier Zhang Ka*[34] and *The Little Groom and Uncle 'Big Leather Boots'*,[35] are novels about young soldiers during the Anti-Japanese War. These are stories for older children. In both stories, the young soldiers are poor. Zhang Ka's parents have died and the Little Groom's father has been captured and his mother killed in the war. Both soldiers fight with the Communist Eighth Route Army and eventually become Party members. They are likeable young heroes who live through exciting but dangerous adventures with the army, much in the manner of the earlier classic, *Feather Letter*. Both stories offer models for children in a narrative that glorifies the Party's role before 1949. Indeed, the war period is a fitting and historic setting for depicting heroic characters, who develop the requisite qualities of bravery, resolution and a keen class consciousness in the midst of 'revolutionary struggle'.

Xu Guangyao, the author of *Little Soldier Zhang Ka,* also won a first-prize for his script that adapted the novel into a film. The film's directors likewise won a first prize. This story—whether film or fiction—was therefore one of the most successful works of the time in this genre.

Table 6.5 Prize-winning Works in Children's Literature (1957–65)*

Author	Title	Genre
Liu Houming	'The Gosling Returns to the Flock' ('Xiaoyan Jifei')	Play
Ren Rongrong	'Tell Me What My Father Does?' ('Nimen Shuo Wo Baba Shi Gan Shenme de?')	Poem
Xu Guangyao	*Little Soldier Zhang Ka* (*Xiaobing Zhangka*)	Story
Yan Yiyan	*The Little Groom and Uncle 'Big Leather Boots'* (*Xiaomaguan he 'Dapixue' Shushu*)	Story
Yuan Jing	*The Story of Little Black Horse* (*Xiao Heima de Gushi*)	Story
Yuan Jing	'Liu Wenxue' ('Liu Wenxue')	Poem
Zhang Youde	'Little Sister Goes to School' ('Meimei Ruxue')	Story

*The shortness of this list belies the extent of material available in this period. For example, in 1958 and 1959 folk stories for children were common.

Whereas the above two stories were set in the pre-Liberation period, Yuan Jing's *The Story of Little Black Horse* extends into post-Liberation China. The central character, Little Black Horse, is also of lowly status but with few redeeming qualities. He is a victim of 'old' society who turns to begging and stealing until he is cared for in a children's home in 1950. Like *Sanmao* and 'The

Watch', which Lu Xun translated in the thirties, the story contrasts two kinds of lives: 'unfortunate and shameful' before Liberation and 'active and energetic builders of socialism' after Liberation.[36] These lives are as different as hell and heaven, wrote one reviewer.

> Who gave Little Black Horse his childhood happiness? Who washed away the scars on his soul? Who changed his tragic fate? The Communist Party and the people's government.[37]

All three stories have returned to types developed in revolutionary literature in the thirties and forties. The heroes are lively and the plots are action-packed. There is a very clear contrast between the 'bitterness' of the old society and the 'happiness' of the new and the pervasive influence of the Party.

Another model, an actual martyr, is celebrated in Yuan Ying's poem 'Liu Wenxue'. Yuan Ying is one of the writers who had earlier defended the fairytale. Here, he wrote of Liu Wenxue whose story was then very contemporary news. In 1959, when he was fourteen years old, Liu Wenxue was killed by a landlord who he found stealing the commune's crops at night. The landlord epitomized all the feudal elements and class enemies in society who wished to destroy the new egalitarian China. Liu Wenxue was portrayed as a hero, as one of Mao Zedong's staunch supporters, and as an embodiment of the highest qualities in children under socialism. Like Lei Feng and Liu Hulan, he was held up as a communist model for all children. Yuan's poem describes Liu Wenxue as 'unyielding' even when facing death.

> You are a green pine on the mountain top,
> Facing rosy clouds above the morning sun.
> You are not afraid of the wild wind and rain,
> You are staunch and unyielding even at death's door.[38]

Liu's story was featured in most literary forms and for all ages of children. He Yi, a prize-winning author, wrote a story of the same name and praised the same staunch spirit. For example, in He Yi's story, when the landlord is confronted by Liu Wenxue, the landlord tries to bribe him. When this fails, the landlord lures the boy to a dark, deserted part of a nearby orchard and smiling—like a cat watching a bird and with an ugly green light in his eyes, in He Yi's version—he offers Liu life for silence, or death (Illustration 6.5)!

Illustration 6.5

from *Liu Wenxue*

Here was the stance of the true revolutionary, seen in the model Beijing operas of the later part of this period and the following period. Whether the hero was male or female, there was a constant maternal care for the collective, coupled with a warrior vigilance against any enemy who wanted to destroy it. Any psychological development or element of self discovery has shifted to the individual character's growing awareness of the revolutionary forces in which he or she had a role to play. Model heroes in Chinese children's literature never wavered:

> (Liu Wenxue) did not retreat one step. He thought of the landlord's oppression when he was young, the Party's teaching when faced with a class enemy, his beloved mother telling him how to be upright, his instructors and comrades' bringing him up as a Young Pioneer, and he thought of the glorious example of the many heroes and revolutionary martyrs—he hated the landlord's cruelty. . . (and his) eyes shone with a fearless determination.
> 'Don't think I'm one of you! I'll fight to the end against rotters and counter-revolutionaries! Kill me, I'm still not afraid!'[39]

Such stories were typical of children's literature in this period. In 1961, Mao Dun published his findings after a survey of works for children in all the books and magazines published in 1960 by two of the major children's publishing houses. There were ninety books in all. He wrote that most of the books he analyzed were 'real' stories, including those about heroes, and the remainder mostly featured children working for socialism in the factories and countryside.[40]

As we have said, Mao Dun claimed that under the semblance of variety, all stories were basically the same. Diény's analysis of Chinese children's books, collected between 1964 and 1966, confirmed that Mao Dun's conclusion was not limited to 1960 publications. Diény reduced the plots of the books he surveyed to six schemas which revolved around a combination of four elements. These elements were a 'model' character who was positive or heroic; a 'friend' who was a 'middle character', fundamentally good but either ignorant, or the subject of 'bad' influences; an enemy 'of the people and of socialism'; and finally an 'event' that was the actual situation in which the three character types found themselves.[41] Diény claimed that these six schemas were 'all constructed on the universal principle of struggle, which rules the world of fiction just as it explains reality'.[42] 'True' stories, he added, are arranged according to the same political principle, complete with an abundance of facts and photos to render them convincing.[43]

In contrast to the above prize-winning examples of revolutionary realism and revolutionary romanticism, two other prize-winners of this period, 'Little Sister Goes to School' and 'The Gosling Returns to the Flock', were more akin to works describing children's daily lives in the first period. Such themes dominated the children's literature scene in the early fifties but gradually disappeared until, by the end of this second period in the mid-sixties, Diény characterized these works as a 'counter-current'. In the interim, concerted ideological campaigns had cast any literature that ignored revolutionary ideology as 'bourgeois', a mortal sin in Mao's China.

However, this emphasis on daily life is the theme of one of the most famous fairytales of this period, Zhang Tianyi's *The Magic Gourd* (1958). It is a fairytale within a dream, but it is set in an everyday family and school environment. Like many early fifties' stories, it advocates work not play, study not laziness. Wang Bao is a middle character in this tale: an ordinary schoolboy who loves stories, hates washing and dreams of owning a magic gourd. He finally finds one, 'not one of those feeble creatures in a fairytale that can grant you three or four wishes only',[44] but a gourd that can grant everything, even his unformed wishes. As a boy, he is granted food, lots of it so he is never hungry, and toys. The gourd also does all his homework and examinations. In the beginning it was fun:

> As a matter of fact, I've got a good imagination and one thing easily makes me think of another. So I found myself holding a handful of peanuts. The next minute two apples had rolled to my feet. While I was picking them up two toffee apples sprang up from the grass, shining and splendid.
>
> I hastily warned myself: 'That's enough! Don't think of anything else!. . .'[45]

Illustration 6.6

from *The Magic Gourd*

The magic gourd was an externalization of a boy's fancies, but in the story the gourd also has a distinct personality of its own: efficient, logical, self-righteous and sometimes querulous. Wang Bao eventually discovers that the magic gourd has stolen all the things Wang has been given. He finds himself isolated from his friends, telling lies, and eventually avoiding people. The secret of the gourd is in not telling anyone about it, but after many difficulties, Wang Bao tells his teacher and his father and becomes an ordinary boy again. In line with the then current campaign against superstition, Zhang Tianyi took the magic out of magic because, according to a critique by Yuan Ying, the gourd deprived Wang Bao 'of something more important than its gifts—the satisfaction a child of new China finds in community life and working with his friends. . . true happiness lies in study and hard work.'[46]

In one sense, Zhang Tianyi's story put forward an interpretation of magic and fairytales that was increasingly common in the late fifties. At that time a slogan was coined referring to the social irrelevance of much of children's literature: 'Ancients and animals fill the sky, who remembers the poor workers, peasants and soldiers?' (*Guren dongwu mantian fei, kelian jimo gong, nong, bing*).[47] The argument developed against fairytales, in particular, was that they spread superstition, led to confused thinking, and divorced children from revolutionary struggle and real life. This is a re-working of earlier Confucian criticisms of the form. In *The Magic Gourd*, dreams, imagination and magic cut Wang Bao from his family, friends, school and the true happiness of hard work. In the end, Wang Bao decides never to dream that sort of dream again.

Debates in Children's Literature Between 1957 and 1965

In this period, the debates were one-sided—hardly debates at all—as the Party controlled all state institutions, including the media, the schools, the publishing houses and the very institutions that gave writers their livelihood. Policy initiatives moved from debate and persuasion to open attack. The focus of these attacks within children's literature was on fairytales as a form, and on bourgeois concepts—relics of the May Fourth period—in the educational theories that informed the field.

With the Anti-Rightist Campaign, criticism was directed not only at individual fairytales, such as 'Discernment', but at the ideology underlying the fairytale form. In particular, fairytales and concepts of childhood which had been current in 1956 (and inherited from the May Fourth period) came under challenge. By 1960, the ideas of Chen Bochui, a fairytale writer and historian of children's literature, were singled out as the focus for attack. While his major work was a collection of twenty articles on children's literature published in 1959, *A Brief Discussion of Children's Literature* (*Ertong Wenxue Jianlun*), a shorter version of the text that first appeared in 1956, was published in 1957, and republished in 1958. Of particular importance was a 1956 essay, reprinted as 'A Discussion of Fairytales' ('Shitan "Tonghua"') in the 1959 work.[48]

Chen Bochui explained his views on fairytales in this essay:

> Through fantasy based on real life, they use imaginative or symbolic forms to express the supernatural power of things or phenomena. Although fairytales are imaginary and untrue stories, they are still realistic. Furthermore they must be works which integrate revolutionary realism and revolutionary romanticism.[49]

This last sentence was an addition for the 1959 publication and sat uneasily with the body of Chen's argument. His realism was 'real life' and not revolutionary realism as we have already explained it. Fantasy, in Chen's essay, was the core of the fairytale and the wings that carried children to a beautiful life and a beautiful future. It had little in common with revolutionary romanticism, which served the interests of class struggle. Chen Bochui was accused of placing artistic criteria before political criteria, and of advocating fantasy in the same way that capitalists used it to 'lead people to ignore class struggle and to abandon ideology'.[50] Basically, Chen was reiterating May Fourth and mainstream fifties' views on fairytales and fantasy, views that were labeled 'revisionist' and capitalist after the launching of the Anti-Rightist Campaign that stunted growth of children's literature in these years.

The problem, as Mao Dun stated in 1961, was that there were no clear guidelines as to the styles and themes of fairytales which would 'instil socialist and communist ideas'. He noted the debilitated state of the fairytale in 1960 and its limited range of themes, partly blaming the intense ideological attacks in that year for the demise of the fairytale. In fact, because the fairytale used symbolic settings, as Chen said, it had become a politically subversive tool in the hands of great writers, such as Ye Shengtao and Zhang Tianyi. It was difficult for officialdom to police allegory, even in a China that had outlawed satire. In a regime of revolutionary romanticism, fairytales were therefore proscribed.

The second major attack in 1960, which impacted on fairytales, centered on concepts of childhood and their influence on children's education and literature. Essentially Chen Bochui had argued that there was a 'children's world'. He claimed children were to be distinguished from adults by their levels of knowledge and age. Chen did not claim that children were in any way separated from the rest of society. He stated that the distinctive feature of children's literature, its educational significance, was dependent on writers' knowledge of actual children and the particular age of the intended audience. In short, he accepted the concept of stages in childhood development and a 'child-centered' children's literature.

> A successful writer must stand with children, be able to begin from their point of view, listen with their ears, see with their eyes and, in particular, understand their spirit.[51]

Left-wing critics equated this perspective with the capitalist 'cult of childhood innocence' (*tongxinlun*) and the separation of the world of childhood (*ertong benweilun*), both of which were influential theories in the founding of children's literature in China in the twenties, but had lost some credibility among reformers in the thirties. It was claimed, with considerable justification, that these ideas were similar to Western theories of education which were grounded in child psychology and children's perceived needs (*ertong zhongxinlun*). The most influential Western spokesperson for this view in pre-war China was John Dewey. As we noted in the historical introduction, Dewey had argued for a child-centered education system. It was this 'bourgeois' philosophy that was challenged in China in the early fifties and attacked, through Chen Bochui's work, in 1960. A 'child-centered' education system was seen as the antithesis of children's education based on an analysis of class struggle.[52] In these attacks, Chen Bochui was accused of being a capitalist and of presenting theories that were poisonous to China's socialist society.

Mao Dun, in his review of children's literature a year later, stated that one of the factors leading to a literature where 'politics was in command, where the artistry lacked vigor, the plots were stereotyped, the characters were abstractions and the language was dull',[53] was precisely this official refusal to recognize the special features of children's literature: the audience with its differing age groups and needs. Without this recognition, he wrote, writers reduced adolescents to miniature adults and children to miniature adolescents. In short, children were treated as 'little adults', which was Lu Xun and Zhou Zuoren's criticism of Confucian children's books at the beginning of the century.

Children's Literature from 1966 to 1976

The eruption of the Great Proletarian Cultural Revolution in November 1965 convulsed all of China over the next decade. At the outset, libraries and schools were closed down and the institutions governing children's literature were 'smashed'. Party headquarters were 'bombarded' by Red Guards, bands of youth who roamed China to 'make revolution'. Children were urged to 'follow Chairman Mao's instruction and "go out and face the world and brave the storm", tempering themselves and transforming themselves in the mighty storm of class struggle'.[54] Children's education as 'revolutionary successors' was to come from experience, not literature.

The intense political and ideological struggles in the Great Proletarian Cultural Revolution resonated powerfully through policy statements on children's education. At issue, according to the Maoists, was the very future of the Chinese revolution. Which group in the 'two-line struggle' between socialists and capitalists, revolutionaries and reactionaries, the proletariat and the bourgeoisie, would control children's upbringing and therefore control China's future?

What kind of successors should we bring up our younger generation to be? We want to bring up successors to the cause of the proletarian revolution while the bourgeoisie wants to bring up their own successors.[55]

To bring up successors to the proletarian revolution required stern controls over children's education to prevent them walking the 'vile road' of 'counter-revolutionary restoration'.

We should have a firm grip on (children's) education and strict control over children. We should never indulge or dote on our children. Whenever they make a mistake or have any shortcoming, they must be criticized and corrected. This is real protection and love. If we pamper our children and let them do bad things, they will be led onto a vile road and will turn into one of the evil roots of counter-revolutionary restoration.[56]

Ideological control of existing children's literature was managed by simply banning it in the interests of revolutionary education. The previous seventeen years of almost all literature and art—including that for children—were labeled 'revisionist', almost all the major writers and literary bureaucrats were purged, and most works were declared 'black' and taken off the shelves.

As stated in the previous chapter, the model for all new literature and art was the revolutionary model operas produced under the guidance of Mao's wife, Jiang Qing. These epitomized 'revolutionary realism and revolutionary romanticism' and espoused heroic models according to rules that emphasized revolutionary heroes and heroines amongst all characters. A separate literature for children virtually ceased to exist. In 1975 American feminist Roxanne Witke asked Jiang Qing, as the leader of revolutionary culture, about the lack of any children's culture in China. 'Would children continue to be made to perform and thus conform to the standards of the revolutionary operas created for and by adults or would another order be created expressly for them?' Jiang Qing's reply showed a total disinterest in the question: 'We have not taken enough initiative. . . but much has been done already by the masses on their own initiative.' As Witke added wryly, 'What that was remained a mystery'.[57] Diény had said much the same thing when he commented that, in China of the time, children were treated as adults and adults as children. This stance effectively rejected the very basis for the founding of a modern children's literature.

The result was the decimation of children's literature as a field. In 1978, two years after Mao's death, the *People's Daily* published a second major editorial looking at the state of children's literature. In 1977, 192 titles, not just in children's literature, were published in 26,530,000 copies for 200 million literate children. This meant that even if every child had equal access there would be just one book for every thirteen children,[58] further deterioration of a field already acknowledged as impoverished in 1955. Commentator Chen Zijun deplored this literary poverty as the 'four two's': twenty writers and two hundred editors produced two hundred books for two hundred million children; as he saw it, 'a situation too dreadful to contemplate in a large socialist country of 960 million people'.[59]

Major Works in Children's Literature (1966–1976)

The small amount of children's literature produced during the Cultural Revolution was generally stern, militant and overtly political in its content. Reviews and discussions of children's literature were rare, as revolutionary literature was considered much less important than 'making revolution'.[60] Literature at this time was incidental reinforcement rather than incentive or instruction in 'revolution'. A survey of the works produced in this period shows that the virtues to be inculcated in children were usually, but not always, the combatant qualities required in revolutionary struggle: bravery and resoluteness to the point of martyrdom, as in *Liu Wenxue*. In 1980, Yang Qin summed it up:

> We cannot say that children's literature in this period was not very good, just that there was very little of it. Even the relatively good works tended towards stereotypes and narrow themes. It is not even worth mentioning theory.[61]

Several children's works from this period, however, did win second prizes for literature and art in the post-Mao awards (1954-79). Some were films for children. Very few films were produced during the years of the Cultural Revolution and because of the cost of film production and the fact that all film studios were state-run enterprises in this period, the films made for children were those considered officially to be the best works, those exemplifying the revolutionary spirit required of model heroes. Filming of *Sparkling Red Star*, originally a story by Li Xintian, continued the earlier practice of filming outstanding written works for children—such as *Feather Letter*, *Sanmao* and *Little Soldier Zhang Ka*—for wide-spread national dissemination. This practice was particularly appropriate for rural China where books were scarce and many children were illiterate. If a village had no cinema, the audience sat on their folding chairs in the fields to watch these movies.

Works for children selected for discussion in this section are those that were considered excellent by critics in both the Cultural Revolution period and in the post-Mao awards. Two works stand at the forefront: *Sparkling Red Star* and 'The Chirruping Grasshopper' (Table 6.6).

The film, *Sparkling Red Star,* is discussed here as typical of Cultural Revolution films and stories for children. The only publication I have found that reviewed works for children and was published within the Cultural Revolution period (a time when I lived in Beijing and had access to all publications) devoted 60 of its 110 pages to discussing this film. It was hailed as a triumph of Chairman Mao's 'proletarian line on literature and art'.

> The creation of the color film, *Sparkling Red Star,* is a test of our study of model revolutionary operas. Its birth is the fruit of the Party's intimate care and constant support; it is a revolutionary product of the operas' ascent to the screen and stimulation of the art of film. In a word, it was created through studying and tempering under the brilliance of Chairman Mao's proletarian line on literature and art.[62]

Table 6.6 Selected Prize-winning Works (Second Class) in Children's Literature (1966–76)

Author/Director	Title	Form
Directors: Li Jun, Wang Ping and Li Ang	*Sparkling Red Star* (*Shanshan de Hongxing*)	Film based on the story by Li Xintian
Hao Ran	'The Chirruping Grasshopper' ('Laduzi Guoguo')	Story

Li Xintian's story was in the tradition of *Feather Letter* and *Little Soldier Zhang Ka*. It followed the life of a boy, Dongzi, in the years 1931–37 when the Communist Party was forced underground. His father fought with the Communist guerrilla forces and his mother burned herself alive rather than capitulate to the enemy and betray the peasants. Dongzi wails stoically, 'Mummy is a Party member and cannot let the masses suffer— that's what she said'.[63] Dongzi is cared for by the peasants and, through his struggles and resourcefulness, he grows from a member of the Children's Corps to become a Red Army soldier. He is a typical hero for Chinese children. The plot is both compelling and exciting, as is the case in the best of these revolutionary adventure stories. I showed the film (with subtitles) to primary school children in Australia in 1978. This audience of Western children sat enthralled throughout and then went outside to play 'Little Red Soldiers' in the playground. Ideology and entertainment merged in this film.

While all of literature's revolutionary heroes were based on those from the operas, the short stories for children by Hao Ran returned to fifties' themes and characterization, with an added dollop of May Fourth pastoral bliss. The main characters were often 'middle characters'. Hao Ran was said to be the major, if not the only, fiction writer for adults or children in this period. His books for adults have long, complicated plots about agricultural collectivization. His stories for children present mostly idyllic rural scenes with 'apple-cheeked' girls, a boy 'skipping out of the door like a lamb that has been locked in the fold all night',[64] and laughs of happiness.

Hao Ran's stories differ significantly from those of the May Fourth period. Hao Ran's children's tales describe an idyllic, rural life in China of the time. When May Fourth children's literature propagated a pastoral idyll, it was to present a dream in contrast to the bleakness of their own society at that time. It was a dream for the future. In Hao Ran's stories, the dream is realized.

In 'The Chirruping Grasshopper', young Er Wang sees his friend's fat grasshopper and wants one for himself. His older brother, Da Wang, promises to catch one for him but is overtaken by more urgent tasks for the commune. Er Wang decides to catch one himself.

> The sound of grasshoppers shrilling came from all over the field. But they were all in hiding and Er Wang could not see even one. Wherever he went they would suddenly fall silent. As soon as he was gone they would start up again. Wherever the chirruping was, there Er Wang would turn over the beanstalks, pile after pile, but he could not find a single grasshopper. He was still at it, very excited, throwing himself onto the piles of beanstalks and combing through each.
>
> Da Wang's joy at finding his lost brother changed to anger when he saw what Er Wang was doing. Dashing up he yelled, 'Who told you to come here?'
>
> Er Wang was startled by this sudden shout from behind. 'Look, Brother, grasshoppers...', he stammered, beaming.
>
> 'Don't talk rubbish!' Da Wang planted his hand on his hips and roared. 'Look at the beans you've trampled and thrown around. You... you...'
>
> 'I'm catching grasshoppers,' said Er Wang, still puzzled. I'm not doing anything to the beans.'[65]

When Er Wang realizes he has trampled the commune's beans he is sorry, and he and Da Wang pick up the beans together. When he arrives home, he finds Da Wang has made a cage, caught a grasshopper and 'how wonderfully that big-bellied grasshopper could sing'.[66] The lesson about care

Illustration 6.7

from 'The Chirruping Grasshopper'

for the collective is painless, there is no moralizing about catching grasshoppers despite the many previous stories on the subject, there is love and understanding between a small boy and his capable elder brother, and the language is simple and lively (Illustration 6.7). Hao Ran's work is marvelous for its colloquialisms and dialogue. Cyril Birch has noted Hao Ran's assimilation of many of the techniques of the old story-tellers: expert use of dialogue within a predictable plot.[67]

Hao Ran also wrote about children's literature, repeating many of the Party cliches, such as that revolutionary literature 'occupied the camp of ideology and culture to nurture and bring up revolutionary successors'.[68] But when asked about writing for children during an interview with him at Beijing University in 1975, Hao Ran expressed naive surprise, answering simply: 'I just know lots of children and I tell them stories'.

Thus, despite all the rhetoric, the model writer of fiction for all audiences in China of this period ignored overt preaching, revolutionary propaganda, and model heroes in writing his children's stories. His works resurrected fifties' stories on children's work and play, even including the fighting crickets, but without the moral message that play was bad and work was good. An adult world does not impinge on Er Wang's world of chirruping grasshoppers.

While the above works were prize-winners in the children's literature produced in the Cultural Revolution period, as judged from a post-Mao perspective, they exclude, as a sample, the songs and poems that were a major literary form at that time. Diény's survey of children's literature published between 1964 and 1965, for instance, included songs as a major literary form for children. To demonstrate the range of themes and styles in this form, we will consider two representative examples from *The Anthology of Children's Poems 1949-79* (*1949-79 Ertong Wenxue Shi Xuan*).

The first example is a song, 'Collecting Conches' (1973).

> At low tide
> Collecting conches,
> One for you,
> One for me
> Not beautiful but big ones.
> The Young Pioneers are oh so happy.
> Why
> Choose big ones?
> For bugles

To play war songs.
Patrolling the island's beaches,
We don't miss a blade of grass, a single tree. . .[69]

The second example is the first verse of Part 10 of a very long poem about Liu Hulan, a revolutionary martyr. Its style is reminiscent of *Liu Wenxue* in the previous period. It was published in 1974.

> Hulan had packed and just gone out,
> When enemies into the village swarmed,
> Red eyed, mad, man-eating dogs,
> Lunging, grabbing people round about.[70]

Here, as with the prize-winning literature already discussed, we see that much of the literature for children was imbued with the militant ideology of the Cultural Revolution. Surprisingly, this was balanced by Hao Ran's work describing rural bliss.

Debates in Children's Literature Between 1966 and 1976

There were really no debates *within* the field of children's literature in this period, as Yang Qin noted. As he said, there was no literary theory of the field. Policy outlined in the introduction to this section—particularly educational policy—dominated children's literature. This policy was imposed, not debated.

Commentary on children's literature produced during the Cultural Revolution came from the early post-Mao reassessment of the field. Most commentary focussed on the educational theories that informed it. Critics blamed Maoist educational practices for the sorry state of children's literature and children's education. For example, the playwright, Liu Houming, lamented the lack of an education 'in emotion and feeling':

> Some students have openly said, 'Relations between people are just like those between wolves'. Ten years of catastrophe [during the Cultural Revolution] have sown seeds of 'hate' and 'struggle' in children's hearts and so they do not believe that beautiful feelings can exist between people. Our duty as writers is to nurture children in happy feelings.[71]

Mao Dun blamed the narrow educational philosophy deployed in children's literature throughout the thirty years of the People's Republic. In 1961, he had called the current crop of children's works the 'force-feeding method of education'.[72] In 1978, Mao Dun was just as direct.

> After Liberation, those involved in children's literature paid particular importance to a work's educational significance but this so-called 'educational significance' was interpreted very narrowly and equated with politics so that it was felt that there was very little to write about.
> This really is getting caught in one's own web.[73]

In the immediate post-Mao period, the Cultural Revolution was condemned roundly. Those who spent their childhood caught in its grip were called 'the lost generation' as they had been denied a sound, conventional education. But at that time in China, the Cultural Revolution had its own logic and considerable attraction. Our survey of children's literature in this chapter offers an indication of one of its attractions to children. The Cultural Revolution offered them adventure. Life for children as part of the vanguard, actually *making* the revolution, was more exciting than the stifling embrace of earlier state policies that regulated children's thoughts and behavior.

A strong current of paternalism—benign or strident—ran through literary and artistic works for children from 1949. There was little humor or fun. Moral overseers circumscribed the lives of the young. Children were exhorted to be 'good' revolutionary successors. They were told for decades that they were the 'future' of China and asked to sacrifice themselves for that distant future. Then Mao Zedong in the Cultural Revolution destroyed the institutions that governed their lives, told them that they owned not just the future, but also the present, and unleashed them to make revolution. Red Guard enthusiasm in the first few years was not contrived but understandably genuine. In one sense, revolutionary action was an escape from the tedium of revolutionary literature and the world it represented. In fact, children's literature was simply unimportant in this period.

Conclusion

It is impossible to understand children's literature in Mao Zedong's People's Republic outside the policy context that governed its production. These policies were steeped in Party politics, emerging out of factional power struggles and the commitment to ideological transformation that lay at the heart of the Communist Party platform. As a state enterprise after 1949, production of children's literature was subject to policy shifts and nationwide political campaigns that frequently sought to rid the field of specific aspects that were unacceptable to those who held sway in the Party at any particular period. Yet the field was not uncontested.

The principal contest in the field was between revolutionary literature, in its various guises, and both traditional and May Fourth literature. Traditional literature was labeled as 'feudal' and May Fourth literature was labeled as 'bourgeois'. Both were considered reactionary within the governing Maoist framework and under official fiat were ultimately purged from the field. In retrospect, it is clear that the short-term victor was a narrow version of the school of revolutionary children's literature.

Our surveys of literary works for children over the three periods of the Mao era show that much was purged and very little in terms of new forms or genres was developed in children's literature. This was consistent with the uneven pattern of development in other areas of the arts, as well as with the erratic political machinations of the Communist Party leadership.

In the first period to 1957, when compared to children's literature before Liberation, 'old' feudal literature had been selectively re-invented for children, through folktales, picture books and animation. Literature with a social purpose remained but it was domesticated into stories of 'good' children. No new, outstanding works celebrated heroic, militant action, although earlier works in this vein were reprinted. Literature in the May Fourth style, with its emphasis on self-discovery and fantasy, also remained, but—with the exception of 'At the Seaside' and Gao Shiqi's poems—this style was diluted into animal stories or diverted into folktales. Pastoral romanticism had disappeared. Satire of contemporary society was clearly prohibited. In the prewar period, satire had given stories like Ye Shengtao's fairytales or Zhang Tianyi's rollicking fantasy, *Big Lin and Little Lin*, their bite, their edge, their black humor. In the new People's Republic of China, the debates and then attacks on the satirical fairytale, 'Discernment', enforced the dictum Mao had delivered in the Yan'an 'Talks': satirical literature about communist society would not be tolerated.

In the second period from mid-1957–65, the fairytale was further debilitated and Maoists attacked the very basis of pre-Communist children's literature of the May Fourth school: recognition of a 'children's world' and children as a distinctive audience. Traditional literature was suspect unless it was a popular form, reworked for children. In the late fifties, folktales abounded but did not win any literary prizes. The only prize-winning work in this category of traditional literature was Wan Laiming's famous animation, *Havoc in Heaven*, adapted from the classic novel, *Journey to the West*. As we saw in the previous chapter, this novel was politically sanctioned at the very top, as Mao Zedong himself had declared Monkey a 'wonder-worker'. The only new genre was stories celebrating revolutionary martyrs, and revolutionary adventure stories re-emerged for older children. However, the dominance of the revolutionary school of children's literature was achieved at the expense of variety, quality and entertainment. Mao Dun pronounced this literature as stereotyped, simplified and dull.

In the third period, the decade of the Cultural Revolution from 1966–76, the rhetoric of revolutionary children's literature and education dominated all public discourse. In practice, there was very little literature for children. What was published complied with the political dictates of class struggle and proletarian literature. However, in an oddly ironic twist, the only 'model' writer of the time returned to the apolitical pastoral bliss of children's daily life in the countryside. Throughout the People's Republic, therefore, the rhetoric *about* children's literature never quite matched the actual practice *of* children's literature.

The triumph of the revolutionary school of children's literature was hollow and short-lived. Post-Mao assessment of the field rehabilitated writers and works purged in the Cultural Revolution. The return of theory reinstated concepts from the fifties and the May Fourth period. Literary awards honored writers, like Ye Shengtao and Bing Xin, whose work extended back to the earliest beginnings of a modern Chinese children's literature. Indeed, the post-Mao critique of the field established that children's literature in the People's Republic of China cannot be properly understood outside its foundations before 1949. The literature after 1949 clearly had its roots in pre-Liberation China.

Notes

1. Glendon, M.A., Gordon, M.W., and Osakwe, C., *Comparative Legal Traditions*, (St. Paul, Minn., 1985), p. 715.
2. Chen Zijun, 'Quanguo Shaonian Ertong Wenyi Chuangzuo Pingjiang Yougan', op. cit., p. 20.
3. Yan Wenjing, 'Xu', *Ertong Wenxue Xuan*, January 1954–December 1955 (Beijing, 1956) p. 1.
4. Editorial reprinted in Chen Zijun, 'Quanguo Shaonian Ertong Wenyi Chuangzuo Pingjiang Yougan', op. cit., p. 21.
5. Yang Li, 'Ertong Wenxue Zatan', *Wenyibao*, Nos 65–6 (1952), p. 28.
6. Ibid., p. 28.
7. Ibid., p. 77.
8. Jiang Feng, *Zhongguo Ertong Wenxue Jianghua*, op. cit., p. 74.
9. Ren Dalin, 'Xishuai', *Xishuai* (Beijing, 1979). Translated in *Chinese Literature*, No 1 (1957).
10. Gao Xiangzhen, 'Xiao Pang he Xiao Song', Zhongguo Zuojia Xiehui (ed.), *Ertong Wenxue Xuan*, January 1954–December 1955 (Beijing, 1956).
11. Ke Yan, '"Xiaobing" de Gushi', in Zhongguo Zuojia Xiehui (ed.), *1956 Ertong Wenxue Xuan* (Beijing, 1958), p. 394.
12. Xiao Ping, 'Haibin de Haizi', in Zhongguo Zuojia Xiehui (ed.), *Ertong Wenxue Xuan*, January 1954–December 1955, op. cit., p. 164.
13. Bing Xin, 'Xiao Judeng', *Xiao Judeng* (Beijing, 1957).
14. Hu Qi, *Wucai Lu* (Beijing, 1957), p. 158.
15. For more on his life see Ye Yonglie, *Gao Shiqi Yeye* (Shanghai, 1979).
16. Gao Shiqi, 'Juner de Zizhuan', *Zhongxuesheng*, No. 62 (1936).
17. Gao Shiqi, 'Taiyang de Gongzuo', in Zhongguo Zuojia Xiehui (ed.), *Ertong Wenxue Xuan*, January 1954–December 1955, op. cit., p. 373.
18. Gao Shiqi, 'Shijian Bobo', Zhongguo Zuojia Xiehui (ed.), *Ertong Wenxue Xuan*, January 1954–December 1955, op. cit., p. 370.

19.   Gao Shiqi, Women de Turang Mama', in Zheng Wenguang (ed.), *1949–1979 Kexue Wenyi Zuopin Xuan,* Shang (Beijing, 1980), p. 492.

20.   Qin Zhaoyang, 'The 10,000 Li Flight of Two Little Swallows', translated by Hu Mengxiong in Modern Chinese Authors, *The Magic Flute and Other Children's Stories* (Beijing, 1958), p. 45.

21.   Ge Cuilin, 'The Wild Grapes', in Modern Chinese Authors, *The Magic Flute and Other Children's Stories,* op. cit.

22.   Hong Xuntao, 'Ma Liang and His Magic Brush', in Modern Chinese Authors, *The Magic Flute and Other Children's Stories,* op. cit.

23.   Ruan Yuanjing, 'Jinse de Hailuo', Zhongguo Zuojia Xiehui (ed.), *Ertong Wenxue Xuan,* January 1954–December 1955, op. cit., p. 385.

24.   Ibid., p. 402.

25.   He Yi, 'Jiu "Jinse de Hailuo" Tantan Jige Tonghua de Teshu Wenti', in Changjiang Wenyi Chubanshe (ed.), *Ertong Wenxue Lunwen Xuan* (Wuhan, 1956).

26.   Yuan Ying, 'Zhengqu Shaonian Ertong Wenxue Chuangzuo de Fanrong', in *Zhongguo Qingnian Wenxue Chuangzuohe Huiyi Baogao, Fayanji* (Beijing, 1956), p. 207.

27.   Ou Yangshan, 'Huiyan', *Zuopin,* No. 1 (1956).

28.   Chen Shanwen, 'Guanyu Tonghua "Huiyan" de Yixie Wenti', *Zuopin,* No. 9 (1956), p. 55.

29.   Chen Bochui, *Ertong Wenxue Jianlun,* (Wuhan, 1959), pp. 127–8.

30.   Hsu Kai-yu and Wang Tin, *Literature of the People's Republic of China,* (Bloomington, 1980), p. 59.

31.   'Take Another Step Forward in Work to Foster and Educate the New Generation', Editorial, *Renmin Ribao* (1 June 1959), translated in *Survey of the Chinese Mainland Press,* No. 2028 (1959), p. 7.

32.   'Foster Communist Heirs with Better Care', Editorial, *Renmin Ribao,* (1 June 1960), translated in *Survey of the Chinese Mainland Press,* No. 2277 (1960), pp. 3–4.

33.   Mao Dun, '60 Nian Shaonian Ertong Wenxue Mantan', op. cit., p. 498.

34.   Hsu Guangyao, *Little Soldier Chang Ka-tse* (Peking, 1974).

35.   Yan Yiyan, *Xiao Maguan he 'Dapixue' Shushu* (Beijing, 1959).

36.   Yuan Jing, *The Story of Little Black Horse* (Peking, 1979), pp. 1, 202.

37.   Liu Houming, 'Du Xiaoheima de Gushi', *Renmin Wenxue,* No. 6 (1962), p. 80.

38.   Yuan Ying, 'Liu Wenxue', Yuan Ying et al. (eds), *Ertong Wenxue,* in *Shixuan,* Shang (Beijing, 1978), p. 238.

39.   He Yi, *Liu Wenxue* (Shanghai, 1965), p. 238.

40.   Mao Dun, '60 Nian Shaonian Ertong Wenxue Mantan', op. cit., p. 497.

41.   Diény, J. P., *Le Monde est à Vous,* op. cit., p. 89.

42.   Ibid., p. 93.

43.   Ibid., p. 94.

44.   Zhang Tianyi, 'Bao Hulu de Mimi', in *Gei Haizimen* (Beijing, 1979), p. 6.

45.   Ibid., p. 40.

46.   Yuan Ying, 'On Zhang Tianyi', *Chinese Literature,* No. 6 (1959), p. 139.

47.   Chen Zijun, 'Quanguo Shaonian Ertong Wenyi Chuangzuo Pingjiang You Gan', op. cit., p. 23.

48.   Chen Bochui, 'Houji', in *Ertong Wenxue Jianlun* (Wuhan, 1959), p. 301. See also Chen Bochui, 'Shitan "Tonghua"', *Ertong Wenxue Jianlun* (Wuhan, 1958), pp. 22–37.

49. Ibid., pp. 58–9.

50. He Si, 'Shenmeyang de Chibang, Wang Nar Fei?', *Renmin Wenxue*, No. 6 (1960), pp. 124, 128.

51. Chen Bochui, *Ertong Wenxue Jianlun*, op cit., p. 22.

52. He Li, 'Ertong Tedian yu "Tongxinlun"', in Yang Qin et al., *Ertong Wenxue Lunwen Xuan*, op. cit., pp. 115–6.

53. Mao Dun, '60 Nian Shaonian Ertong Wenxue Mantan', op. cit., p. 497.

54. 'Use Mao Tse-tung's Thought to Educate Children to Become Proletarian Revolutionaries', Editorial, *Chieh-fang Rih-pao* (*Jiefang Ribao*), translated in *Survey of the Chinese Mainland Press*, No. 3961 (1967), p. 24.

55. 'Actively Guide Teenagers and Children to Receive Tempering and Grow Up in the Great Proletarian Cultural Revolution', Editorial, *Kuang-min Jih-pao* (*Guangming Ribao*), translated in *Survey of the Chinese Mainland Press*, No. 3720 (1966), p. 15.

56. 'Use Mao Tse-tung's Thought to Educate Children to Become Proletarian Revolutionaries', op. cit., p. 25.

57. Witke, R., *Comrade Chiang Ch'ing* (Boston, Toronto, 1977).

58. 'Nuli Zuohao Shaonian Ertong Duwu de Chuangzuo he Chuban Gongzuo', *Renmin Ribao*, 18 November 1978, p. 1. Reprinted in Yang Qin et al., (eds), *Ertong Wenxue Lunwen Xuan*, op. cit., p. 14.

59. Chen Zijun, 'Quanguo Shaonian Ertong Wenyi Chuangzuo Pingjiang Yougan', op. cit., p. 21.

60. The author studied in China between January 1974 and June 1976 and collected all relevant materials available in newspapers and book stores around Beijing.

61. Yang Qin, 'Xuyan', in Yang Qin et al. (eds), *Ertong Wenxue Lunwen Xuan*, op. cit., p. 8.

62. 81 Dianying Zhipianchang Shanshan de Hongxing Chuangzuo zu Yingzhizu, 'Zai Yinmushang wei Wuchanjieji Zhengguang', in Tianjin Renmin Chubanshe (ed.), *Yao Tichang Wei Haizimen Chuangzuo* (Tianjin, 1975), p. 62.

63. Lan Wenlong, 'Tongguo Dianxinghua de Tujing Suzao Wuchanjieji Yingxiong Dianxing', in Tianjin Renmin Chubanshe (ed.), *Yao Tichang Wei Haizimen Chuangzuo* (Tianjin, 1975), p. 84.

64. Hao Ran, 'The Chirruping Grasshopper', in *The Call of the Fledgling and Other Children's Stories* (Peking, 1974), p. 1.

65. Ibid., pp. 12–13.

66. Ibid., p. 16.

67. Goldman, M. (ed.), *Modern Chinese Literature in the May Fourth Era*, op. cit., p. 399.

68. Hao Ran, 'Women yao Nuli wei Haizimen Chuangzuo', in Renmin Chubanshe (ed.), *Yao Tichang Wei Haizimen Chuangzuo* (Tianjin, 1975), p. 7.

69. Liu Meng, 'Jian Hailuo', in Yuan Ying et al. (eds), *1949-1979 Ertong Wenxue Shi Xuan*, op. cit., p. 456.

70. Li Xuebie, 'Liu Hulan de Songge', in Yuan Ying et al. (eds), op. cit., p. 456.

71. Gao Hongbao, 'Wei Shaonian Ertong Tigong Gengduo Genghao de Jingsheng Shiliao', *Wenyibao*, No. 10 (1981), p. 3.

72. Ibid., p. 487.

73. Mao Dun, 'Zhongguo Ertong Wenxue shi Dayou Xiwangde', Yang Qin et al. (eds), *Ertong Wenxue Lunwen Xuan*, op. cit., p. 20.

7

The Post-Mao Canon

Across the twentieth century, children's literature in China developed its own infrastructure, writers, works and vast readership. In Mao's China, a quarter century of Communist rule challenged the very concept of a children's literature that evolved so painfully in the previous decades. By the time of Mao's death, most of the literary works that had marked the history of this literature were purged. It was only after Mao's death that critics were able to reconstruct the field, unfolding continuities, affirming contested forms, such as the fairytale, and honoring major writers and their works with national awards (Table 6.2).

These writers and their works are at the core of a modern canon of children's literature in China. The term 'canon' is ambiguous, though as stated in the introduction, in literature, a canon refers variously to major authors, a list of major works, or fundamental principles that govern literary criticism and judgement. An authoritative list of major writers and works develops 'by a cumulative consensus' over time.[1] In China, the foundation of the story of modern children's literature is the replacement of the centuries-old Confucian canon by a modern literary canon for children.

The formation of this literary canon is part of the big picture of Chinese history in the twentieth century. Reformers struggled to develop a children's literature through imperialism, war, revolution, isolation and China's emergence as a powerful state in the global community. This struggle has given the canon of children's literature its historical contours, its political color and its literary forms. Indeed, the history of this canon resonates loudly with the twentieth-century political history of the nation.

The Canon: Its Historical Development

The canon of modern Chinese children's literature is steeped in China's nation-building efforts this century. A concern with China's strength as a nation echoes throughout the literature and its guiding theories. Major writers have frequently displayed an explicit sociopolitical purpose, and often a tangible enemy, in their works. Themes of revolution, modernization and transformation—of self, of society and of the Chinese nation—dominate the major works in the field. Indeed, children's literature itself was a response to China's humiliations in the early twentieth century.

The genesis of modern children's literature in China was the aftermath of World War I when China's weakness as a nation was highlighted by the Versailles Treaty. Under the direction of victor nations, the Treaty ignored China as an ally and ceded Chinese territory (Taiwan) to Japan. Chinese reformers recognized China's international insignificance in this act. Building on earlier efforts at national reform, they sought to modernize China throughout the May Fourth period, named after public demonstrations on May 4, 1919 against the Treaty decision. This movement became part of a literary renaissance that spawned a children's literature to help 'save' China and build a new society. Children's literature flourished. Lu Xun, China's foremost modern writer, was the spokesperson for children's literature in the May Fourth period and is now recognized as the founding father of the field. Many of the canonical authors—the older generation—began writing for children and adults as separate audiences at this time. These writers of literature specifically for children had a grand purpose: to transform China.

Aspects of the new children's literature were reshaped and redirected by Marxists as part of the 'cultural front' in the armed struggle for national liberation. Mao Zedong advocated and enforced a revolutionary, popular literature to mobilize China's masses and, in his words, 'push history forward'.[2] This stream, with its own stable of authors and works, added to May Fourth children's literature and to commercialized children's books that flourished in the cities. With the Communist victory in 1949, Maoist cultural guidelines alone governed children's literature. The alleged 'First Golden Age' of children's literature in the mid-fifties was really a golden age of organization when bureaucratic institutions controlled children's education (including the books children read) to propagate a singular and statist version of Chinese history in which the young were cast as future actors. In the subsequent international isolation of China under Mao, children's literature was cannibalized by a distortion of the educational theories that had nurtured it. These tumultuous times embroiled children's literature—and all of China—in constant change.

After Mao's death, when the entire history of this literature was reassessed, there was sufficient certainty and stability to overview the field. Post-Mao critics endorsed writers who had been considered important throughout the twentieth century until their proscription during the Cultural Revolution. These writers, their works, and the criteria that govern their selection as preeminent, constitute a canon of children's literature in its formative period from Lu Xun to Mao Zedong. The major works are now included in anthologies, institutionalized through the education system, and frequently reprinted.

The post-Mao reassessment made clear that future developments in children's literature would build on this foundation. Famous authors and artists—such as Ye Shengtao, Bing Xin, Zhang Tianyi, Zhang Leping and Wan Laiming—were honored for their contributions to the field in the People's Republic. But as these writers were also involved in the earlier history of children's literature, public recognition of their work also signaled a continuity in children's literature from the May Fourth to the post-Mao periods. It also gave an authoritative endorsement of major works, major themes and major trends in Chinese children's literature beyond the artificial divide of the year 1949 as opening Lu Xun's 'gates of darkness' leading to a sunlit socialist world. Indeed, literature for children in the People's Republic emerged out of pre-1949 literature, and its concerns hearkened back to the earlier period. In this sense, the two national awards that symbolized public recognition of children's writers and writings served an important instrumental function in the formation of this literary canon.

Canon Formation: The Politics of Education

Children's literature in China has been about the politics of education. In all the debates this century, educational theories imported a moral universe which was, in turn, a function of particular ideologies. The politics of children's literature in the period of this study was about the educational, and therefore the ideological, principles that informed the books that children read and, potentially at least, shaped children's values and beliefs. Because competing forces explicitly espoused opposing political ideologies, often in situations of armed conflict, children's literature was highly, if not savagely, politicized.

Lu Xun and many other reformers initially fought for a modern children's literature to combat Confucianism. Within a framework of Social Darwinism, they saw the effects of Confucian education as outmoded, pernicious, and ultimately leading the Chinese race to at least symbolic extinction in any world order. Thus early children's literature was as much about the retrogressive degeneracy of 'old' Chinese society as it was about the evolutionary possibilities of a revitalized China. In Lu Xun's stories, the child usually featured as part of a man-eating Confucian 'civilization'. In his translations and essays on children's literature, however, the child was a potent symbol of China's possible future as a just and modern society. This symbol reverberated throughout the following decades. Chinese children became the future China. Therefore, their literature mattered. It was judged on this basis.

In revolutionary rhetoric, children's beliefs were increasingly grounded only in factional politics which generated shifting policies. Under Mao, the nexus between present and future was pulled intolerably tight. The nexus was fed by educational theories that crudely posited a direct relationship between political belief and revolutionary or counter-revolutionary action. This assessment of the relationship justified the strict state control of children's literature. Primarily, however, this politicized literature was very dull. As Jiwei Ci wrote, the Cultural Revolution offered a 'long and exciting holiday' from routine and repression which, we have suggested, included the corpus of revolutionary children's literature itself. Jiwei Ci argued that the Cultural Revolution therefore satisfied 'a deep psychological need' and functioned like 'wars, carnivals, and witch hunts in other times and places'.[3] But even this 'carnival' was rationalized as an education in revolutionary action.

The post-Mao reassessment of children's literature has criticized Maoist educational practices. These practices have been called 'force-feeding', narrow and wrong. But no-one has really criticized the educational imperative, with its emphasis on children as the future, as the dominant rationale for a children's literature itself. While post-Mao practices have been widened, relaxed and diversified, education through children's literature remains one mode of political control and the main criterion for officially, at least, judging major works.

Concerns about social values among children in the late eighties, for example, led the Party to resurrect one of the most obedient, most contrived, and most ascetic models for children from the sixties: Lei Feng. Exhibitions were held and books on his life were handed out to children at school. While the Communist Party rules China, the politics of education are likely to continue to shape both children's literature and critiques of the field. In short, this study suggests that the broad principles governing canon formation in children's literature from Lu Xun to Mao Zedong are continuing to color children's literature in China after Mao.

The Canon: Privileged Literary Forms and Genres

Our survey of major works in modern literature for children has demonstrated that some forms and genres have been privileged over others in the literary canon. It has been argued that this arose partly from the alignment of certain schools of children's literature with competing political forces. Each school had favored forms and genres that supposedly supported its educational thrust. However, while the distinctive features of these schools have an explanatory role in any history of Chinese children's literature, the schools shared writers and works. They also had loose and shifting boundaries and, in fact, borrowed openly from each other.

Thus, the rhyming form and classical language of *The Three Character Classic* belongs unmistakably to Confucian children's texts. It was adapted for revolutionary purposes in the war period. The fairytale lay at the heart of May Fourth children's literature. It was transformed, by many of the same writers who first introduced it, into a powerfully subversive, early form of revolutionary literature. Realistic adventure stories were prefigured in the emphasis on fiction in the earliest children's literature. Comics were a commercialized form developed originally for children and co-opted into mass revolutionary literature for popularization purposes. An inclusive version of revolutionary literature dominated the field by 1949, partly because its writers had appropriated and reworked the most popular literary forms from other schools. Mao Zedong, in 1938 and 1942, had even claimed Lu Xun—minus his satire—as part of China's revolutionary tradition. The post-Mao pronouncement of a canon was also inclusive; a synthesis that included all the modern literary forms developed before 1949. As we approach the end of the twentieth century, the synthesis incorporates, albeit very marginally so far, the important early contributions of Lu Xun's brother, Zhou Zuoren.

Children's literature after Mao has not necessarily privileged the forms and genres favored in the formative period. The emphasis on the politics of education in children's literature has masked the fact that most of these forms emerged out of industrial publishing techniques. Chinese education had always emphasized the written text. Western-style commercialized publishing and distribution networks, mainly based in Shanghai, were the vehicle for the early flowering of written children's literature and comics through journals and books. This period was probably the First Golden Age of children's literature. Support for the comic book reasserted an emphasis on visuality, traditionally communicated through elite or popular forms such as painting or opera. But comics primarily adapted written works. Film in the period of this study also adapted its themes from written works and its styles from opera. It was a 'word-bound' form.[4] The Communists were able to control production of this literature and art, and who read or saw it, because they controlled the infrastructure.

In the post-Mao period, 'technologicalized visuality'[5] has transformed what Chinese children like to read and watch. Chinese cities and increasingly the Chinese countryside are wired for sound and images. At the same time, much of the communications network has been commercialized, global programs are more and more accessible, and children have become active consumers with their own preferences, not merely a passive audience to be fed a prescribed diet. Technological revolution has changed the children's literature industry at the end of the twentieth century, including favored forms and genres, just as commercialized publishing changed this literature at the beginning of the century. Detailed study of post-Mao children's literature and art will inevitably need to consider the radical changes wrought by global technologies and visual communication.

Conclusion

Dramatic change in the political and technological environments inside China does not dilute the significance of the canon of children's literature formed in the period from Lu Xun to Mao Zedong. The works of canonical writers are constantly reprinted and recirculated. A technologized media adapts old works into new forms, a strategy long recognized by Chinese Marxists. The canon of children's literature is therefore further disseminated just as it is institutionalized in its written and audio-visual forms as part of the post-Mao education system. Children's literature is cumulative and the post-Mao canon includes the corpus of major works published in the period between Lu Xun's first translations in 1903 and Mao Zedong's death in 1976.

Children's literature in this period was about great dreams of a future China. It was constructed in the hope of recreating the nation, with a more egalitarian society and a stronger international position. It was 'read' as shaping imagined futures. It was, thus, explicitly functional. In this sense, the drama of children's literature acts out its own story of China's transformation in the twentieth century.

Notes

1.   Abrams, M.H., *A Glossary of Literary Terms*, op. cit., p. 20; Simpson, J.A., and Weiner, E.S.C., *The Oxford English Dictionary*, Second Edition, Vol II (Oxford, 1989), pp. 338–9.
2.   McDougall, Bonnie S., *Mao Zedong's 'Talks at the Yan'an Conference on Literature and Art': A Translation of the 1943 Text with Commentary*, op. cit., p. 70.
3.   Ci Jiwei, *Dialectic of the Chinese Revolution: From Utopianism to Hedonism* (Stanford, 1994) p. 77.
4.   Leyda, Jay, *Electric Shadows: An Account of Film Audience in China* (Cambridge, Mass., 1972) cited in Chow, Rey, *Primitive Passions: Visuality, Sexuality, Ethnography, and Contemporary Chinese Cinema* (New York, 1995) p. 16.
5. Chow, Rey, *Primitive Passions: Visuality, Sexuality, Ethnography and Contemporary Chinese Cinema*, op. cit., p. 16.

Bibliography

A Ying, *Zhongguo Lianhuantuhua Shihua* (Beijing, 1957).

Abrams, M.H., *A Glossary of Literary Terms*, 5th ed. (New York, 1988).

'Actively Guide Teenagers and Children to Receive Tempering and Grow Up in the Great Proletarian Cultural Revolution', Editorial, *Kuang-min Jih-pao (Guangming Ribao)*. Translated in *Survey of the Chinese Mainland Press*, No. 3720 (1966).

Ai Lu, 'Ertong Duwu Zhong de Jige Wenti', *Wenyibao*, No. 63 (1952).

Anderson, Hans Christian, *Fairytales and Other Stories by Hans Christian Andersen*. Revised in part and newly translated by Craigie, W.A. and J.K. (London, 1914).

Aries P., *Centuries of Childhood*. Translated by B. Baldick (Edinburgh, 1962).

Ba Jin, 'Introduction', in *Changsheng Ta* (Shanghai, 1955).

Benton, G, 'The Yenan "Literary Opposition"', *New Left Review*, No. 88 (1975).

Bi Keguan and Huang Yuanlin, *Zhongguo Manhua Shi* (Beijing, 1986).

Bi Qingyu, 'Zhigen yu Renmin—Tantan Bai Qiuen Zai Zhongguo ji qi Zuozhe', *Lianhuanhuabao*, No. 2 (February 1981).

Bing Xin, *Ji Xiao Duzhe* (Shanghai, 1933).

Bing Xin, 'Zishu', in Yao Nailin (ed.), *Xiandai Zhongguo Wenxue Quanji* (Aomen, 1972).

Bing Xin, 'Xiao Judeng', in *Xiao Judeng* (Beijing, 1957).

Birch, C., 'Change and Continuity in Chinese Fiction', in Goldman, M. (ed.), *Modern Chinese Literature in the May Fourth Era* (Cambridge, 1977).

Bodde, D. (ed.), *A Short History of Chinese Philosophy by Feng Yu-lan* (Toronto, 1948).

Bouskova, M., 'The Stories of Ping Hsin', in Prusek, J. (ed.), *Studies in Modern Chinese Literature* (Berlin, 1964).

The Cathay ('a fortnightly bulletin issued for the guidance and entertainment of guests of Cathay and Metropole Hotels and Cathay Mansions. . . gratis to guests', IV:48 (16 December, 1933).

Cao Xueqin, *The Story of the Stone*, Vol. 1. Translated by D. Hawkes (Harmondsworth, 1973).

Chang, Parris H., 'Children's Literature and Political Socialization', in Hsu, F.K.L. and Chu, Godwin C., *Moving a Mountain: Cultural Change in China* (Honolulu, 1979).

Chang Tien-i, *The Magic Gourd* (Peking, 1979).

Chen Bochui, *Ertong Wenxue Jianlun* (Wuhan, 1958).

Chen Bochui, 'Shitan "Tonghua"', in *Ertong Wenxue Jianlun* (Wuhan, 1958).

Chen Bochui, *Ertong Wenxue Jianlun* (Wuhan, 1959).

Chen Bochui, 'Houji', in *Ertong Wenxue Jianlun* (Wuhan, 1959).

Chen Bochui, *Zuojia yu Ertong Wenxue* (Tianjin, 1957).

Chen Guang, *Danao Tiangong* (Shanghai, 1961).

Chen Shanwen, 'Guanyu Tonghua "Huiyan" de Yixie Wenti', *Zuopin,* No. 9 (1956).

Chen Xiao, 'Jiaqiang dui Xin Lianhuantuhua Bianhui yu Chuban Gongzuo de Sixiang Lingdao', *Wenyibao,* No. 55 (1952).

Chen Xiu, 'Dalu Ertong Wenxue Jinkuang', *Zhangwang,* 265 (1973).

Chen Zijun, 'Quanguo Shaonian Ertong Wenyi Chuangzuo Pingjian Yougan', in Dierci Quanguo Shaonian Ertong Wenyi Chuangzuo Pingjiang Weiyuanhui Bangongshe (ed.), *Ertong Wenxue Zuojia Zuopin Lun* (Peking, 1981).

Chesneaux, J., *China: The People's Republic, 1949–1976.* Translated by P. Auster and L. Davis (Hassocks, 1979).

Chesneaux, J., *The Political and Social Ideas of Jules Verne.* Translated by T. Wikeley (London, 1972).

Chi Cheng, 'New Serial Pictures', *Chinese Literature,* No. 2 (1974).

Chiang Wei-pu, 'Chinese Picture Serial Books', *Chinese Literature,* No. 3 (1959).

Chow, Rey, *Primitive Passions: Visuality, Sexuality, Ethnography and Contemporary Chinese Cinema* (New York, 1995).

Ci, Jiwei, *Dialectic of the Chinese Revolution: From Utopianism to Hedonism* (Stanford, 1994).

Coveney, P., *The Image of Childhood, the Individual and Society: A Study of the Theme in English Literature* (London, 1967).

Croizier, R.C. (ed.), *China's Cultural Legacy and Communism* (New York, 1970).

Croll, E., *Feminism and Socialism in China* (London, 1978).

Darton, F.J.H. (Harvey), *Children's Books in England: Five Centuries of Social Life* (Cambridge, 1958).

Darwin, Charles, *On the Origin of Species* (New York, publication year not recorded).

De Bary, W.T. et al. *Sources of Chinese Tradition,* Vols I and II (New York, 1964).

De la Mare, W., *Lewis Carroll* (London, 1970).

Dewey, J., 'The School and the Life of the Child', in Martin S. Dworkin, *Dewey on Education* (New York, 1959).

Diény, Jean-Pierre, *Le Monde est à Vous: La Chine et les Livres pour Enfants* (Paris, 1971).

Dianying Zhipianchang Shanshan de Hongxing Chuangzuo zu Yingzhizu, 'Zai Yinmushang wei Wuchanjieji Zhengguang', in Tianjin Renmin Chubanshe (ed.), *Yao Tichang Wei Haizimen Chuangzuo* (Tianjin, 1975).

Dierci Quanguo Shaonian Ertong Wenyi Chuangzuo Pingjiang Weiyuanhui Bangongshe (ed.), *Ertong Wenxue Zuojia Zuopin Lun* (Beijing, 1981).

Dujian Shan, adapted from the color film, Dujuan Shan (Beijing, 1975).

Eagleton, T., *Criticism and Ideology: A Study in Marxist Literary Theory* (London, 1978).

Eagleton, T., *Literary Theory: An Introduction* (Oxford, 1983).

Engle, Hualing-Nieh and Engle, Paul (eds and translators), *The Poetry of Mao Tse-tung* (London, 1973).

Ertong Wenxue Gailun Bianxiezu (eds), *Ertong Wenxue Gailun* (Chengdu, 1982).

'Ertong Wenxue Yanjiu' Bianjishe (ed.), *Ertong Wenxue Yanjiu*, Vols I and II (Shanghai, 1959).

Farquhar, M.A., 'Monks and Monkey: 'A Study of "National Style" in Chinese Animation', *Animation Journal*, 1:2, Spring, 1993.

Feng Hsueh-feng, *Fables* (Peking, 1953).

'The Film "An Orphan on the Streets" Abroad', *China's Screen*, No. 1 (1982).

'Finding Out About the Population', *Australia-China Review*, No. 10 (November, 1982).

Fokkema, D., 'Lu Xun: The Impact of Russian Literature', in Goldman, M. (ed.), *Modern Chinese Literature in the May Fourth Era* (Cambridge, Mass., 1977).

'Foster Communist Heirs with Better Care', Editorial, *Renmin Ribao*, 1 June 1960. Translated in *Survey of the Chinese Mainland Press*, No. 2277 (1960).

Franke, W., *A Century of Revolution 1851–1949* (Oxford, 1970).

Gao Hongbao, 'Wei Shaonian Ertong Tigong Gengduo Genghao de Jingshen Shiliao', *Wenyibao*, No. 10 (1981).

Gao Shiqi, 'Shijian Bobo', in Zhongguo Zuojia Xiehui (ed.), *Ertong Wenxue Xuan, January 1954–December 1955* (Beijing, 1956).

Gao Shiqi, 'Taiyang de Gongzuo', in Zhongguo Zuojia Xiehui (ed.), *Ertong Wenxue Xuan, January 1954–December 1955* (Beijing, 1956).

Gao Shiqi, 'Juner de Zizhuan', *Zhongxuesheng*, No. 62 (1936).

Gao Shiqi, 'Women de Turang Mama', in Zheng Wenguang (ed.), *1949–1979 Kexue Wenyi Zuopin Xuan, Shang* (Beijing, 1980).

Gao Xiangzhen, 'Xiao Pang he Xiao Song', in Zhongguo Zuojia Xiehui (ed.), *Ertong Wenxue Xuan, January 1954–December 1955* (Beijing, 1956).

Ge Cuilin, 'The Wild Grapes', in Modern Chinese Authors (eds), *The Magic Flute and Other Children's Stories* (Beijing, 1981).

Giles, H., *San Tzu Ching* (Taipei, 1972).

Glendon, M.A., Gordon, M.W. and Osakwe, C., *Comparative Legal Traditions* (St Paul, Minnesota, 1985).

Goldman, Merle, *Literary Dissent in Communist China* (New York, 1971).

Goldman, Merle (ed.), *Modern Chinese Literature in the May Fourth Era* (Cambridge, Mass. and London, 1977).

Gorky, M., 'How I Learnt to Write', in *On Literature* (Seattle, 1973).

Gorky, M., 'On Themes', in *On Literature* (Seattle, 1973).

Gorky, M., 'To Anton Chekhov', in *On Literature* (Seattle, 1973).

Gorky, M., 'To H.G. Wells' (1916), in *On Literature* (Seattle, 1973).

Gu Yuanqing, 'Jinyibu Fanrong Shaonian Ertong Wenyi Chuangzuo', in Tianjin Renmin Chubanshe (ed.), *Yao Tichang Wei Haizimen Chuangzuo* (Tianjin, 1975).

Guo Moruo, 'Wei Xiao Pengyou Xiezuo, Dierci Quanguo Shaonian Ertong Gongzuo Ganbu Dahuishang de Jianghuade Zhaiyou', *Renmin Ribao,* 1 June 1950.

Guo Moruo, *Shaonian Shidai: Wode Tongnian 1892–1902* (Shanghai, 1953).

Hao Ran, 'The Chirruping Grasshopper', in *The Call of the Fledgling and Other Children's Stories* (Peking, 1974).

Hao Ran, 'Women yao Nuli wei Haizimen Chuangzuo', in Tianjin Renmin Chubanshe (ed.), *Yao Tichang Wei Haizimen Chuangzuo* (Tianjin, 1975).

Hao Ran, *Youmiaoji* (Beijing, 1973).

Haviland, V., 'A New Internationalism', in Haviland, V. (ed.), *Children and Literature: Views and Reviews* (London, 1973).

Haviland, V., *Children's Literature: A Guide to Reference Sources* (Washington, 1966).

Hayward Scott, D., *Chinese Popular Literature and The Child* (Chicago, 1980).

Hazard, Paul, *Books, Children and Men.* Translated by M. Mitchell (Boston, 1963).

He Li, 'Ertong Tedian yu "Tongxinlun"', in Xi Jin et al. (eds), *Ertong Wenxue Lunwen Xuan 1949–1979* (Beijing 1981).

He Qi, 'Ertong Wenxue Chuangzuo de Xin Chengjiu', *Wenyibao*, No. 366 (1980).

He Si, 'Shenmeyang de Chibang, "Wang Nar Fei?"', *Renmin Wenxue*, No. 6 (1960).

He Yi, 'Jiu "Jinse de Hailou" Tantan Jige Tonghua de Teshu Wenti', in Changjiang Wenyi Chubanshe (ed.), *Ertong Wenxue Lunwen Xuan* (Wuhan, 1956).

He Yi, *Liu Wenxue* (Shanghai, 1965).

He Yi, *Tonghuaxuan* (Shanghai, 1978).

He Yi, *Xiaobaihuayuanding Zashuo* (Shanghai, 1979).

Hong Xuntao, 'Ma Liang and His Magic Brush', in Modern Chinese Authors (eds), *The Magic Flute and Other Children's Stories*. Translated by Xu Mengxiong (Beijing, 1981).

Hsia, C.T., *A History of Modern Chinese Fiction* (New Haven and London, 1961).

Hsiao Ping, 'At the Seaside', *Chinese Literature*, No. 1 (1977).

Hsu, F.K.L. and Chu, Godwin, C. (eds), *Moving a Mountain: Cultural Change in China* (Honolulu, 1979).

Hsu Guangyao, *Little Soldier Chang Ka-tse* (Peking, 1974).

Hsu Kai-yu and Wang Tin, *Literature of the People's Republic of China* (Bloomington, 1980).

Hsu Kuang-yao, *Little Soldier Chang Ka-tse* (Peking, 1974).

Hu Congjing, 'Wo Guo Geming Ertong Wenxue Fazhan Shilue (1921–1937)', in *Wenxue Pinglun* (1963).

Hu Qi, *Wucai Lu* (Beijing, 1957).

Hua Guozhang and Liu Dawei (illustrators), *Xiao Qishou* (Huhehot, 1975).

Hua Kuo-chang and Liu Ta-wei (illustrators), *Young Riders on the Grassland* (Peking, 1977).

Hua Sanchuan, *Baimaonu* (Shanghai, 1961).

Hua Shan, *Jimao Xin* (Shanghai, 1972). Translated in *Haiwa the Shepherd Boy* (Peking, 1974).

Huang Zhiqing, *Zhou Zuoren Lunwenji* (Hongkong, 1972).

Isaacs, Harold, *Straw Sandals: Chinese Short Stories 1918–1933* (Cambridge, Mass., 1974).

Jen Ta-lin, 'Crickets', *Chinese Literature*, No. 1 (1977).

Jiang Feng, *Ertong Wenxue Gailun* (Changsha, 1982).

Jiang Feng, *Lu Xun Lun Ertong Jiaoyu he Ertong Wenxue* (Shanghai, 1961).

Jiang Feng, 'Guanyu "Ertong Wenxue"', *Wenxue,* I:6 (February 1935).

Jiang Feng, 'Guanyu Ertong', *Wenxue,* IV:1 (December 1935).

Jiang Feng, *Zhongguo Ertong Wenxue Jianghua* (Nanjing, 1959).

Jiang Feng, 'Guanyu "Ertong Wenxue"', *Zhongxuesheng,* 6:2 (1936).

Johnson, Kinchen, *Folksongs and Children's Songs from Peiping,* Vols I and II (Taipei, 1971).

'Kangzhan Wenyi Zai Bianqu', *Kangzhan Wenyi,* 1:7 (1938).

Keenan, B., *The Dewey Experiment in China: Educational Reform and Political Power in the Early Republic* (Cambridge Mass. and London) 1977.

Kessen, William (ed.), *Childhood in China* (New Haven and London, 1975).

Ke Yan, '"Xiao Bing" de Gushi', in Zhongguo Zuojia Xiehuhui (ed.), *1956 Ertong Wenxue Xuan* (Beijing, 1958).

Koestler, A., *The Sleepwalkers: A History of Man's Changing Vision of the Universe* (New York, 1963).

Kuo Mo-juo, 'Smash the Gang of Four', *Chinese Literature,* No. 1 (1977).

Laing, D., *The Marxist Theory of Art* (Sussex, New Jersey, 1978).

Lang, Andrew, *Literary Fairytales* (London, 1895).

Lang, Olga, *Ba Jin and His Writings* (Cambridge, Mass., 1967).

Lao She, *Bao Chuan* (Beijing, 1979).

Lao She, 'Xin Aimier', *Wenxue: Ertong Wenxue Teji,* VII:I (1936).

Lao Xiang, 'Guanyu Kangri Sanzi Jing', *Kangzhan Wenyi,* 1:7 (1938).

Lavrin, J. (ed.), *Russian Stories: Pushkin to Gorky* (London, 1946).

Lee, Leo Ou-fan, 'Genesis of a Writer', in Goldman, M. (ed.), *Modern Chinese Literature in the May Fourth Era* (Cambridge, 1977).

Lee, Leo Ou-fan (ed.), *The Lyrical and the Epic: Studies of Modern Chinese Literature by Jaroslav Prusek* (Bloomington, 1980).

Lee, Leo Ou-fan, *The Romantic Generation of Modern Chinese Writers* (Cambridge, Mass., 1973).

Leyda, J., *Electric Shadows: An Account of Film Audience in China* (Cambridge, Mass., 1972).

'Lianhuanhuabao de Yijian Xishi', *Lianhuanhuabao*, No. 3 (1981).

Li Keruo, 'Xianming de Duizhao—Ping "Sanmao Jinxi"', *Ertong Wenxue Yanjiu,* No. 1 (1959).

Li Ming and Ling Xiao, 'Lianhuantuhua Gaizao Gongzuo, Shanghai Tongxun', *Wenyibao*, 1:6 (1949).

Li Qun, 'Ping "Dazhongtuhua Chubanshe" de Lianhuantuhua', *Wenyibao*, 384:2 (1951).

Li Subo, 'Bing Xin de *Ji Xiao Duzhe'*, in Li Xitong (ed.), *Bing Xin Lun* (Shanghai, 1932).

Li Xitong (ed.), *Bing Xin Lun* (Shanghai, 1932).

Li Xuebie, 'Liu Hulan de Songge', in Yuan Ying et al. (eds.), *1949–1979 Ertong Wenxue Shi Xuan* (Beijing, 1981).

Lin Ke, 'Cong "Liu Wenxue" Tanqi', *Wenyibao*, No. 10 (1960).

Lin Kehuan, *Baotong* (Beijing, 1978).

Liu Houming, 'Du Xiaoheima de Gushi', *Renmin Wenxue,* No. 6 (1962).

Liu Jiyou, *Dongguo Xiansheng* (Beijing, 1973).

Liu Meng, 'Jian Hailuo', in Yuan Ying et al. (eds.), *1949–1979 Ertong Wenxue Shi Xuan* (Beijing, 1981).

Liu Yu, 'Jiefangqu Diyizhang Ertongbao', *Ertong Wenxue Yanjiu,* 2 (1959).

Liu Zheng, Song Jian et al., *China's Population: Problems and Prospects* (Beijing, 1981).

Lu Bing, 'Duhua Zagan', in "Ertong Wenxue Yanjiu" Bianjishe (ed.), *Ertong Wenxue Yanjiu,* Vol. 1 (Shanghai, 1959).

Lu Bing and Chen Qiucao (illustrators), *Little Tadpoles Look for their Mother* (Shanghai, 1980).

Lu Hsun, *A Brief History of Chinese Fiction.* Translated by Yang Hsien-i and Yang, Gladys (Peking, 1976).

Lu Hsun, *Dawn Blossoms Plucked at Dusk.* Translated by Yang Hsien-i and Yang, Gladys (Peking, 1976).

Lu Xun, *Old Tales Retold.* Translated by Yang Hsien-i and Yang, Gladys (Peking, 1972).

Lu Xun, Postscript of 'Chunye de Meng', *Chenbao Fukan*, 22 October 1921.

Lu Xun, *Selected Stories of Lu Xun*. Translated by Yang Hsien-i and Yang, Gladys (Peking, 1972).

Lu Xun, *Silent China*. Translated by Yang, Gladys (London, Oxford, New York, 1973).

Lu Xun, 'Yonggan de Yuehan', in Jiang Feng (ed.), *Lu Xun Lun Ertong Jiaoyu Yu Ertong Wenxue* (Shanghai, 1961).

Lu Xun, *Lu Xun Quanji*, Vols 1–20 (Beijing, 1973).

Lu Xun, 'Guxiang', in *Lu Xun Quanji*, Vol. 1 (Beijing, 1973)

Lu Xun, 'Kuangren Riji', in *Lu Xun Quanji* Vol. 1 (Beijing, 1973).

Lu Xun, 'Moluo shi li shuo', in *Lu Xun Quanji*, Vol. 1 (Beijing, 1973).

Lu Xun, 'Nahan', in *Lu Xun Quanji*, Vol. 1 (Beijing, 1973).

Lu Xun, 'A Zhang yu Shanghai Jing', *Lu Xun Quanji*, Vol. 2 (Beijing, 1973).

Lu Xun, 'Suigan Lu, 25', in *Lu Xun Quanji*, Vol. 2 (Beijing, 1973).

Lu Xun, 'Wushiqi Xiandai de Tushazhe', in *Lu Xun Quanji*, Vol. 2 (Beijing, 1973).

Lu Xun, '"Pengbi" Zhiyu', in *Lu Xun Quanji*, Vol. 3 (Beijing, 1973).

Lu Xun, 'Wusheng de Zhongguo', in *Lu Xun Quanji*, Vol. 4 (Beijing, 1973).

Lu Xun, 'Disanzhong Ren', in *Lu Xun Quanji*, Vol. 5 (Beijing, 1973).

Lu Xun, '"Lianhuantuhua" Bianhu', in *Lu Xun Quanji*, Vol. 5 (Beijing, 1973).

Lu Xun, 'Shanghai Ertong', in *Lu Xun Quanji*, Vol. 5 (Beijing, 1973).

Lu Xun, 'Women Xianzai Zenme Zuo Fuqin', in *Lu Xun Quanji*, Vol. 5 (Beijing, 1973).

Lu Xun, 'Kantu Shizi', in *Lu Xun Quanji*, Vol. 6 (Beijing, 1973).

Lu Xun, 'Lianhuantuhua Suotan', in *Lu Xun Quanji*, Vol. 6 (Beijing, 1973).

Lu Xun, 'Lianhuantuhua Xiaotan', in *Lu Xun Quanji*, Vol. 6 (Beijing, 1973).

Lu Xun, 'Ewen Yiben "A Q Zhengzhuan" Xuji Zuozhe Zishu Zhuanlue', in *Lu Xun Quanji,* Vol. 7 (Beijing, 1973).

Lu Xun, 'Meng', in *Lu Xun Quanji,* Vol. 7 (Beijing, 1973).

Lu Xun, 'Ershisi Xiaotu', in *Lu Xun Quanji,* Vol. 11 (Beijing, 1973).

Lu Xun, 'Yuejie Luxing', in *Lu Xun Quanji,* Vol. 11 (Beijing, 1973).

Lu Xun, 'Ailuoxianke Tonghua Ji', in *Lu Xun Quanji,* Vol. 12 (Beijing, 1973).

Lu Xun, 'Chibian', in *Lu Xun Quanji,* Vol. 12 (Beijing, 1973).

Lu Xun, 'Diao de Xin', in *Lu Xun Quanji,* Vol. 12 (Beijing, 1973).

Lu Xun, 'Biao: Yizhi de Hua', in *Lu Xun Quanji,* Vol. 14 (Beijing, 1973).

Lu Xun, 'Eluosi de Tonghua', in *Lu Xun Quanji,* Vol. 14 (Beijing, 1973).

Lu Xun, 'Xiao Bide', in *Lu Xun Quanji,* Vol. 14 (Beijing, 1973).

Lu Xun, 'Xiao Yuehan', in *Lu Xun Quanji,* Vol. 14 (Beijing, 1973).

Lun yu, *The Analects of Confucius,* XVIII, 6. Translated and annotated by Waley, A. (London, 1949).

Mackerras, C., 'The Taming of the Shrew: Chinese Theatre and Social Change Since Mao', *Australian Journal of Chinese Affairs,* No. 1 (1979).

Mao Dun, 'Zhongguo Ertong Wenxue shi Dayou Xiwangde', in Yang Qin et al. (eds.), *Ertong Wenxue Lunwen Xuan* (Beijing, 1980).

Mao Dun, '60 Nian Shaonian Ertong Wenxue Mantan', in *Mao Dun Wenji Pinglun Ji* (Beijing, 1981).

Mao Dun, 'Gei Tamen Kan Shenmo Hao', in *Mao Dun Wenji,* Vol. 9 (Hong Kong, 1966).

Mao Dun, 'Lianhuantuhua Xiaoshuo', in *Mao Dun Wenji,* Vol. 9 (Hong Kong, 1966).

Mao Dun, 'Gaoerji he Zhongguo Wenxue', in *Mao Dun Wenji,* Vol. 10 (Hong Kong, 1966).

Mao Dun, 'Yizhide Yaoqiu he Xiwang', *Wenyibao,* No. 1 (1949).

Mao Tse-tung, 'Talks at a Meeting with Chinese Students and Trainees in Moscow (17 November 1957)'. Translated in *English Quotations from Chairman Mao Tse-tung* (Peking, 1976).

Mao Tse-tung, *Five Documents on Literature and Art* (Peking, 1967).

Mao Tse-tung, *Poems* (Peking, 1976).

Mao Tse-tung, 'On Practice'. Translated in *Selected Works of Mao Tse-tung*, Vol. I (Peking, 1975).

Mao Tse-tung, 'In Memory of Norman Bethune'. Translated in *Selected Works of Mao Tse-tung*, Vol. II (Peking, 1975).

Mao Tse-tung, 'On New Democracy'. Translated in *Selected Works of Mao Tse-tung*, Vol. II (Peking, 1975).

Mao Tse-tung, 'Talks at the Yenan Forum on Literature and Art'. Translated in *Selected Works of Mao Tse-tung*, Vol. III (Peking, 1975).

Mao Tse-tung, 'On the Correct Handling of Contradictions Among the People'. Translated in *Selected Works of Mao Tse-tung*, Vol. V (Peking, 1975).

Mass Criticism Group of Beijing and Qinghua Universities, 'Negating the Revolution in Literature and Art Aims at Restoring Capitalism', *Peking Review*, 22 (28 May 1976), cited in Mackerras, C., *The Performing Arts in Contemporary China* (London, 1981).

McDougall, B.S. *Mao Zedong's Talks at the Yenan Conference on Literature and Art: A Translation of the 1943 Text with Commentary* (Ann Arbor, 1980).

McDougall, B.S. (ed.), *Popular Chinese Literature and Performing Arts in the People's Republic of China 1949–1979* (Berkeley, Los Angeles and London, 1984).

Meizi, 'Duo Duo Chuangzuo Ertong Wenyi Duwu', *Wenyibao*, No. 63 (1952).

Mills, H.C., 'Lu Xun: Literature and Revolution From Mara to Marx', in Goldman, M. (ed.), *Modern Chinese Literature in the May Fourth Period* (Cambridge, Mass. and London, 1977).

Mu Mutian, 'Kangzhan Wenyi Yundong de Judian', *Kangzhan Wenyi*, 1:6 (1938).

Munroe, D., *The Concept of Man in Contemporary China* (Ann Arbor, 1977).

Nebiolo, G. 'Introduction', in Chesneaux, J., *The People's Comic Book: Red Women's Detachment, Hot on the Trail and Other Chinese Comics.* Translated by Endymion Wilkinson (Garden City, N.Y., 1973).

'Nuli Zuohao Shaonian Ertong Duwun de Chuangzuo he Chuban Gongzuo', *Renmin Ribao,* 18 November 1978.

Nunn, R., *Publishing in Mainland China* (Cambridge, Mass., 1966).

O'Dell, F.A., *Socialization Through Children's Literature: The Soviet Example* (Cambridge, 1978).

Opie, Iona and Opie, Peter, *The Classic Fairy Tales* (London and New York, 1974).

Orwell, G., 'Boys Weeklies', in Orwell, S. and Mackay, J. (eds), *The Collected Essays, Journalism and Letters of George Orwell, Vol. 1: An Age Like This 1920–1940* (Harmondsworth, Middlesex, 1970).

Ou Yangshan, 'Huiyan', *Zuopin,* No. 1 (1956).

Pan Yu-ch'un, 'A Reader's Complaint', in Crozier, R. C. (ed.), *China's Cultural Legacy and Communism* (London, 1970).

Pellowski, Anna, *The World of Children's Literature* (New York, London, 1968).

Pickard, P.M., *I Could a Tale Unfold: Violence, Horror and Sensationalism in Stories for Children* (London, 1961).

Pickowicz, P., 'Ch'u Ch'iu-pai and the Chinese Marxist Conception of Revolutionary Popular Literature and Art', *China Quarterly,* 70 (June 1977).

Pickowicz, P., *Marxist Literary Thought in China: The Influence of Ch'u Ch'iu-pai* (Berkeley, Los Angeles and London, 1981).

Ping Lin, 'Nan Tongyao', *Kangzhan Wenyi,* 1:2 (1938).

Population Census Office Under State Council, Department of the State Statistical Bureau, *The 1982 Population Census of China* (Hong Kong, 1982).

Prusek, J., 'Yeh Sheng-t'ao and Anton Chekhov', *Archiv Orientalni,* 38 (1970).

Prusek, J. (ed.), *Studies in Modern Chinese Literature* (Berlin, 1964).

Prusek, J., 'Subjectivism and Individualism in Modern Chinese Literature', *Archiv Orientalni*, 25 (1957).

'Qianyan Lianhuanhua yu Lianhuanhuajia', *Lianhuanhuabao*, No. 7 (1979).

Qin Zhaoyang, 'The 10,000 Li Flight of Two Little Swallows', in Modern Chinese Authors (eds), *The Magic Flute and Other Children's Stories* (Beijing, 1981).

Qu Qiubai, 'The Question of Popular Literature and Art'. Translated by Pickowicz, P., in Berninghausen, J. et al., *Revolutionary Literature in China: An Anthology* (New York, 1976).

Ren Dalin, *Xishuai* (Peking, 1979).

Renmin Ribao, Editorial, 15 June 1948.

Renmin Ribao, Editorial, 9 September 1955.

Renmin Ribao, Editorial, 28 May, 1978.

Ridley, C. P., Godwin, P. H. B. and Doolin, D. J., *The Making of a Model Citizen in Communist China* (Stanford, 1971).

Ruan Yuanjing, 'Jinse de Hailuo', in Zhongguo Zuojia Xiehui (ed.), *Ertong Wenxue Xuan, January 1954–December 1955* (Beijing, 1956).

Schram, S., *Mao Tse-tung: Political Leaders of the Twentieth Century* (Harmondsworth, Middlesex, 1967).

Schurmann, F., *Ideology and Organization in Communist China* (Berkeley and Los Angeles, 1968).

Shen Congwen, 'Lun Bing Xin de Chuangzuo', in Li Xitong (ed.), *Bing Xin Lun* (Shanghai, 1932).

Shen Wu (ed.), *Zhonghua Gushi,* Vols. I-XII (Shanghai, published at various times between 1915 and 1941).

Shen Zhen and Chen Jian, 'Ye Shengtao Xiansheng de "Zide" Zhexue', *Zuopin*, No. 8 (1957).

Simpson, J.A. and Weiner, E.S.C., *The Oxford English Dictionary*, Second Edition, Vol II (Oxford, 1989).

Su Su, *Xiao Jianxi* (Canton, 1947).

Sun Qinyang, *Chunfeng Lailiao* (Shanghai, 1933).

Sun Youjun, *The Adventures of a Little Rag Doll.* Translated by Delia Davin (Beijing, 1980).

'Sun Wukong Sanda Baigu Jing', in Chuangzuo Zu, *Sun Wukong Sanda Baigujing* (Shanghai, 1973).

'Take Another Step Forward in Work to Foster and Educate the New Generation', Editorial, *Renmin Ribao,* 1 June 1959. Translated in *Survey of the Chinese Mainland Press*, No. 2028 (1959).

Tian Haiyan, 'Suqu Ertong Geyao', *Ertong Wenxue Yanjiu*, 1 (1959).

Townsend, J.R., *Written for Children: An Outline of English Language Children's Literature* (Harmondsworth, Middlesex, 1974).

Trimmer, S., 'On the Care which is Requisite in the Choice of Books for Children', in Haviland, V. (ed.), *Children and Literature: Views and Reviews* (London, 1973).

'Use Mao Tse-tung's Thought to Educate Children to Become Proletarian Revolutionaries', Editorial, *Chieh-fang Rih-pao* (*Jiefang Ribao*). Translated in *Survey of the Chinese Mainland Press*, No. 3961 (1967).

van Eeden, F., *Little Johannes*. Translated by Clara Bell (London, 1895).

Verne, J., *Journey to the Center of the Earth* (New York, 1959).

Wagner, R.G., 'Lobby Literature: The Archaeology and Present Functions of Science Fiction in China', in Kinkley, J. C. (ed.), *After Mao: Chinese Literature and Society 1978–1981* (Cambridge, Mass. and London, 1985).

Wang Kelang, 'Chuban Shiye de Puji Wenti', *Wenyibao*, No. 22 (1950).

Wang Linqui, *Baimuji de Gushi* (Beijing, 1955).

Wang Meng, 'Butterfly', *Chinese Literature,* No. 1 (1981).

Wang Shuyuan et al., 'Azalea Mountain', *Chinese Literature,* No. 1 (1974).

Wang Tongzhao, 'Xiao Hong Denglong de Meng', *Wenxue: Ertong Wenxue Teji*, VII:1 (1936).

Wei Junyi, 'Cong Ertong Wenxue Kandao de Jige Wenti', *Wenyibao*, No. 3 (1953).

Williams, R., *Marxism and Literature* (Oxford, 1977).

Williams, R., *The Long Revolution* (Harmondsworth, 1965).

Williams, R., *Keywords* (Glasgow, 1976).

Williams, R., *Culture* (Glasgow, 1981).

Witke, R., *Comrade Chiang Ch'ing* (Boston, 1977).

Wolff, E., *Chou Tso-jen* (New York, 1971).

Wu Han, 'Do Fairy Plays Spread Superstition?'. Translated in *Survey of China Mainland Magazines*, No. 278 (1961).

Wu Nong and Li Lu, 'Huiqi Huabi zai Changzheng', *Lianhuanhuabao*, No. 10 (1979).

Wylie, M., *Children of China* (Hong Kong, 1962).

Xi Jin, 'Xuyan', in Xi Jin, Guo Dasen, Cui Yi (eds.), *Ertong Wenxue Lunwenxuan 1949–1979* (Peking, 1981).

Xi Jin, Guo Dasen, Cui Yi (eds.), *Ertong Wenxue Lunwenxuan 1949–1979* (Peking, 1981).

Xia Yan, 'Daixu', in Zhang Leping, *Sanmao Liulangi* (Shanghai, 1978).

Xiao Ping, 'Haibin de Haizi', in Zhongguo Zuojia Xiehui (ed.), *Ertong Wenxue Xuan, January 1954–December 1955* (Beijing, 1956).

Xin Shi, 'Geming Yingxiong Gushi dui Xiaoxuesheng Daode Yishi Xingcheng de Zuoyong de Chubu Yanjiu—wen du Duhou Gan', *Xinlinxue Bao,* No. 2 (1966).

Xiong Foxi, 'Tongshen II', *Chenbao Fukan,* 20 November 1927.

Xiong Foxi, 'Tongshen III', *Chenbao Fukan,* 27 November 1927.

Xu Guangping, 'Guanyu Lu Xun de Shenghuo', in Jiang Feng (ed.), *Lu Xun Lun Ertong Jiaoyu yu Ertong Wenxue* (Shanghai, 1961).

Xu Xingkai, 'Ertong yu Jiating, Ertong Yanjiu zhi Yi', *Chenbao Fukan,* 17 January 1926.

Yan Wenjing, 'Xu', *Ertong Wenxue Xuan*, January 1954–December 1955 (Beijing, 1956).

Yan Yiyan, *Xiao Maguan he 'Dapixue' Shushu* (Beijing, 1959).

Yang, Gladys (ed. and transl.), *Silent China: Selected Writings of Lu Xun* (London, 1973).

Yang Hsien-i and Yang, Gladys (transl.), *A Brief History of Chinese Fiction* (Peking, 1976).

Yang Hsien-i and Yang, Gladys (transl.), *Dawn Blossoms Plucked at Dusk* (Peking, 1976).

Yang Hsien-i and Yang, Gladys (transl.), 'Shanghai Children', in *Lu Xun: Selected Works,* Vol. III (Beijing 1959).

Yang Hsien-i and Yang, Gladys (transl.), *Old Tales Retold* (Peking, 1972).

Yang Hsien-i and Gladys Yang, *Selected Stories of Lu Xun* (Peking, 1972).

Yang Li, 'Ertong Wenxue Zatan', *Wenyibao*, Nos 65–66 (1952).

Yang Qin, *Ertong Wenxue Lunwen Xuan* (Beijing, 1980).

Yan Yiyan, *Xiao Maguan he 'Dapixie' Shushu* (Beijing, 1978).

Ye Shengtao, 'The Scarecrow', in *Chinese Literature*, 1 (1961).

Ye Shengtao, 'The Seed', *Chinese Literature*, 1 (1961).

Ye Shengtao, 'Daocaoren', in *Daocaoren* (Shanghai, 1949).

Ye Shengtao, 'Huamei Niao', in *Daocaoren* (Shanghai, 1949).

Ye Shengtao, 'Xiaobai Chuan', in *Daocaoren* (Shanghai, 1949).

Ye Shengtao, 'Yike Zhongzi', in *Daocaoren* (Shanghai, 1949).

Ye Shengtao et al., *Ertong Wenxue Yanjiu, Dierji* (Shanghai, 1979).

Ye Shengtao, 'Rang Shao'er Duwu ru Meihua Shengkai, Quanguo Shaonian Ertong Duwu Chuban Gongzuo Zuotanhui Fayanxuankan' in Ye Shengtao et al., *Ertong Wenxue Yanjiu, Dierji* (Shanghai, 1979).

Ye Shengtao, *Gudai Shixiang de Yingxiong* (Shanghai, 1949).

Ye Shengtao, 'Gudai Shixiang de Yingxiong', in *Gudai Shixiang de Yingxiong* (Shanghai, 1949).

Ye Shengtao, 'Huangdi de Xinyi', in *Gudai Shixiang de Yingxiong* (Shanghai, 1949).

Ye Shengtao, '"Lingdao" *zhege Ci'er. Geren,* Ziji de Zhexue', *Wenyibao*, No. 10 (1957).

Ye Shengtao, *Ye Shengtao Duanpian Xiaoshuo Xuanji* (Peking, 1954).

Ye Shengtao, *Ye Shengtao Tonghua Xuan* (Peking, 1956).

Ye Shengtao, 'Houji', in *Ye Shengtao Tonghua Xuan* (Peking, 1956).

Ye Shengtao, 'Huochetou de Jingli', in *Ye Shengtao Tonghua Xuan* (Peking, 1956).

Ye Shengtao, 'Niaoyan de Hua', in *Ye Shengtao Tonghua Xuan* (Peking, 1949).

Ye Shengtao, 'Guoqu Suitan', *Zhongxuesheng*, IV (January 1951).

Ye Yonglie, *Gao Shiqi Yeye* (Shanghai, 1979).

Ye Yonglie, *Xiaolingtong Manyou Weilai* (Shanghai, 1978).

Yi, 'Zai Tan Ertong Wenxue', *Wenxue*, VI:1 (1 January 1936).

Ying Can, 'Ertong Nian de Ertong Wenxue', *Zhongxuesheng*, 62 (February, 1936).

Ying Xiuren, *Qizi de Gushi* (Shanghai, 1961).

Yu Dafu, 'Zhongxuesheng Nali Zou', *Zhongxuesheng*, VI (July 1930).

Yuan Jing, *The Story of Little Black Horse* (Peking, 1979).

Yuan Jing, *Xiao Heima de Gushi* (Beijing, 1959).

Yuan Ying, 'On Zhang Tianyi', *Chinese Literature*, No. 6 (1959).

Yuan Ying, 'Liu Wenxue', in Yuan Ying et al. (ed.), *Ertong Wenxue Shixuan, shan* (Beijing, 1978).

Yuan Ying, 'Liu Wenxue' in Zhongguo Zuojia Xiehui (ed.), *Ertong Wenxue Xuan 1959–1963* (Shanghai, 1963).

Yuan Ying, 'Zhengqu Shaonian Ertong Wenxue Chuangzuo de Fanrong', in *Zhongguo Qingnian Wenxue Chuangzuozhe Huiyi Baogao, Fayanji* (Beijing, 1956).

Yun Geng, 'Lianhuantuhua de Gaizao Wenti', *Wenyibao*, 1:5 (1949).

'Zai Guoji Shuji Yishu Zhanlanhui Shang, Siben Ertong Duwu de Jiang', *Ertong Wenxue Yanjiu*, 2 (1959).

Zhang Leping, *Sanmao Congjunji* (Chengdu, 1983).

Zhang Leping, *Sanmao Liulangji* (Shanghai, 1978).

Zhang Songlin, 'China's Animated Cartoon Films', *China Reconstructs*, 30: 2 (1981).

Zhang Tianyi, *Big Lin and Little Lin* (Peking, 1958).

Zhang Tianyi, 'Bing Xin', in Li Xitong (ed.), *Bing Xin Lun* (Shanghai, 1932).

Zhang Tianyi, *Da Lin he Xiao Lin* (Peking, 1956).

Zhang Tianyi, 'Bao Hulu de Mimi', in *Gei Haizimen* (Beijing, 1959).

Zhang Tianyi, *Luo Wenying de Gushi* (Peking, 1962).

Zhang Tianyi, *Zhang Tianyi Xuanji: Xiandai Zuowen Ku* (Shanghai, 1936).

Zhang Tianyi, 'Mifeng', in *Zhang Tianyi Xuanji: Xiandai Zuowen Ku* (Shanghai, 1936).

Zhang Xin, 'Lianhuanhua yu Dianying Yishu', *Lianhuanhuabao* (October, 1977).

Zhang Youde, *Meimei Ruxue* (Beijing, 1961).

Zhang Zhigong, *Chuantong Yuyan Jiaoyu Chutan* (Shanghai, 1962).

Zhao Jingshen, *Tonghua Lunji* (Shanghai, 1929).

Zhen Guangzhong and Fan Qilong, 'Zhou Zuoren yu Ertong yu Ertong wenxue', *Sichuan Shifan Daxue Xuebao*, Vol. 4, 1986,

Zheng Wenguang, *Fei Xiang Renmazuo* (Beijing, 1979).

'Zhongguo Chubanjie zhi Xianshi Yibie', *Zhongxuesheng*, 41 (January 1934).

Zhongguo Ertong Duwu Zuozhe Xiehui (ed.), *Ertong Wenxue Chuangzuo Xuanji 1948* (Shanghai, 1949).

'Zhongguo Quanguo Wenxue Yishujie Lianhehui, 1950 Nian Gongzuo Gongzuo Zongjie ji 1951 Nian Gongzuo Jihua', *Wenyibao*, No. 35 (1950–1).

'Zhongguo Quanguo Wenxue Gongzuozhe Xiehui Quanguo Weiyuanhui, Guanyu Zhenglie, Zuzhi, Gaijin Gongzuo de Fangan', *Wenyibao*, No. 57 (1952).

Zhongxuesheng, Editorial, 1 January 1930.

Zhonghua Gushi, Vol. 6 (Shanghai, 1935).

Zhou Enlai, 'Zhou Enlai on Questions Related to Art and Literature', *Chinese Literature,* No. 6 (1979).

Zhou Yang, 'The Path of Socialist Literature and Art in China', in Kai-yu Hsu, *Literature of the People's Republic of China* (Bloomington and London, 1980).

Zhou Zuoren, 'Our Own Garden', in Wolff, E., *Chou Tso-Jen* (New York, 1971).

Zhou Zuoren, 'Jinghua Lu', *Ziji de Yuandi* (Shanghai, 1923).

Zhou Zuoren, 'Ertong de Wenxue', in Huang Zhiqing (ed.), *Zhou Zuoren Lunwenji* (Hong Kong, 1972).

Zhou Zuoren, 'Ertong de Shu', *Ziji de Yuandi* (Shanghai, 1923).

Zi Yu, 'Jiben Ertong Zazhi', *Wenxue*, IV:3 (1935).

Index

adolescent books, 23
Adolescents and Children's
 Publishing House, 253
Adolescents and Children, 253
adventure stories, 143, 304
 in Civil War, 183
Aesop's Fables, 20
All-China Federation of Literature
 and Art Circles, 252
All-China Resist-the-Enemy
 Federation of Writers and Artists,
 172
Ancient Stone Hero, The, 105–11,
 114, 153
'Ancient Stone Hero, The', 106–8
Andersen, Hans Christian, 34, 91–2,
 101, 105, 109–11, 125, 126, 128,
 138, 265
*Animal Behavior of American
 Soldiers, The,* 216
'Animal Talk', 111, 113–4
animal stories, 266
*Anthology of Children's Poems
 1949–79, The,* 290
Anti-Japanese War, 7, 91, 144, 166,
 183, 273–4
 adventure stories of, 183
Anti-Rightist Campaign, 250, 255,
 270, 280
'At the Seaside', 258, 261–3, 294
Austen, Jane, 123
'Autobiography of a Germ, The',
 264
awards *see* national prizes for
 children's literature
Azalea Mountain, 236–8

Ba Jin, 22, 25, 27, 153, 155–8, 159
 fairytales, 155–8
Bao Lei, 256

Barrier, 104
'Barrier', 104
'Beside the Pond', 65, 66–7
Bethune, Norman, 238–42
Big Lin and Little Lin, 148, 153,
 159–62, 294
'Big Nose', 198
Bing Xin, 27, 35, 92, 97, 124, 136,
 138, 181, 255, 256, 263, 295,
 301
 idealization of love, 117
 influence of Tagore, 118, 122
 Letters to Young Readers, 35, 92,
 115–22, 136
 new artistic sensibility, 116
 pathos, 116
 subconscious aspects of writing,
 122
Blake, William, 97, 101, 102, 105
Book of Hills and Seas, The, 63
Book of Rites, The, 17
Bows Against the Barons, 132
*Brief Discussion of Children's
 Literature, A,* 281
Bureaucratic planning of literature,
 212

Call to Arms, 53
Canon of children's literature, 4, 5,
 299–305
CCP, *see* Chinese Communist Party
censorship, 150, 213–8
Ch'i Cheng, 236
Chekhov, Anton, 82
Chen Bochui, 45, 84, 153, 167, 181,
 256, 270–1, 280–3
Chen Zijun, 272, 285
Chesneaux, Jean, 6, 8, 230
Chiang Kai-shek, *see* Jiang Jieshi
Child Without a Country, 153, 162

Mary Ann Farquhar teaches China studies and Asian law at Griffith University in Brisbane, Australia. She studied at Beijing University in the seventies, graduating from the Department of Language and Literature. She also has a law degree. Her main publications are in Chinese culture, especially literature, cinema, and law.